DROP DEAD

DROP DEAD

How a Coterie of Corrupt Politicians,
Bankers, Lawyers, Spinmeisters,
and Mobsters Bankrupted New York,
Got Bailed Out, Blamed the President,
and Went Back to Business as Usual
(*And It Might Be Happening Again*)

RICHARD E. FARLEY

Regan Arts.

This is a work of nonfiction. The research for this work was extensive and was drawn from various sources, including published materials and interviews. The views and opinions expressed in this book are those of the author and do not necessarily reflect the official policy or position of any other agency, organization, employer, or company. Assumptions made in the analysis do not reflect the position of any entity other than the author—and, since he is a critically thinking human being, these views are always subject to change, revision, and rethinking at any time.

Regan Arts is committed to publishing works of quality and integrity. We are proud to publish this book; however, the story, the experiences, and the words are the author's alone.

First Regan Arts hardcover edition 2025
Library of Congress Control Number: 2024902652
978-1-68245-230-1 (Hardcover)
978-1-68245-231-8 (eBook)

FRONT COVER: *Left-, center- and right-hand photos:* Gerald Ford Presidential Library/NARA; *2nd front left:* Ronald Reagan Presidential Library/NARA; *2nd from right:* Bernard Gotfryd Photograph Collection/Library of Congress.
BACK COVER: AP Photo

Design by Neuwirth & Associates, Inc.

Printed in the United States of America
1   3   5   7   9   10   8   6   4   2

*To Bernie Nussbaum, Andy Maloney, Sid Zion, Milton Mollen,
and the other dearly departed members of Jerry Finkelstein's Kitchen
Cabinet, who clued me into a great deal of what follows herein.*

SKEETERS: If it wasn't for graft, you'd get a very low type of people in politics. Men without ambition.

CATHERINE: Especially since you can't rob the people anyway.

SKEETERS: Sure . . . how was that?

CATHERINE: What you rob, you spend, and what you spend goes back to the people. So, where's the robbery?

—*The Great McGinty* by Preston Sturges

CONTENTS

SAINT ANTHONY
AND THE MONK

IT IS UNDERSTANDABLE THAT MANY OF OUR FELLOW CITIZENS take false comfort in the notion that "misinformation" and "fake news" first infected our public life with the arrival on the national political scene of Donald Trump, Twitter, the Steele Dossier and the Hunter Biden laptop. Those same citizens nod solemnly when Michael Beschloss or some other "serious historian" laments the days when reasonable men and women of the Democratic and Republican Parties would get together and compromise and find reasonable solutions to the nation's problems. They are nostalgic for a simpler time in our national discourse when Walter Cronkite told us the nightly news, and he—and most of the rest of the press—gave it to us straight. I hope those troubled souls read farther herein, for if they do, they will find real solace, as the republic has survived scoundrels in high places with much more intelligence, cunning, wit, and charm than can be found on the target lists of today's special prosecutors.

"The past remembers better than it lived," the great political scientist Jackie Gleason once observed. The first in-the-bag journalist was not named Maddow or Hannity. Cleisthemes likely had an Athenian town crier or two on the take. Even in the heyday of so-called responsible political and media behavior—those halcyon days just after Halberstam blew the lid off Vietnam and Woodward and Bernstein brought down Nixon—the politicians shamelessly pulled the wool over the voters' eyes with the willing assistance of their ink-stained lackeys. It was just easier back then. With only three television networks, a handful of national circulation newspapers, and another handful of newsweeklies, back in 1975, they could afford to be subtle. Now, in addition to the three networks, we've got CNN, Fox News, MSNBC, Newsmax, NewsNation, Bloomberg, and a few more on the television; hundreds of blogs and podcasts; and hundreds more Substacks and YouTubes. To message through the racket these days, you must pick a lane and go full Howard Beale.

YOU MAY HAVE SEEN SERIOUS, UNSMILING EXPERTS ON PUBLIC television lecturing you on the causes of the New York City fiscal crisis of 1975—the demographic changes the city experienced after World War II, the loss of manufacturing jobs, and the increase in public-sector union employment. If those experts were liberals, they droned on about the need to understand that a compassionate New York City helped its poor more than other large, less compassionate American cities. If the experts were conservative, they intoned on the maze of accounting gimmicks, fiscal chicanery, deficit spending, and irresponsible borrowing by New York City liberals.

It is likely you fell asleep before either the liberal or conservative experts finished speaking their peace about the New York City fiscal crisis. Had you stayed awake, no matter which camp of experts you believed, you still wouldn't understand how the disaster happened.

A real understanding cannot come by listening to those who misspent the days of their youth in prestigious universities accumulating advanced degrees and their careers thinking great thoughts at fancy think tanks. Proper understanding can only come from listening to those few remaining souls who know the cadence of the political clubhouse, now long defunct. Those who can tell you of Meade Esposito, Carmine DeSapio, Bill Shea, Roy Cohn, and Bunny Lindenbaum can let you in on what was actually done and by whom because just about everything you think you know and may have been told about the 1975 New York City fiscal crisis is likely not quite what actually happened, *Daily News* headlines notwithstanding.

To begin to understand how the whole debacle could have happened, you need to carefully consider the careers of two New York City characters from that era: John Patrick Scanlon, public relations man, and his first prominent client, convicted felon and labor leader, Anthony M. Scotto.

ANTHONY SCOTTO, THE PRESIDENT OF LOCAL 1814 OF THE International Longshoremen's Association in Brooklyn and a vice president of the national union, found himself in dire need of public relations expertise in August 1969 when the US Department of Justice identified him as a captain in Carlo Gambino's organized crime family. Senator John McClellan of Arkansas published that finding in the *Congressional Record*, which was thereafter duly reported by the nation's newspapers. This revelation, however embarrassing, did not come as a complete shock to the residents and workers on the Brooklyn waterfront as Scotto had taken over Local 1814 from his father-in-law, Anthony "Tough Tony" Anastasio, the brother of Albert Anastasia, cofounder and boss of "Murder, Inc.," the Mafia organization that later became the Gambino crime family.

At first blush, John Scanlon would be an unlikely conscript in any effort to clean up the public persona of a mobbed-up union boss. Born in 1935 in an Irish enclave near Yankee Stadium, Scanlon graduated from Catholic University in Washington, joined a religious order, and spent six years teaching in Roman Catholic schools. After leaving the religious order, he taught high school for a while, sold textbooks, and became a full-time activist against the Vietnam War. In 1968, he went "Clean for Gene" and joined the antiwar presidential campaign of Senator Eugene McCarthy. Scanlon worked for a stint as a speechwriter for New York City Mayor John Lindsay. After that, he went into the public relations business.

The second Scanlon laid eyes on Anthony Scotto, he knew he had something to work with. Scotto stood up and came from behind his desk at Local 1814. He looked Scanlon right in the eye with a warm smile of perfect white teeth and offered his hand. Tall, dark, and handsome, Scotto looked like Tony Bennett's brother, if Tony Bennett had a brother who went to Harvard Business School and worked at Chase Manhattan Bank. Elegantly but conservatively dressed, articulate and intelligent, Scanlon could hardly believe this guy was Anthony Scotto, the Gambino capo. And when he met Scotto's wife, Marion, equally attractive, beautiful, blond, vivacious, and dignified, it was done, as far as Scanlon was concerned.

Scanlon's PR strategy for Scotto was as bold as it was brilliant. There would be no "keeping a low profile," skulking around the Brooklyn docks like an ordinary, old-school wiseguy. No, Anthony Scotto would be made a pillar of the New York establishment, a power broker, a man-about-town, colorful and quotable. He and Marion were seen on the black-tie charity ball circuit, mixing with Charlotte Ford and Lee Radziwill. He got himself appointed to the Board of Trustees of the Brooklyn Academy of Music. He even lectured at Harvard University on labor relations. With his union pension fund campaign contributions and rank-and-file members ready to canvass, Scanlon's cleaned-up Scotto was most welcomed by politicians come election time. He was on a first-name basis with Teddy Kennedy, Hubert Humphrey, Jimmy Carter, Mayors Lindsay and Wagner, and fellow Brooklynite Hugh Carey. Local 1814 was one of the largest donors to Carey's 1974 gubernatorial campaign, and Scotto was seated front and center at Carey's $500-a-plate inauguration gala at the Waldorf Astoria hotel.

With Scanlon feeding him lines, Scotto was soon a darling of the New York media as well. "I can buy any reporter in town for a cup of coffee," Scotto quipped to Pulitzer Prize–winning journalist Murray Kempton, who took no offense and loved the copy. Pete Hamill, a Scanlon pal and the laureate of the New Left was another admirer. The *New York Times*' John L. Hess was *not* an admirer. He took notice of Scanlon's clean-up campaign and referred to Scotto sarcastically as "Saint Anthony of the Docks."

IN JUNE 1975, AMID THE FISCAL CRISIS, THE MUNICIPAL Assistance Corporation (MAC) was formed to sell bonds backed by New York State to finance New York City's operations because the market was oversaturated with New York City debt securities. The MAC board, appointed by Governor Carey, was made up of business leaders advertised as having the highest character and integrity who would judiciously dole out the money to New York City only if it made progress toward ending its profligate ways and shady practices. New York City, the investment community believed, had become captured by special interests, particularly the unions.

The MAC, under the leadership of Felix Rohatyn, the cosmopolitan and refined white-shoe M&A banker from Lazard Frères, with the prodding of Governor Hugh Carey, hired as one of its first executives none other than John P. Scanlon, mouthpiece for Anthony Scotto, the Gambino-linked union boss. In his interview with Rohatyn, Scanlon had insisted on a few unorthodox conditions to his agreeing to work for Rohatyn at the MAC: he must be allowed to continue to represent two clients, David Buntzman and Albert Schwartzberg, both of whom figured prominently in corruption matters being investigated by grand juries impaneled in New York. That Rohatyn didn't throw Scanlon out of his office reveals much about both men. The Monk had the gift of gab, he did. That rare ability, so prevalent among certain of the Irish, to spin a tale of absolute bullshit that leaves even those of education and high IQs wondering if the fellow jawboning them might actually have it right. With his bow tie, white beard, twinkling eyes, and sonorous voice, Scanlon looked and sounded like an Irish C. Everett Koop. Before long, Rohatyn was unconcerned about Scanlon's side gigs. After a pleasant chat with Scanlon, MAC's general counsel, Daniel Goldberg, said he saw no conflict of interest either. But when the *New York Times* found out about Scanlon's moonlighting in February 1976 and wrote all about it, those concerned reconsidered and thought it might be best if Scanlon resigned, which he soon did.

JOHN SCANLON DID NOT SUFFER LONG FROM THE MAC EMBARrassment. Scotto was a good client. And the Monk soon found many other clients: alleged sex offender Reverend Bruce Ritter of Covenant House; the felonious investment bank Drexel Burnham Lambert; Credit Suisse, after it was accused of keeping hundreds of millions of dollars rightfully belonging to Holocaust victims; and Brown & Williamson, the tobacco company accused of making cigarettes more addictive. Some may find these associations unsavory, but not the New York power elite. Until his death, Scanlon remained a member in good standing of that club.

ANTHONY SCOTTO HAD THE MISFORTUNE OF FIGURING PROMInently in 1,100 hours of tapes from FBI wiretaps gathered during its investigation of racketeering on the Brooklyn waterfront, culminating in his indictment on January 25, 1979. Not all of Scotto's friends abandoned him. Former Mayor John V. Lindsay testified at Scotto's RICO trial as a character witness, calling him "a man of high integrity." A week later, former Mayor Robert F. Wagner also testified, calling Scotto "a man of integrity and ability—and a darned good labor leader." But the climax of the trial came two days later, when Carey, the sitting governor of New York, took the witness stand, and Scotto's counsel, the mob lawyer James M. LaRossa, asked the governor about Scotto's reputation. Carey said: "He is trustworthy, energetic, intelligent, effective, and dedicated." After the jury retired to deliberate, Scotto pal Pete Hamill wrote a column supporting his friend entitled: "Our National Bird, not the Eagle, but the Stool Pigeon." Hamill wrote: "There is something inherently dangerous about the growing practice of using wired stool pigeons . . . Yesterday, as Anthony Scotto waited for the jury to make the decision that would affect the rest of his life, it was difficult to root for anyone but Scotto."

The jury had other rooting interests, convicting Scotto on thirty-three charges after which he was sentenced to five years in federal prison.

AS YOU WILL SEE, THE ROOT CAUSE OF THE FISCAL CRISIS WAS not President Ford telling the city to "Drop Dead" (in fact, it was Ford who, with no better option, bailed the city out), but rather the corruption of the city's politically privileged. A governing culture that ignored conflicts of interest and shrugged off vouching for known criminals could hardly be expected to insist on propriety in balancing its accounts. The two conventional narratives that explain the crisis—on the left, that the Nixon-Ford conservatives harnessed a racist backlash against urban America in the mid-1970s and punished New York City for its progressive, humane treatment of the poor; and on the right, that a spendthrift, incompetent liberal-controlled city bankrupted itself through giveaways to unions and welfare cheats—leaves those that held power at the time, whatever their ideology, off too easy. Liberals and conservatives, Democrats and Republicans, bankers and union leaders, columnists and cardinals all liked to get their parking tickets fixed. And still do.

THE DAMAGE LEFT IN THE WAKE OF NEW YORK CITY'S FISCAL crisis included not only a dirtier, less safe, and more chaotic city but also the destroyed career of a mayor—Abe Beame, who only wanted to show the city that old-fashioned clubhouse politics that took care of working people was still viable in the 1970s—and shattered the aspirations of three men—Gerald Ford, Nelson Rockefeller, and Hugh Carey—hoping to be elected president of the United States. The competing ambitions of these men, the strength of their personalities, their cunning, personal flaws, and weaknesses affected the outcome of the crisis and their own fates, as much as the unemployment rate, accounting gimmicks, falling tax revenue, the bonds that wouldn't sell, or the votes they had in Albany or in Washington, DC.

This is the real story of how it all went down.

CHAPTER ONE

ELECTING YOUR OWN BOSS

HE WAS SHORT. ALMOST COMICALLY SO, AT FIVE FEET, TWO inches. That was the first thing anyone who first met Abe Beame noticed, and he was well aware of this. There are some fields for which diminutive stature is not a handicap, and Abe Beame, before running for political office for the first time at the advanced age of fifty-five years old, had worked in some of those fields for he very rarely had held fewer than two jobs. But high political office had become a tall man's game by the 1960s. Besides being the shortest man ever elected New York City mayor, Beame was also the oldest at sixty-seven years old and the first practitioner of the Jewish faith. He was not new to politics, however, when he first ran for city comptroller in 1961. He had joined the Madison Democratic Club in Brooklyn in 1929, fresh out of college. Waiting his turn, paying his dues, and deferring to leadership did not trouble Abe Beame.

Beame was born Abraham Birnbaum in London, England, in 1906. His father, Philip, owned a restaurant in Warsaw, which was part of the Russian Empire then, and Philip was active in the anti-Tsarist revolutionary movement there. After Tsar Nicholas II's secret police got wind of Philip's activities that year, Philip thought it wise to skip town and sent his pregnant wife to London while he set sail for New York with plans to send for her after he settled in. Before she could join him in his cold water flat on Manhattan's Lower East Side, Abraham was born. Mother and child joined Philip in New York months later.

In 1912, the year the family name was changed, Abe's mother died. While attending elementary school at PS 160, young Abe got his first job: waking up neighbors in the tenement who could not afford alarm clocks by knocking on their doors before he left for school each morning. Abe was a good student and was accepted to the High School of Commerce in Manhattan at Tenth Avenue and West 58th Street. After school, he worked the 4:00 p.m. to midnight shift in the paper factory where his father was foreman. Abe went on to City College of New York, the "poor man's Harvard," from which he graduated with honors with a business degree in 1928. Before his senior year, he married his high school sweetheart, Mary Ingerman. Abe got a job right out of college—a job he would hold for seventeen years—teaching accounting at Richmond High School in Queens. He and Mary leased an apartment in Crown Heights, Brooklyn.

While Abe's father's politics were radical and leftist, Abe's ran far more moderate, which explains why Abe walked the short distance from his apartment to the Madison Democratic Club and offered his services. For a budding clubhouse politician, a better time and place could not have been matched. The Madison Democratic Club was founded in 1905 by John H.

McCooey, who succeeded Hugh McLaughlin as the Democratic boss in Brooklyn the prior year. As those names would indicate, the Brooklyn Democratic Party was controlled by the Irish in those days, but by the end of World War I, the Jews were leaving the Lower East Side and moving in large numbers to Brooklyn. In 1919, Irwin Steingut, the son of the Manhattan Tammany Hall Jewish boss Simon Steingut, moved to Brooklyn and joined McCooey's organization. It was, as they say, a marriage made in heaven, or at least Boss Tweed's image of heaven. The Irish and the Jews of Brooklyn formed the most united and powerful political organization of the next half century, not just in New York City or even in New York State, but in the entirety of the United States (with the possible exception of the first Richard Daley's Cook County machine).

For seventeen years, Abe Beame licked envelopes, manned phone banks, and canvassed his Crown Heights neighborhood until his first payoff came. In 1946, Mayor William O'Dwyer appointed Beame as assistant city budget director. With the increase in salary over his high school teaching job, Beame no longer needed his second job—teaching night classes at Rutgers University in New Jersey—which meant more time at home with Mary and their two sons. After six more years of loyal service to the party, Beame was promoted to city budget director by Mayor Vincent Impellitteri.

In 1961, Beame was given his first shot at elective office. After failing to get the nod to become Brooklyn borough president, he was tapped by Brooklyn boss Joseph T. Sharkey to be the party's candidate for New York City comptroller that year. For New York City politics, 1961 was a watershed year, for that was the year that Mayor Robert F. Wagner Jr., son of Tammany legend US Senator Robert Wagner Sr., broke with Manhattan boss Carmine DeSapio and won in a landslide despite the opposition of the citywide Democratic organization. Beame gladly accepted DeSapio's support and won his race easily, making him the highest-elected clubhouse politician in the city.

In 1965, having burned a great many bridges, Mayor Wagner announced he would not seek reelection for a fourth term. That set off a four-way scramble for the Democratic nomination among Paul Screvane, the City Council president and Wagner's preferred successor; Paul O'Dwyer, a city councilman, the brother of the former mayor, and a progressive firebrand; William Fitts Ryan, a congressman from the Upper West Side of Manhattan and a good-government reformer; and Beame, the city comptroller and the chosen candidate of the clubhouse bosses. Beame won comfortably with 45 percent of the primary vote.

In the general election, Beame faced Congressman John V. Lindsay, the nominee of the Republican and Liberal Parties, and William F. Buckley Jr., the nominee of the Conservative Party. Perhaps if the race had taken place before the television cameras chose our leaders, the result may have been different.

Lindsay, fifteen years younger than Beame, was an exemplar of WASP perfection: movie star handsome; articulate; son of a respected lawyer and investment banker whose ancestors came to New York in the seventeenth century; graduate of the Buckley School, St. Paul's School, and Yale (Scroll and Key); heroic war service during World War II with five battle stars; and the four-term congressman from the Silk Stocking District of Manhattan's Upper East Side. Lindsay was also six feet, four inches tall.

Buckley Jr., nineteen years younger than Beame, was even WASPier than Lindsay, an incredible accomplishment given that Buckley was an Irish Catholic. The son of a fabulously wealthy oil man, Buckley also graduated from Yale (Skull and Bones) in 1950. The year after graduating, Buckley wrote his first book, *God and Man at Yale,* criticizing the Yale faculty and administration as wayward proponents of atheism and socialism and establishing himself as the nation's leading conservative public intellectual. Four years later, he founded *National Review,* the influential conservative political magazine. Buckley stood a shade under six feet, two inches tall.

Besides these two tall, handsome, verbally adept scions of wealth and privilege, Beame, whose speech bore the unmistakable accent of the first-generation immigrant New Yorker, looked and sounded second-rate. The viciously funny Buckley—who said if he won the race, he would demand a recount—repeatedly teed off on Beame as a marionette of the bosses. Looking up at Buckley at candidates' forums, Beame had no clever ripostes, only an exasperated, sputtering, earnest defense of his record as comptroller. Beame's lack of humor was legendary. A friend of Beame's said his best jokes could be funny—if told by someone else.

Beame lost the race to Lindsay by four percentage points.

At sixty years old and out of elective office, Beame took a job as a financial analyst with American Trust Company and finally made some decent money for the first time in his life. It bored him to tears. In 1969, his successor as comptroller, Mario Procaccino, announced he would challenge Lindsay for mayor in that year's city election, and Beame let it be known among the bosses that he wanted his old job back. In part because he was a loyal clubhouse man, but in larger part because he would win, the bosses agreed, and Beame got another term as comptroller.

In 1973, Beame would once again be the choice of the bosses for mayor, and the outcome would be different than in

1965. New York City in 1973 was very different from the city of 1965. In the heady, Great Society, War on Poverty days of the mid-1960s, many New Yorkers took to John Lindsay and his Ivy League–educated, idealistic, long-haired liberal lieutenants. The economy was strong, Wall Street was go-go, and the money was flowing into the city from Lyndon Johnson's poverty programs. Eight years later, those days seemed like a mirage. The city had been ravaged by riots in the aftermath of the Martin Luther King assassination. New York Senator Robert F. Kennedy had also been assassinated. The war in Vietnam had demoralized and divided New Yorkers. Radical groups of every stripe were setting off bombs in the city on nearly a monthly basis. Wall Street was in a prolonged bear market. The economy was in recession. The Nixon administration was scaling back aid to the cities. John Lindsay turned out to be an ineffective administrator, not at all up to the challenges of the times. After eight years of labor unrest and fiscal chaos, New Yorkers were ready to trade in the tall and handsome Yalie for the dull, short accountant from Brooklyn. Beame defeated Congressman Herman Badillo in the Democratic primary run-off, 60.8 to 39.2 percent, and handily defeated Republican John Marchi in the general election.

On election night, five floors below the ballroom in the Biltmore Hotel where his supporters celebrated, the bosses—Meade Esposito of Brooklyn, Patrick Cunningham of the Bronx, Frank Rossetti of Manhattan, Matthew Troy of Queens, and James Smith of Staten Island—crowded into Beame's four-room suite with the rest of Beame's inner circle. Beame's campaign chairman, eighty-five-year-old party warhorse James A. Farley, told stories of the old FDR days with his pal Jack Dempsey, the seventy-eight-year-old former heavyweight boxing champion, laughing loudly. A cynical press called it Beame's elderly rebellion to Lindsay's youth revolution. Beame didn't care. He was not ashamed of these men, he was proud of them. He was proud of the Tammany tradition, for these men and Tammany brought Beame to where he was that night. The clubhouse, where patience, experience, loyalty, and hard work were rewarded, was a far better proving ground than Yale, as far as Beame was concerned. Reformers? They made speeches, attended protest marches, and made a lot of noise, but what had they actually accomplished? Liberals claimed they loved the Blacks and the Puerto Ricans, but who gave those communities real power? Hadn't Carmine DeSapio made Hulan Jack the first Black borough president? The clubhouse had made them all, elevated them all, without regard to race or creed. The Irish McCooey begat the Jew Steingut, who begat the Italian Esposito. The Madison Democratic Club way was the American way. That was true progress, thought Beame, and he would show the city that it still worked in 1973 as well as it did in 1929.

JANUARY 1, 1974, WAS INAUGURATION DAY IN NEW YORK CITY. The weather forecast for the day, bitterly cold and overcast, was not conducive for a long speech, so Beame settled on a short address—no longer than twelve minutes. He would make no attempt at eloquence. It would be a very businesslike address, and the day's events would be short on pomp and circumstance. He descended the stairs of City Hall bareheaded in the cold, impeccably dressed and groomed as always, looking bankerly in his Chesterfield overcoat and dark tie, with Mary by his side, looking elegant and beaming as her husband was sworn in as the 104th mayor of New York City. After taking the oath, Beame

approached the lectern, put on his thick horned-rim glasses—
which immediately made him look not like a banker but like
an accountant from Brooklyn—and began his short address.
Bess Myerson, the former Miss America and city commissioner
of consumer affairs who was the mistress of ceremonies for
the Inauguration Day events, had trouble hearing Beame and,
looking around at the other spectators, could see they couldn't
hear Beame very well either. She looked at Beame and immediately knew the cause of the problem: the microphones on the
lectern had not been lowered, remaining at a height appropriate
for John Lindsay. An attractive young assistant was quickly sent
over, and she discreetly adjusted the microphones downward.
The new mayor didn't skip a beat. This had happened to him
countless times over the years. Preoccupied with remembering
his speech, like so many times before, he had forgotten to lower
them himself.

THE CITY JOHN LINDSAY LEFT BEAME WAS IN VERY ROUGH SHAPE.
The national recession of 1973–1974 hit New York City and
the other older, industrial cities of the Northeast and Midwest
particularly hard, and its effects lasted longer there, continuing beyond the end of the national recession. The unemployment rate in New York City rose from 6.0 percent in 1973 to
12.0 percent in July 1975.[1] Inflation rose from a 3.6 percent
annual rate in January 1973 to an 11.8 percent annual rate in
January 1975. Inflation is particularly damaging to municipal
finances as a city's costs feel the full effect of price increases,
but its revenues (disproportionately real estate taxes) often fall
as property values decline because of high mortgage rates. The
one-two punch of recession and inflation hit New York City at a

time of historic vulnerability. The city had experienced radical demographic and economic changes over the preceding three decades, leaving it with challenges that it had not addressed particularly well.

Following World War II, New York City remained—briefly— the industrial powerhouse of the nation, but its peak in terms of industrial employment occurred in 1947. Thereafter, slowly at first but growing more rapidly by the late 1950s, manufacturing jobs began to leave New York City, first to the surrounding suburbs, then to the sunbelt states, and finally overseas. In 1947, New York City was home to over a million manufacturing jobs. By 1975, the number had shrunk to 529,000.[2] The rise of the automobile, the government subsidization of home ownership in the suburbs with the G.I Bill mortgages, and the quest for lower taxes and labor costs enabled this exodus of jobs. But not everyone got the memo.

Just as the low-skilled manufacturing jobs were leaving New York, a flood of unskilled labor arrived. The acceleration of the mechanization of agriculture in the South after World War II, combined with the unremedied racial segregation, fueled the great internal migration of mostly unskilled Blacks to northern cities, including New York. The increased affordability of airplane travel during the 1950s also enabled hundreds of thousands of Puerto Ricans to leave their impoverished island for a better life in New York. Between 1950 and 1970, New York City's population remained about the same (7.9 million). However, nearly a million upper- and middle-income residents (mostly white) had left the city, replaced by an equal number of lower-income Blacks and Puerto Ricans. During the 1970s, this white flight would accelerate, with over 850,000 people, disproportionately middle-income and white, leaving New York City. The city was also getting older. In 1950, 8 percent of the city's population was sixty-five or older. By 1975, it was over 13 percent.[3]

New York City was not unique among American cities, however, in experiencing these trends. Deindustrialization, "white flight," and aging populations affected most northern industrial cities during this period, some more dramatically than New York. These factors alone do not explain why New York City went broke. The fact that New York City provided more services to its citizens than did other cities does partially explain the straits it found itself in. More impactful was the fact that it was a city—rather than a state—that was paying for those services. For example, New York City ran a free municipal hospital system with nineteen hospitals. This may have made sense prior to 1965, but the federal government enacted Medicaid that year allowing poor people access to private hospitals. Thereafter it made much less sense, and the city-run hospitals were noteworthy for their subpar care and inefficiencies. In 1974, one-fourth of the city's hospital beds were vacant. What the city hospital system did provide was thousands of jobs that city politicians could hand out to politically connected administrators, doctors, nurses, and orderlies.

Similarly, New York City ran its own courts and prisons, functions assumed by states or counties elsewhere. These too provided thousands of jobs that city politicians could dole out to loyal Democrats; but if those functions were taken over by the state, those jobs would be doled out to loyal Democrats by politicians in Albany—a much less preferable outcome as far as the city politicians were concerned. Unique among American cities, New York had its own university system, providing tuition-free higher education to all city residents—a very popular perk among the city's middle-class residents. Among its professors and administrators the politically connected were well represented as well. The New York City transit system, the largest in the country, was also operated and funded by the city until 1968. It employed over 35,000 workers, a bonanza of patronage for city politicians.

Overly generous welfare benefits were a common complaint among those lamenting New York City's fiscal woes. The truth regarding the role of welfare payouts in the city's fiscal demise is complicated. New York City's benefits were less generous than those in Boston, Los Angeles, and San Francisco. However, unlike most cities, New York City was required to bear a por-tion of the cost of its citizens' welfare benefits—25 percent, the largest contribution of any city in the nation. And New York still received the lowest federal subsidy for welfare costs—50 percent (Mississippi, for example, had a 70 percent federal subsidy).[4] When the recession hit in 1973, payrolls were cut as welfare rolls expanded. In 1974, 1.5 million New Yorkers were on welfare, triple the number ten years earlier. The great internal migration had become a great financial burden. Nearly two-thirds of all welfare recipients in New York City were born outside of New York State.[5]

Since so many of those welfare recipients were born in the South or Puerto Rico, they were citizens of the United States, and, accordingly, they were entitled, as residents of New York City, to vote for the candidates of the Democratic Party in New York City elections. This was a reality not lost on Carmine DeSapio, the longtime Manhattan Democratic Party boss, well aware that Harlem was located in Manhattan. It was also not lost on Meade Esposito, the Brooklyn Democratic Party boss, equally aware as he was that Bedford-Stuyvesant was located in Brooklyn. During the 1960s and early 1970s, powerful Black and Puerto Rican politicians emerged in New York City, and the bosses, mostly Irish and Italian, made way for and promoted them, even if begrudgingly at times. Those bosses had not forgotten how to count, and self-preservation is a more powerful political instinct than racism. Hulan Jack, J. Raymond Jones, Adam Clayton Powell Jr., Basil Patterson, Denny Farrell, Percy Sutton, David Dinkins, Shirley Chisolm, Carl McCall, Charlie Rangel, and Herman Badillo in short order became among the most powerful political figures in the city. When they united, they could harness the Black and Puerto Rican votes and determine the outcome of any citywide election. Accordingly, any Democrat running for mayor advocating for a cut in welfare benefits might as well cut his or her own throat, for that was an issue that would unite the aforementioned power brokers.

A popular vote-winning middle-class giveaway that helped bankrupt the city was rent control. Originally implemented as a federal wartime measure in 1943 to temper inflation, it was rescinded nationally in 1948. But not in New York. New York State passed its own temporary rent control law in 1950, and, in 1962, the state granted New York City the power to enact its own rent control measure, which turned out to be most definitely not temporary. Middle-class New Yorkers—and some upper-middle-class New Yorkers—loved rent control. In 1974, Congressman Ed Koch lived in a rent-controlled Greenwich Village apartment paying $250 per month, half what it would go for on the open market.[6] But rent control lowered the value of residential buildings, reducing tax revenues and incentives for landlords to improve properties to make them more valuable.

The cost of the city's payroll dwarfed the cost of welfare benefits and rent control. The proximate cause of this was the unionization of the municipal workforce. Prior to 1958, New York City employees were not legally permitted to bargain collectively.

That changed on March 31 of that year when Mayor Wagner signed an executive order granting the unions the right to collective bargaining—to negotiate with the city on behalf of municipal employees. As the power of the political clubhouse waned during the 1960s, the union hall filled that vacuum. Union dues found their way into the coffers of pro-labor politicians, and union members staffed their campaign office phone banks and canvassed their neighborhoods. If you counted all of the city's public employee union members and their adult immediate family members who were registered voters, you quickly calculated that they cast enough votes to elect the winner of every mayoral Democratic primary. As Victor Gotbaum, president of District Council 37 of the American Federation of State, County and Municipal Employees, New York City's largest union, stated in 1965: "We have the ability, in a sense, to elect our own boss."

ON JANUARY 1, 1966, THE DAY JOHN LINDSAY WAS INAUGURATED, Michael Quill, the sixty-year-old, fiery Irish-born founder and president of the Transit Workers Union, proceeded to call a strike, stopping dead in their tracks the city's subways. The strike was illegal, and on January 4, Quill was ordered arrested by New York State Supreme Court Judge Abraham N. Geller. When the police arrived to arrest Quill before the television cameras, he shook his fist in defiance and spat: "The judge can drop dead in his black robes and we would not call off the strike!" Two hours later, in jail, Quill collapsed with a heart attack. He died two weeks later. Shaken, Lindsay caved to the transit workers' demands, and the city agreed to a generous new contract. It would only be the first lucrative pact agreed to by Lindsay to buy labor peace, and it set the template for union negotiating strategy for the rest of his administration: Request outrageous increases in salaries and pension benefits and favorable work rules, threaten to strike, and settle for very generous increases and improvements to work rules.

With compliant mayors in City Hall, the unions grew more emboldened and successful, winning ever-higher wages, overtime pay, and, most costly, pensions, with the city picking up an ever-increasing share of pension costs. Over time, retirement ages for pension qualification were lowered as benefits increased. For example, by 1974, most New York City teachers were not required to make any contributions at all to their pensions.

It is not surprising, then, that New York City in the mid-1970s spent more per capita—$1,224—than any other city in the country. Boston, the next highest, spent $858. When only taking into account traditional municipal functions, New York City was not the biggest spender, however. It spent $435 per capita, less than Boston, Newark, San Francisco, and Baltimore. While the number of New York City employees increased by nearly 70 percent from 1940 to 1974, and it employed more people per 10,000 residents (585) than any other city except Washington, DC (737), when adjusted to take into account only employees in traditional municipal functions, New York dropped behind Newark, Philadelphia, San Francisco, and Baltimore. Obviously it was the nontraditional operations that accounted for New York City's bloated payroll. Of course, where Ivy League good-government types saw bloat and frowned, a Brooklyn politician's eyes would gleam with joy, as all he saw were patronage jobs and votes.

New York City residents certainly were not undertaxed. Only residents of Boston paid more city taxes. Over 10 percent of all personal income of city residents was paid in taxes to New York City.[7] But since the majority of those taxes went to pay for city employees who could elect their own boss, the political cost of high taxes was more than offset by the votes of loyal union members.

BEAME GENUINELY BELIEVED THAT THE CITY WOULD MAKE IT through those tough times—somehow it would find the money. There was one legacy Beame was hell-bent not to leave. He was not going to be the mayor who shredded the safety net of programs assembled by Fiorello La Guardia, Al Smith, and Franklin Roosevelt that made life for poor people tolerable in New York City (and provided tens of thousands of jobs to be doled out to loyal Democrats). To those who questioned whether New York City needed its own university system in addition to the large New York State University system, Beame would stiffen up to his full sixty-two inches and proudly declare that he would not be where he was today—mayor of New York City—had he not been given a free college education at CCNY. To those who questioned the power of the municipal employee unions over city government, Beame would reach into his wallet and produce his honorary United Federation of Teachers union card and speak of how hard it was to raise a family of four on a teacher's salary before collective bargaining. To those who would bemoan the welfare queens, Beame would dismiss them with a swift wave of the back of his hand and recall what life was like on the Lower East Side before public assistance for impoverished children of single-parent households like himself. Whether he had to beg, borrow, tax, or steal, somehow the money would be found.

15

By the time Beame settled in at City Hall, New York City had lived well beyond its means for over a decade. The city was legally obligated to have a balanced budget—and it was not supposed to be able to borrow to pay ordinary course operating expenses. But somehow it did.

CHAPTER TWO

A BAD DEBT IS BETTER
THAN A GOOD TAX

BEAME'S CLOSEST ADVISORS WERE TWO MEN, FRIENDS FOR decades, also from Brooklyn, one of whom worked for the New York City government his entire career and the other who worked the city government to his advantage his entire career. The man who worked for the city was James A. Cavanagh, and once Beame became mayor, Cavanagh would become first deputy mayor, the number-two man at City Hall. Cavanagh was fifty-nine years old at the time and a thirty-five-year veteran of the New York City civil service, starting as a $15-a-week clerk in the Department of Housing and Buildings. Three years later, Cavanagh transferred to the City Budget Bureau where he soon caught the eye of the legendary civil servant John Carty, who mentored a tight-knit group of protégés known as the "Irish Mafia" who controlled the Budget Bureau well into the 1970s. Born in Bergen Beach, Brooklyn, Cavanagh never lived outside the borough, moving to the slightly nicer neighborhood of Mill

Basin, one mile away, when he advanced up the civil service pay scale.

Beame met Cavanagh in the 1940s when both men worked in the Budget Bureau, and the two quickly developed a genuinely close friendship—as close as brothers, colleagues remembered. Like Beame, Cavanagh was often underestimated because of his physical appearance. If Beame looked like the prototypical short, Jewish accountant from Brooklyn, Cavanagh looked like the fat, amiable, Irish political hack from Brooklyn. Forever struggling with his weight, red-faced and with a shock of white hair, Cavanagh lumbered about the Budget Bureau in baggy brown suits, in turn grandfatherly and kind or stone-cold with barely concealed rage, depending on the budget numbers. And since, like Beame, he was neither glib nor articulate, he made due with as few words as possible when reporters were around. He never attended college, a fact about which he was deeply insecure, as more and more of the Budget Bureau employees arrived from Columbia and NYU in the 1960s. But Cavanagh had a PhD in loyalty, and he was a wizard with numbers.

Cavanagh's special brilliance was finding creative ways to "balance" the New York City expense budget. This talent was especially valued by New York City mayors, for New York City mayors, like mayors everywhere, like nothing more than spending money the city did not have. To so spend was something New York City mayors were not supposed to be able to do, but Cavanagh always seemed to find a way. That was why, in 1970, Mayor Lindsay appointed Cavanagh to head the Budget Bureau.

There were many long-standing public finance laws in New York that made the deficit spending that Cavanagh enabled legally impossible. But what is possible need not be strictly legal.

Like most cities, New York had two budgets: an expense budget and a capital budget. The expense budget set forth the revenues and expenses for the city's operations for the applicable fiscal year. The capital budget provided for the acquisition and improvement of the city's capital assets—buildings, bridges, and the like—with a useful life longer than one year and the financing thereof, often using long-term debt. The expenses in the operating budget were not legally permitted to be financed with long-term debt—only with short-term debt that would be repaid with revenues received in the same fiscal year. The New York City Charter required the city to balance its expense budget, meaning that no borrowing not to be repaid intra-year was to be used to finance expenses during any fiscal year. The New York City Charter also required the City Council to set the annual real estate tax at a level that would produce a balanced expense budget. This taxing authority was not unlimited, however, as the New York State Constitution capped the real estate tax rate at two and one-half percent of the five-year average valuation of taxable real estate in the city.

By law, the mayor was required to submit the expense budget to the City Council and the Board of Estimate by April 15 of each year (New York City's fiscal year began on July 1 and ended on June 30 of the succeeding year). The City Council and the Board of Estimate then had the opportunity to modify the expense budget, but the mayor could reject the proposed modifications by veto. It required a two-thirds majority in both the City Council and the Board of Estimate to override the mayor's veto. The capital budget went through essentially the same approval procedure.

Another law that made the 1975 fiscal crisis legally impossible was the New York State Constitution's municipal general debt limit. Article 8, Section 5, of the New York State Constitution limited the amount of long-term debt New York City could issue for any purpose to 10 percent of the latest five-year average valuation of taxable real estate in the city. There were, however, important exceptions to the general debt limit—exceptions that were abused, illegally at times, by the city to borrow beyond its means.

New York City was permitted under the New York State Constitution to issue short-term debt to smooth out the mismatch in timing between operating expenses—which were payable at roughly equal monthly amounts throughout the year—and revenues—which were much more lumpy, as various taxes were due annually or quarterly, and federal and state government aid to the city was also paid unequally throughout the year. To "smooth out" these timing mismatches, the city would issue tax anticipation notes (TANs) and revenue anticipation notes (RANs), intended to be repaid when the corresponding tax or federal or state aid revenue was received later in the fiscal year.

The New York State Constitution provided for another exception to the general debt limit for debt incurred to finance low-rent housing, nursing homes for low-income patients, and urban renewal projects in an amount not to exceed two and one-half percent of the latest five-year average valuation of taxable real estate in the city.

A third exception was debt incurred by city government-sponsored entities that technically was not a debt obligation of the city. For example, debt issued by a stadium authority created by the city to be paid by turnstile revenue and concession revenue and not backed by the "full faith and credit" of the city would not be counted as debt for purposes of the constitutional general debt limit.

The legal requirement for a balanced municipal budget is, even in the best of fiscal times, aspirational. Budgets are by their nature a guess or projection, only as useful as the good faith that goes into preparing them, and good faith was in short supply in New York City budget making during the decade leading up to the fiscal crisis. For example, you may in good faith budget average snow removal costs for a year that ends up with record snowfall and be very wrong, or you might in bad faith budget for no snow removal costs to help balance an actually unbalanced budget and also be very wrong. Revenues too can be budgeted in bad faith. For example, in the midst of a recession with soaring unemployment, it could be assumed that income tax receipts won't decline. Cavanagh routinely budgeted for 100 percent payment of real estate taxes when actual payment rates were consistently less than 95 percent.

Other, more creative gimmicks were used by Cavanagh to "balance" the New York City expense budget. Long-term borrowing to finance the capital budget was as perfectly legal and proper as borrowing to finance the expense budget was illegal and improper. Article VIII of the New York State Constitution prohibited the city from issuing long-term debt with a maturity longer than the useful life of the asset purchased with the proceeds of that debt. Notwithstanding the legalities, over time, more and more expense items were mischaracterized as capital improvements and shifted from the expense budget into the capital budget. In the eleven-year period through 1975, over $2.4 billion of expenses were stuffed into the capital budget, $722 million in 1975 alone. While a school building is clearly a capital asset and, perhaps, textbooks as well, paying teachers' salaries clearly is not. No matter. Cavanagh's Budget Bureau deemed a portion of teachers' salaries to be "teacher training," useful over the entire career of a teacher—magically, therefore, a capital expenditure and not an expense—justifying more long-term New York City bonds to finance teachers' salaries. To get air cover for many of these specious characterizations, the city, time and again, obtained legislation from Albany legally and conclusively deeming ordinary goods and services to have multiyear useful lives so that they could be included in the capital budget rather than the expense budget and financed with the proceeds of long-term debt.[1]

The constitutional general debt limit exception for short-term debt to smooth over timing differences between when revenues were received and expenses paid was also abused to mask deficit spending. TANs were properly issued in anticipation of real estate tax payments. But if real estate tax receivables were no good—say, the owner of the building was bankrupt—those receivables should be written off and certainly not borrowed against.

Cavanagh did borrow against bad receivables, and worse. He included tax-exempt properties—like foreign embassies—on the tax rolls, issued phony tax bills for those properties, and borrowed against them. And what happened when those phony taxes were never paid? The city just rolled over the unpaid balance into another TANs issue, finding more uncollectible real estate taxes to support the notes. This was playing with fiscal fire even in the low-interest rate environment of the 1960s, but it was explosive in the high-interest rate 1970s, as the accrued interest on the TANs, properly issued or not, had to be repaid. The fraud and manipulation of the real estate tax rolls got so bad that by June 30, 1975, the New York State Comptroller, after auditing the city's tax rolls, found that 80 percent of the unpaid real estate taxes recorded on the city's books was uncollectible.[2]

Unfortunately, the city had issued $380 million of TANs supported in reality by only $106 million in collectible real estate taxes.[3] Later, on August 29, 1975, the Municipal Assistance Corporation required the city to write-off even that $106 million as doubtful as to collection.

Cavanagh played similar games with state and federal aid, which together accounted for approximately 40 percent of city revenues. RANs were originally intended to smooth out revenue and expense mismatches by borrowing short term to cover expenses until the related federal or state aid payments in the current fiscal year were paid. That limited borrowing to one year's aid at most. That changed in 1965 when Mayor Wagner, finding to his sorrow but not surprise that the city was broke, went hat in hand to Albany to ask for a slight change in the public finance law that would help solve the city's money problems: allow the city to issue RANs not just backed by the current fiscal year's anticipated aid, but also the following fiscal year's. Enabling legislation from Albany soon followed.[4] Only Standard & Poor's (S&P) and Moody's seemed to notice, temporarily downgrading the city's credit rating to Baa from A as a result of this fiscal sleight of hand.

One problem that Cavanagh had in borrowing against state and federal aid to be received was that he had no accurate estimate of what that aid might actually be. Each department of city government conducted its own negotiations for federal and state aid grants, and there was no central accounting for any of it. And like real estate tax receivables, federal and state aid receivables stayed on the books—and were borrowed against—long after they were obviously uncollectible. For example, the city would borrow one hundred cents on the dollar for every claim for Medicaid reimbursement submitted to the federal government when experience showed that a significant portion of those claims would be disallowed. By 1975, hundreds of millions of dollars of questionable Medicaid receivables remained on the books and were borrowed against. Of course, overestimating federal and state aid also made balancing the expense budget easier, so no one blew the whistle on this until it was too late. By 1975, $963 million of the city's accumulated budget deficit of $5.1 billion was attributable to uncollected (and uncollectible) federal and state aid receivables.[5] By June 30, 1975, New York City had $2.56 billion of RANs outstanding.[6] In Cavanagh's immortal words: "A bad loan is better than a good tax."[7]

The city further abused its debt issuing powers by creating agencies such as the Educational Development Fund, the Housing Development Corporation, and the Transit Construction Fund to issue off-balance-sheet debt not subject to the constitutional general debt limit. In 1974, the city petitioned Albany to form the Stabilization Reserve Corporation (SRC) to help the city refinance its short-term debt by the issuance of up to $500 million of ten-year bonds. The legality of the SRC was challenged in court, and it never issued any bonds. Nevertheless, Cavanagh, to help balance the expense budget, established a $150 million receivable on the city's books from the SRC in 1974 for the proceeds of those bonds that were never issued and a $370 million receivable in 1975 for proceeds of SRC bonds that likewise would never be issued.

The city also manipulated the financing of the middle-income state housing program, Mitchell-Lama, to artificially reduce financing costs. After a housing development was completed, its rents were supposed to cover the costs of its long-term mortgage bonds. Pending completion, the city helped finance projects by issuing short-term bond anticipation notes (BANs), notes intended to be refinanced with long-term mortgage bonds after the project had been completed and tenants began paying rent. The interest rates on the short-term BANs were typically lower than the interest rates on long-term mortgage bonds, so the city simply kept rolling over the BANs into more BANs long after projects were completed and fully occupied in order to keep rents lower and tenants (i.e., voters) happy.

Another honeypot for fiscal chicanery was the city's public employee pension funds. Perhaps the most egregious larceny involving the city's pensions was their underfunding. Cavanagh used actuarial assumptions about mortality not updated since the 1930s, when life expectancies were many years shorter. The city also funded its pensions every two years, in arrears, rather than annually, effectively a permanent one-year loan from the pension funds to the city. By 1975, the cumulative deficit of pension funding was $12.2 billion. The city also paid to itself from the pension funds what it called "excess interest"—any return on pension fund assets in excess of 4 percent in any year. While this may have been tolerable during the low inflation, low interest rate era before the late 1960s, in the high inflation, high interest environment of the 1970s, a 4 percent return wouldn't keep pace with inflation. This "excess interest" in 1975 transferred $261 million from the pension funds to the city. It wasn't the pensioners that were put at risk because of this maneuver—the city was obligated under the New York State Constitution to pay retirees their pensions regardless of whether there were enough assets in the pension funds to do so—it was future taxpayers who would foot the bill.

A balanced budget only has meaning if the accounting principles used in preparing it are fair and reasonable. The New York City expense budget for years before the crisis was prepared by Cavanagh in accordance with accounting principles later described as "accrual basis for revenues and cash basis for expenses." For example, in 1973, the city decided to bill in advance eighteen months of water use charges, rather than the usual twelve months, yielding an additional $52.5 million in revenue, and Cavanagh recognized all of it in fiscal 1973, even though one-third of the expenses of providing the water would be borne by the city in the next fiscal year. In 1974, the city had the sewer bills for fiscal 1975 payable on June 30, 1974, rather than July 1, 1975, allowing Cavanagh to book all of fiscal 1975's sewer bill revenue in fiscal 1974. The city then issued TANs against these future fiscal year tax revenues as well, further cannibalizing future cash flows. The city would also delay expenses by pushing them into the next fiscal year. For example, Cavanagh decided that teachers would be paid on July 1, covering the second half of June, if the regular two-week pay cycle had that payment occurring the last week of June. City vendors would see June—and with growing frequency May and April—bills not paid until July. All of these gimmicks, of course, only made matters worse for the eventual day of reckoning.

And when all of Cavanagh's tricks failed to "balance" the expense budget, city politicians would again go hat in hand to Albany and request a state law that overrode the New York City Charter provision prohibiting borrowing to balance the expense budget and to give them authority to issue debt on an emergency basis to alleviate a cash crunch. Requesting this emergency debt, referred to as series bonds or budget notes, became a more or less annual event. Don't blame just the Democrats. Republican Mayor John Lindsay was as bad as Democrat Mayor Robert Wagner in requesting special debt authority, and Republican Governor Rockefeller and the Republican Senate always obliged. A bad debt is better than a good tax.

But these on-the-record contrivances tell only half the story. For every real estate tax bill issued, there is an appraisal and, quite often, an appeal of that appraisal. At the appeal hearing, a case can be made to lower the value a building is appraised for, thereby reducing the tax the owner pays. For builders proposing new buildings or renovations of existing ones, there is the opportunity to negotiate tax breaks and rebates and other types of city subsidies. For all of those, you need a lawyer, or more particularly, what is referred to as a "land-use" lawyer. Even more particularly, the land-use lawyer to see in New York City in the 1970s (and the 1960s and 1950s, for that matter) was a genial, gregarious fellow named Abraham M. Lindenbaum, known to all as Bunny. And Bunny made it his business to be known to all in New York City government who taxed, zoned, or otherwise affected the value of New York City real estate. All who knew Bunny agreed that he was a man who knew how to return a favor. Bunny also happened to be that second close advisor to and decades-old friend of Beame—the one who worked New York City government to his advantage so successfully.

Bunny, like his friend Beame, was a member of the legendary Madison Democratic Club in Crown Heights, Brooklyn. Bunny too rose to become an election captain there. After Bunny graduated law school in the 1930s, he specialized in real estate law. He first went to work for one of the borough's largest title insurance companies. After ten years there, Bunny opened his own real estate law firm with a partner, Sidney Young, working in a cramped, one-room office. Bunny's life changed when he met an up-and-coming Brooklyn developer named Fred Trump. As Trump's real estate empire took shape, Bunny's practice grew. Soon, Bunny's firm was taking an entire floor of offices at 16 Court Street in downtown Brooklyn.

Fred Trump, born in the Bronx in 1905, inherited a modest real estate business from his father and masterfully took advantage of government financing and subsidies to build an outer-borough real estate empire. During the Great Depression, Trump loaded up on federal government loan subsidies under the National Housing Act of 1934 to build residential housing in Brooklyn and Queens. When World War II came, Trump built housing for the federal government to house workers at the Brooklyn Navy Yard. After the war, Trump built federal- and New York State–subsidized middle-income housing projects for returning veterans in Brooklyn. In the 1960s, Trump built his largest complex, Trump Village in Coney Island. At his peak, Fred Trump owned nearly 30,000 housing units in Brooklyn and Queens. In 1968, Fred's son Donald joined the family business and became its president in 1971.

There is a natural symbiotic relationship between real estate developers and politicians. Land, particularly in New York City, is perhaps the most regulated asset in existence. Local government records determine who legally owns land and who has a valid mortgage thereon. Local zoning laws determine what you can do with the land you own. Local government can take land from one owner by eminent domain and make it available to a developer. In many jurisdictions, the local government itself is one of the largest landowners—it can sell or lease that land to a favored developer or deny it to a disfavored one. Local government also finances itself in large part by the taxes it levies on land and transactions involving it. Governments at all levels have, since the New Deal era, financed the development of land—with mortgages, loan guarantees, tax incentives, and outright grants.

The relationship between real estate developers and politicians is not a one-way street by any stretch. Real estate developers are major employers. Those jobs can be handed out to members in good standing of the Madison Democratic Club. Developers buy, in bulk, concrete and steel and glass and carpeting and dozens of other products, which can be purchased from suppliers in good standing with the party bosses. Developers need insurance of all kinds, and there were many insurance brokers in the clubhouses of Brooklyn. And, of course, real estate developers need lawyers.

At all the points of contact between the government and the real estate developers, Bunny could be found. With an encyclopedic knowledge of the laws, rules, and regulations governing New York City real estate, and the zoning and taxing thereof, and of the human beings who decided that zoning and taxing, Bunny's reputation spread as the man to see in Brooklyn if you wanted to build something. Bunny, wired into the borough of Brooklyn by way of the Madison Democratic Club, could tell a developer which person in the deeds office had a son who needed a summer job cutting grass at one of the developer's buildings, which zoning official had an elderly mother who would really appreciate a ground-floor apartment close to a bus line, which city councilman had a brother-in-law in the food truck business that might do well selling burgers at a construction site.

As Bunny rose up in the Madison Democratic Club, he thought it would be beneficial for all if his client Fred Trump met his friend Beame, and thereafter Fred and Abe were closely acquainted. Through Beame, Bunny met Mayor Wagner in the 1950s, and on the strength of that relationship, Bunny's business entered Manhattan, the world's biggest and toughest game when it came to real estate. Bunny took what he learned in Brooklyn, applied it in Manhattan, and came to even more success.

In 1960, Bunny was appointed by Mayor Wagner to replace Robert Moses on the City Planning Commission, but was forced to resign in 1961 when he was caught doing what earned him the seat on the commission in the first place—soliciting campaign contributions for Wagner from builders who did business with the city.[8] Bunny's law practice did not suffer in the least from what some not knowledgeable about the ways of New York City might call a scandal.

In the ten-year period ending 1975, Bunny's clients received more zoning variances than clients of any other attorney in New York City.[9] Bunny's clients also got the highest proportion of reduced real estate taxes from the City Tax Commission.[10] In addition to Trump, Bunny's clients included developer William Zeckendorf Jr., William Kaufman, Peter J. Sharp, the New York Real Estate Board, the Tisch family, and the Roman Catholic Archdiocese of New York. Like fellow Brooklynite Anthony Scotto, Bunny was a major contributor to Governor Carey's 1974 campaign ($20,000), but not as generous as his client Fred Trump's contribution to Carey's campaign ($25,000).[11]

No one will ever know the true tally of the hundreds of millions of dollars (possibly billions of dollars) of real estate tax revenues New York City never received because of the skillful lawyering of Bunny Lindenbaum. And Bunny was just the best of his breed. There were dozens of other politically connected land-use lawyers providing similar services to lesser developers and landlords.

Beame was impeccably honest in his own personal financial dealings. He had never taken a dime out of the city till that he hadn't honestly earned. But when it came to the practices of others from the clubhouse, the Madison Democratic Club in particular, Beame did not judge. The ends had to be looked at when evaluating the means. It was easy to condemn Cavanagh's machinations when viewed myopically. But the money he was able to produce helped real people in real need. The people want the firehouse down the block to be adequately staffed. They want daily trash pickups. They want the local hospital emergency room open. They want the neighborhood patrolled by the police cars. They want the special education programs for the intellectually disabled children. Was it wrong for Bunny to trade favors for zoning waivers for Fred Trump? Good luck getting a high-rise built in New York City, with all the rules and red tape and environmental impact statements required by the laws the Lindsay good-government types put on the books. But those buildings created affordable housing and offices for good-paying jobs so that working people can afford to live in that housing, and those developers pay taxes on those buildings to pay for the latest lefty do-gooder program. The people do not want a mayor they can canonize; they want a mayor who keeps the city running. Beame was going to keep the city running, as it always had.

CHAPTER THREE

A FACTORY OF LEGAL GRAFT

IT'S NEVER A CRISIS UNTIL THE MONEY RUNS OUT. DESPITE THE demographic deterioration, economic downturn, and fiscal irresponsibility, the municipal bond market kept buying New York City bonds and notes at attractive rates for the city throughout the Wagner and Lindsay administrations. Budget deficits, accounting gimmicks, rating agency admonitions, graft, and waste were all shrugged off by Wall Street, which kept the money pouring in, in ever-increasing amounts. The fiscal crisis didn't arrive until the financial markets—the buyers of the city's debt, particularly its short-term notes—said "no more." That this happened when it did had as much to do with financial market factors as it did with the city's fiscal condition.

The most important factor was simple supply and demand. New York City, with $14 billion of debt, accounted for nearly 10 percent of all municipal debt in the United States by 1975. Its $6 billion of short-term debt accounted for nearly 30 percent of all short-term municipal debt.[1] Simple principles of portfolio diversification dictate that municipal bond funds not hold over 10 percent of their portfolios in one city's debt securities. Simply put, by 1975, New York City had saturated the municipal bond market with its paper, and the limit had been reached.

Another factor was that the financial asset class of municipal bonds was less attractive in 1975 than it was in previous years. Interest on New York City municipal bonds was exempt from federal and New York State income tax, making them attractive investments for investors taxed at high rates, like banks and high-income individuals. Because they were tax-free, municipal bonds carried a lower interest rate than corporate bonds of comparable quality that were taxable. By 1975, after two years of recession and stock and bond market losses, many banks and high-income individuals had losses available to offset taxable income, and lower-yielding tax-free municipal bonds were no longer a good investment for them. By early 1975, banks, historically the largest buyers of municipal bonds, were net sellers of municipal bonds.[2] Despite this pullback, state and local governments and agencies, desperate for cash as a result of the recession, issued 20 percent more debt in the first half of 1975 than they did in 1974.[3] One of the smart things Beame did when he was city comptroller under Mayor Wagner and Mayor Lindsay was to divest the city's public employee pension funds of tax-free New York City bonds, as the pension funds were tax-exempt. In 1962, two-thirds of the assets of those pension funds (approximately $2 billion) were invested in New York City bonds. But that divestment had to be absorbed by the municipal bond market and, by 1975, it had the effect of crowding out demand for new city bond issuances.[4]

In addition to the supply and demand imbalance, there were very real concerns about New York City's short-term debt burden and the possibility that if a market disruption occurred, the city might default on one of its nearly monthly refinancing of portions of that debt. In the six years from 1969 to 1975, New York City increased its short-term debt sixfold.[5] All of that increase took place during a rising interest rate environment, putting additional strain on the city's cash flow. In 1975, 14 percent of the city's expense budget was devoted to debt service.[6]

There were also serious concerns among well-informed institutional investors about where the city's short-term debt would rank as to payment priority in any bankruptcy or debt reorganization. The New York State Constitution provided that bondholders had a "first lien" on all city revenue in the event of default; but many legal experts believed that the "first lien" only applied to debt issued under the constitutional general debt limit or the low-income housing limit. The principal of TANs, RANs, and BANs might rank junior to those other categories of debt.[7] There were also questions as to the legality of TANs issued against phony taxes, RANs issued against nonexistent federal and state aid revenues, and BANs issued after projects were completed. Might those notes be subordinated to debt that was lawfully issued? All these questions troubled the municipal bond market in 1975.

NEW YORK CITY WASN'T ALONE IN ABUSING BORROWING PRIVIleges, it was just the worst offender. The nation's second worst offender was New York State, which had been engaging in its own money tricks for nearly sixteen years with the arrival in Albany of New York's longest-serving governor, Nelson Rockefeller.

Some speculate that Nelson's promiscuous spending on behalf of the state was born out of the circumstances of his birth as the grandson of the richest American of all time, John D. Rockefeller Sr., the nation's first billionaire and the founder of the Standard Oil Company. Nelson, born in 1908, was the second of the five sons, and third of six children, of John D. Rockefeller Jr., the only son of Nelson Sr. and grew up, as one might imagine, in want of nothing, shuttled by limousine between the family's nine-story townhouse at 10 West 54th Street in Manhattan, a 3,500-acre estate at Pocantico Hills in Westchester County and a summer home on Mount Desert Island in Seal Harbor, Maine. The five Rockefeller boys were raised by their philanthropist father to be "muscular Christians," religious, patriotic, and competitive. Nelson did not need encouragement in the competitive department, having believed from early childhood that he was destined for great things. He told his siblings this was so because he had been born on the same day as his grandfather, without question an omen of greatness.

After high school at New York City's Lincoln School, Nelson attended Dartmouth College, where he was active in student government. He ran twice for student body president and lost, although he was elected vice president, an omen that Nelson apparently did not notice. After graduation in 1930, Nelson married Mary Todhunter Clark, a Philadelphia girl from a prominent family he had met four years earlier at Seal Harbor, and went to work in the family office at Rockefeller Center where he spent a decade successfully running a number of business ventures.

In 1940, Nelson received a call from James Forrestal, the Dillon Read investment bank partner on loan to the Roosevelt administration. Nelson's successful business ventures in Latin America had caught FDR's eye, and the president wanted Nelson to serve in the newly created position of coordinator of the Office of Inter-American Affairs (OIAA). With World War II raging, Roosevelt was concerned about Nazi Germany's overtures to Latin American nations, appealing to the anti-American feelings there. Nelson was personally well liked by many leaders in the region, and Roosevelt believed he would be the perfect man to thwart Hitler's influence there. It was at the OIAA where Nelson first acquired a reputation as a big spender: his budget in 1940 was $3.5 million; by 1944, it was $140 million. As the war wound down, Nelson was given the job of assistant secretary of state for American Republic Affairs. But then FDR died, and President Truman's secretary of state, James Byrnes, was not a fan of Nelson's, and Nelson left the State Department in August 1945.

Back in private life, Nelson tended to his numerous business and philanthropic interests during the Truman years. After Eisenhower was elected, Nelson was called to public service again, as undersecretary of the Department of Health, Education and Welfare (HEW). After eight months at HEW, President Eisenhower moved Nelson into the White House as special assistant for Cold War strategy, which was a fancy title for being Ike's eyes and ears at the CIA and FBI. What Nelson really wanted was a cabinet position, preferably secretary of defense. When it became clear to Nelson that he had no path to advancement, he resigned in December 1955. Nelson had already decided his next move.

New York Republicans were salivating at the prospect of running Nelson as their candidate against Governor William Averell Harriman in 1958, and Nelson thought Harriman would be the perfect opponent for him. As the millionaire son of railroad tycoon Edward Henry Harriman, Averell could hardly make an issue out of Nelson trying to buy the election. And Harriman could not run as a "good government" candidate, because he had gotten into bed with Carmine DeSapio and the Tammany machine in order to secure the Democratic nomination in 1954.

Few predicted it, but Nelson was an absolute hit among the working-class voters of New York—he was a natural retail politician. The Puerto Ricans loved him for speaking fluent Spanish to them in East Harlem. The Blacks loved that he campaigned in their neighborhoods on the back of a flatbed truck with a piano—played by Count Basie. The Irish and Italians loved his "Hiya, Fella" greeting and pats on the back as he canvassed their neighborhoods—and the middle fingers Nelson would pitch to his hecklers. The lefty Americans for Democratic Action types could never figure out how their beloved working-class voters went for the larger-than-life millionaire. Despite it being a terrible year for Republicans—Democrats gained forty-nine seats in the US House, fifteen seats in the Senate, and six gubernatorial seats—Nelson beat Harriman by ten percentage points.

As governor of New York—and a Rockefeller—Nelson was immediately a national political figure and a contender for the 1960 presidential Republican nomination. While Nelson decided not to run that year, he made Richard Nixon grovel for his endorsement. Nixon had to come to New York and pay homage to Nelson in his thirty-two-room Fifth Avenue apartment two days before the convention and agree to a number of liberal-leaning changes to the party platform to appease

Nelson. That deal—the "Treaty of Fifth Avenue," the press called it—angered the conservative base of the Republican Party, who thought it more a Republican Munich Treaty. After Nixon lost the razor-thin vote to John F. Kennedy (Kennedy told intimates he would have lost to Rockefeller), Nelson was the odds-on favorite for the 1964 Republican nomination.

Nelson shared a political liability with John F. Kennedy: he was an inveterate skirt chaser. But unlike Kennedy, whose dalliances were never serious, Nelson got smitten. He had taken up with Margaret "Happy" Murphy, wife of a family friend and retainer. On November 18, 1961, Nelson announced he was separating from his wife. In a cruel twist of fate, the next day, Nelson was informed that his son Michael had gone missing in New Guinea and was presumed dead (his body was never found). On May 4, 1963, Nelson and Happy were married. Columnist Stewart Alsop observed that Nelson could become president or remarry, but not both (given the higher moral standards Americans held their presidents to in those days).

Despite the naysayers, Nelson plowed ahead and ran for president in 1964, spending millions in the Republican primaries. But Nelson's millions couldn't shake off the "character issue." Barry Goldwater easily won the nomination. Embittered, Nelson took the fight against Goldwater all the way to the floor of the convention in San Francisco, one of the most divisive in Republican Party history. Conservatives took to calling Rockefeller the "Great Wrecker," not just of the Murphy home in 1961, but of the Republican Party in 1964. Nelson ran again for the presidency in 1968. After Nixon's strong showing in New Hampshire—winning with 78 percent to Nelson's 11 percent—Nelson quickly dropped out. But after Robert F. Kennedy was assassinated in June, Nelson reentered the race, somehow believing he could capture the votes of young people and liberals who backed RFK. His resurrected campaign went nowhere.

Nelson was reelected to a record fourth term as New York governor in 1970, easily beating former Supreme Court Justice Arthur Goldberg by twelve percentage points. But with Nixon in the White House poised for reelection in 1972, time was running out for Nelson, who would be sixty-eight years old in 1976—then thought by some to be too old for the office.

But then came Watergate. And in October 1973, Vice President Spiro Agnew was forced to resign over a bribery scandal. When Nixon selected Congressman Gerald Ford to replace Agnew, Nelson saw one last chance for the presidency. With Agnew out and the accidental Vice President Ford saddled with Nixon's Watergate baggage, the 1976 Republican presidential nomination was up for grabs. While California Governor Ronald Reagan, the favorite of the conservatives, would certainly be in the race, Nelson thought, correctly, that given the shellacking the Republicans took in 1964 with a right-wing candidate, the party would be hesitant to hand the nomination to another right-winger.

But there was the problem of 1974. Nelson was up for reelection, and New York State was facing a looming fiscal catastrophe that he knew better than anyone might hit at any moment. After mulling it over for weeks, Nelson settled on a solution. He would announce that he would not be running for a fifth term in 1974 and, to give his lieutenant governor, Malcom Wilson, his handpicked successor, a leg up for the Republican nomination, he would resign on December 31, 1973, so Wilson could run as the incumbent (and hold the bag when the state's finances went to hell). The 1976 presidential election was three years away. Plenty of time for Nelson to distance himself from New York's problems.

And unfettered with the responsibilities of office, Nelson could campaign full-time, scouring the country for delegates.

To Nelson's delight, Nixon's Watergate problems only worsened during the months following his stepping down as governor. On August 4, 1974, Nixon resigned. Three weeks later, President Ford called and offered Nelson the vice presidency. At the time, many pundits thought Ford, now the accidental president, would not run for a term in his own right in 1976. Nelson would be a heartbeat away and, untainted by Watergate, he would be the obvious choice to fend off Reagan. Nelson quickly accepted. He was easily confirmed vice president by Congress, despite lengthy and intrusive hearings that delayed his swearing in until December 10. The most noteworthy disclosures involved Nelson's wealth: he was "only" worth $218 million. Most estimates in the press before the hearings put the number at ten times that amount. The public was disappointed. They wanted him to be much richer than that. What was the country coming to in 1974, when Rockefellers weren't even billionaires anymore?

On September 8, 1974, Ford pardoned Nixon and his popularity plummeted. The moderate Republicans were looking for a candidate to beat Reagan, memories of 1964 and Barry Goldwater's thrashing by Lyndon Johnson were still fresh in their minds. Nelson was starting to look like a viable candidate, and Nelson started believing that 1976 would be the year his quest for the presidency would be fulfilled. But there was the problem of New York's fiscal mess.

The New York State fiscal crisis coming to a head in 1974 was born out of Nelson Rockefeller's grandiose building plans. Year after year, Nelson would propose gargantuan spending and borrowing for housing programs—to the delight of developers like Fred Trump. Nelson's ambitious plans, however, were often

41

stymied by the voters when they rejected his referenda for new bond issues backed by the "full faith and credit" of the state. For decades, states had created agencies to get around the referendum requirement by having agencies issue debt and not the state. New York State first issued agency debt in 1921, with the creation of the Port Authority of New York. But without credit support from the state, the bond market wouldn't buy the agency's bonds unless they were "self-liquidating," a fancy way of saying the revenues generated by the agency would be more than sufficient to pay the interest and principal on the bonds. That requirement worked when building a bridge or turnpike where tolls would more than cover the debt service costs. It didn't work, for example, when building low-income housing where rents paid by less-than-credit-worthy tenants were to be relied on. The solution to this problem was developed in 1954 by a municipal bond lawyer from New York named John Mitchell, who would later become President Nixon's US attorney general (and, after that, a federal prisoner as a result of his involvement in Watergate).

Mitchell's idea, originally conceived for a federal school building program, was for an agency to issue debt with the state agreeing, if the agency can't repay the debt, to ask the state legislature to approve funds to pay the debt. The state would not be obligated legally to pay the agency's debt, but would have a "moral obligation" to do so. Congress didn't like Mitchell's idea, but Nelson Rockefeller loved it. Five years later when Rockefeller created the New York State Housing Finance Agency (HFA), he had the HFA go to market with an offering of Mitchell's "moral obligation" bonds, and the municipal bond investors bought them. Rockefeller had found a way to finance 125,000 new middle-income housing units each year for the next fifteen years.

Nine years later, Governor Rockefeller wanted to create another housing agency to build low-income housing, called the Urban Development Corporation (UDC). The problem with the UDC was that its occupants would be much greater credit risks than those of the HFA, and the legislature was concerned that the "moral obligation" would soon be an actual one. But Rocky never let a crisis go to waste, and in the wake of the rioting after the Martin Luther King Jr. assassination in April 1968, he made approval of the UDC a racial issue—if you opposed building more ghetto housing, you might well be a bigot. Rocky got his UDC. But by 1974, the UDC was in trouble. It was only a matter of time before the state would have to step in. As the state dithered, UDC bondholders seethed.

To make matters worse, New York State and a number of its agencies were not treating municipal bondholders very well. A major dispute broke out in June 1974 when Governor Malcom Wilson signed legislation that permitted the Port Authority of New York and New Jersey to acquire the money-losing PATH train system. Legislation was required because in 1961, as part of the deal with bondholders to get funding for the construction of the World Trade Center, Governor Rockefeller agreed to a law prohibiting the Port Authority from acquiring any more money-losing railroads, which would degrade the Port Authority's credit rating. Governor Wilson repealed that law to allow the PATH acquisition, even though hundreds of millions of Port Authority bonds had been issued in reliance on Rockefeller's promise. The next day, United States Trust Company, the trustee for $96.5 million of those bonds, filed suit for breach of contract and due process violations. The litigation would continue throughout 1975 and worked itself all the way up to the US

Supreme Court. On April 27, 1977, the Supreme Court ruled in favor of the bondholders.[8]

The SRC's difficulties also spooked the municipal bond market in 1974. As discussed earlier, the SRC was formed as a "moral obligation" entity of the city to assist in refinancing $520 million of short-term debt. The city had no legal obligation to pay the SRC bonds, but if it failed to do so, the state was obligated to pay stock transfer tax revenues owing to the city over to the SRC to service its bonds. A taxpayer filed suit claiming that the SRC was a "mere conduit" formed to circumvent the general debt limit provision of the New York State Constitution and lacked any legitimate corporate purpose. With the legal status of the SRC in limbo, no bonds were ever issued, and by the time the New York Court of Appeals upheld the SRC in 1975, as a result of the city's then-raging fiscal crisis, the SRC's ability to issue bonds was nil. But the SRC legal challenge cast doubt on the theretofore assumed legality of city agency moral obligation debt.

WHAT NEVER WAS LITIGATED IN A COURTROOM OR DRAFTED IN a bond indenture was whether or not all of the billions of proceeds of those bond issuances found their way into uses that produced a public benefit. In truth, many of those proceeds went to sweetheart deals for the politically influential. For example, in 1965, the Pennsylvania Railroad was nearly bankrupt and went looking to the State of New York for a bailout. The state ultimately agreed to buy the Long Island Rail Road (LIRR) from the Pennsylvania Railroad Company for $65 million, $60 million of which was used to repay a loan to Citibank, which would never have been paid in full in a bankruptcy. Arthur Levitt, the state comptroller, later issued a report that the LIRR was not worth $65 million, but because of the liabilities assumed by the state, was worth a negative $65 million and that the state would have to borrow $200 million to modernize the railroad. But bonds were issued, and Citibank got its money back. The deal was proposed by a special state committee formed to consider what to do with the LIRR, and on that committee was Eben Pyne, a senior vice president of Citibank. The lawyer recommended by Governor Rockefeller and selected by the state legislature to negotiate the deal for the state was William A. Shea.[9]

There was no one who believed for a second that Bill Shea was taken to the cleaners in the negotiations over the LIRR purchase. Bill Shea simply did what he always did: delivered what his clients wanted. Although Shea's client was nominally the State of New York in the LIRR matter, he took instructions from the state's legislative leaders in Albany. There are many reasons why those legislative leaders might want to arrange to have the taxpayers of the State of New York State bail Citibank out of a very bad loan. For example, Citibank, one of the nation's largest banks, made many loans each year, some of which might be made to friends and family of those same legislative leaders who might have had trouble obtaining loans elsewhere. Citibank also had a well-respected management training program for ambitious, young college graduates, who might as well be children of those same legislative leaders and their campaign contributors. Retired legislative leaders also become lobbyists, and Citibank paid retainers to many lobbyists.

Bill Shea was born in Manhattan in 1907. After graduating from Georgetown on a basketball scholarship and Georgetown Law School thereafter, he attached himself to the Brooklyn Democratic Party, becoming a protégé of John McCooey, the Brooklyn Democratic party chairman. Like Beame and Lindenbaum, Shea became an election captain. Through Joseph T. Sharkey, one of McCooey's successors, Shea met Mayor Wagner in the mid-1950s. When the Brooklyn Dodgers and the New York Giants both left for California in 1957, Wagner, facing much voter criticism for not retaining a National League baseball team, chose Bill Shea to lead a committee to bring the National League back to New York. Through a series of brilliant maneuvers, Shea delivered, and the New York Mets were born in 1962. Mayor Wagner was so grateful he named the Mets stadium in Queens after Shea.

With that, Bill Shea became the most famous lawyer in New York. He was already its most politically powerful. He was a close friend of Beame from Brooklyn Democratic politics, but equally close with Mayor John Lindsay and perhaps closest of all to Governor Nelson Rockefeller. Shea and Rockefeller owned neighboring townhouses on 54th Street in Midtown Manhattan. True political power is bipartisan, and only a very foolish lawyer lets ideology get in the way of a fee.

Bill Shea operated in the fulcrum of connection between politicians and businesspeople much like Bunny Lindenbaum, but on a much larger scale, as Shea touched all manner of enterprises not simply real estate. His was a world of power breakfasts at the Regency, liquid lunches at the 21 Club, and banquets and dinners five nights a week, interrupted by entertaining clients, judges, and elected officials at one his boxes at Madison Square Garden, Yankee Stadium, and, not least of all, Shea Stadium, as Shea was an obsessive sports fan. Well into his sixties, he still bore a resemblance to the strapping college athlete he once was, albeit with the extra weight from all those dinners. Shea made it his business to know everyone worth knowing in New

York City, Albany, and Washington, and when you already knew most everyone worth knowing, those who matter want to know you, which made it easier for Shea to get to know new people worth knowing.

A very critical key to Bill Shea's success was something he learned early on at the knee of John McCooey. Bill Shea learned how to keep his mouth shut. When word spread that you could tell Bill Shea things, however felonious, that stayed with Bill Shea, many people worth knowing came to Bill Shea with their problems. They did not come to Bill Shea because he was an expert in the intricacies of corporate law. He could not cite for you the minutiae of the Clayton Act. But Bill Shea could call a partner who could. He also had the number of the fellow at the Federal Trade Commission (FTC) who oversaw Clayton Act compliance and the number of the assistant US attorney in the Southern District of New York to whom violations of that act would be referred. He also had the private numbers of the chairmen of the House and Senate committees in Washington in charge of oversight of the FTC. And, most importantly, Bill Shea could tell you what was likely to happen to you as a result of your Clayton Act problem because when he called those numbers, they all called back.

Like Anthony Scotto, Bunny Lindenbaum, and Fred Trump, Bill Shea was a major contributor to fellow Brooklynite Hugh Carey's 1974 gubernatorial campaign, giving more than all of them, $46,000. Shea's law firm, Shea & Gould, was not forgotten by Shea's political friends. The firm did more mortgage financing work for the city than any other law firm, often with loans arranged from one of Shea's banking clients, of which he had many, and on some of whose boards of directors he served. The firm also represented many of the city's unions and their pension funds. Shea's power and the largesse it produced at Shea & Gould led journalist Jack Newfield to call the firm "a factory of legal graft."[10] Shea, of course, would never respond to such talk. He'd have his disheveled, brilliant, temperamental litigation partner Milton Gould handle that. "Politically powerful? Ridiculous," Milton told the *New York Times* in 1978. "We are the most misunderstood law firm in New York. We have never been political. You never met people less political in your life."[11]

CHAPTER FOUR

THE WAY TO WASHINGTON

THE FIRST NINE MONTHS OF MAYOR BEAME'S ADMINISTRATION went more or less as most New York City mayoral administrations begin. He blamed his predecessor for the problems he inherited. Most notable of those problems was an expense budget deficit that Beame estimated to be over a billion dollars (he would be correct). Beame pronounced that through austerity measures and better financial management, he had reduced that deficit to under $200 million (he had not). The new city comptroller, Harrison Jay Goldin, told the press that the remaining deficit was much worse than Beame was acknowledging—closer to a half billion dollars (he was right). Beame told the press that Goldin was being a political opportunist (which he undoubtedly was). Goldin was not of the clubhouse; therefore, he was not someone Beame was inclined to assume was reliable. But like it or not, the political fates of both men would be intertwined to a large extent as a result of the crisis.

Goldin was born to a middle-class family in the Bronx in 1936. He graduated as valedictorian from the prestigious Bronx High School of Science and then *summa cum laude* from Princeton. He went on to Yale Law School where he was an editor of the *Yale Law Journal.* From there, he went to the Kennedy Justice Department where he worked in the civil rights division. After a brief stint at the Davis Polk & Wardwell law firm, he ran for a New York State Senate seat in the Bronx in a special election in 1965 as a reform Democrat with the support of Bobby Kennedy, bucking the Bronx machine of Charles Buckley, and won. He ran for city comptroller in 1969, against Beame, losing in the primary. He went back to the State Senate and ran for comptroller again in 1973 and won. Goldin, with his earnest, intellectual demeanor, out-of-fashion wire-rim glasses and bald pate, had the look of a reformer and a very nerdish one. But he was ruthlessly ambitious and not to be taken lightly. As Stanley Friedman, Beame's deputy mayor for intergovernmental affairs, would later describe him: "He has all the attributes of a masterful politician. He is clever, unscrupulous, vicious, articulate and for his own survival at all costs."[1]

The trading of blows by Beame and Goldin was not particularly alarming to anyone, as this was what New York City mayors and comptrollers had been doing to each other for decades. Beame, the comptroller before Goldin, gave Mayor Lindsay and his predecessor, Mayor Wagner, the same fits that Goldin was now giving him. Budget deficits had, for decades, been resolved one way or another, with state aid from Albany, federal aid from Washington, a cooperative municipal bond market, Jim Cavanagh's alchemy; or some combination of all four.

But as the leaves turned and the cool breezes of October arrived in 1974, there came a realization on the trading floors of Wall Street, at the rating agencies and the editorial desk of the *New York Times* that this time it might be different. It was. And so began the first act of the fiscal crisis. It would be played out in the city, in downtown Manhattan, Beame and Goldin at City Hall battling the banks of Wall Street.

On October 2, 1974, the city sold $420 million of BANs at an interest rate of 7.74 percent, the highest rate of interest the city had ever paid on a BANs issue.[2] Alarmed by this, Goldin called a special meeting of the Comptroller's Technical Debt Management Committee, which was comprised of representatives of the comptroller's office and representatives of the major banks that acted as underwriters for the city's debt offerings. At the meeting, the bankers discussed the reasons for the unexpectedly high interest rate—most responsible was the oversupply of city notes in the market—and offered ways to reduce offerings of city debt in the near term to alleviate the oversupply. The bankers warned Goldin that the market for city debt was saturated, and the day was coming when the city would not be able to sell any debt at anything approaching a reasonable interest rate.[3]

Three days later, matters got materially worse for the market for the city's debt. Fitch Investors Services Inc., the third most influential bond rating agency after S&P and Moody's, lowered its credit rating for New York City bonds from A to BBB for maturities prior to 1980 and to BB for maturities thereafter. This was very troubling because many large institutional municipal bond investors were severely limited in the amount of debt rated below A they could buy. If either S&P or Moody's joined Fitch in a downgrade, those limitations would be triggered, as two of the three top ratings agencies would have the rating below A. Fitch blamed the downgrade on growing real estate tax collection delinquencies, the expense budget deficit, and the city's deferral of maintenance on its property—not surprising, given that the capital budget was stuffed with 53 percent expense items.[4]

Beame and Goldin blamed Fitch. On October 22, they put out an ill-advised statement hoping to calm the rebelling municipal bond investors. Rather than acknowledging the severity of the city's fiscal condition, they tried to pull the wool over the eyes of investors by minimizing the city's problems, hoping to buy time to arrange for more state and federal aid or, at minimum, more taxing authority from Albany. They put out a press release that day that asserted the city's credit position had actually improved, notwithstanding what Fitch had to say. It noted that the value of the city's taxable real estate had risen faster than its debt, and that the city's revenues were nine times its debt service compared with only five or six times in 1955.[5] What Beame and Goldin didn't report was that the city's other expenses had grown much faster than both the value of its taxable real estate and the growth of city revenues, which made the credit statistics they cited meaningless.

Five days later, the *New York Times* published an article quoting a group of fiscal authorities as saying the city was in deeper economic trouble than at any time since the Great Depression. The fiscal authorities cited the city's budget gimmicks and borrowing for ordinary expenses.[6] A week later, the *New York Times* followed with an editorial entitled "Near-Bankrupt City," stating that the current city deficit could run to $1 billion and that the "City is sliding into bankruptcy with dismaying speed."[7] That same day, the city was required to agree to record interest rates averaging 8.3 percent in order sell $500 million of RANs and $115 million of TANs.[8]

IN THE MIDST OF THE MARKET TURBULENCE, NEW YORK STATE held an election. It was an election that would have profound consequences for how the looming fiscal crisis would be resolved. A governor without deep experience in the ways of Congress and personal relationships with House and Senate leadership and the president would be at a disadvantage to one who did. A governor unfettered by the mistakes of the past in New York City and State government would have more room to maneuver than one so encumbered. A governor wily in the ways of the clubhouse, but also wise to the ways of Wall Street and with enough of his own dough to not be beholden to either, would be better equipped than possessing some but not all of those qualities. Ideally, for the crisis fast at hand, you would want a longtime congressman out of the Brooklyn clubhouse with business experience and "fuck-you" money. Luckily for the vested interests in New York City, such a candidate was in the race.

Who the Republican candidate for governor would be was never in doubt, as Governor Wilson was assured of the nomination. The Democratic race was a crowded rodeo, with five candidates joining the contest: Congressman Ogden Reid from Westchester; Joseph Ettinger, a political neophyte from Long Island; Queens Assemblyman Donald Manes; Howard Samuels, the former administrator of the Small Business Administration who lost in the primary to Arthur Goldberg four years earlier; and Congressman Hugh Carey from Brooklyn. By the time of the Democratic state convention in Niagara Falls on June 13, the field had been whittled down to Samuels and Carey. The delegates backed Samuels by a tally of 68 percent to 31 percent, but, critically, since Carey won over 25 percent of the delegates, his name would automatically appear on the ballot for the primary election in September. Nevertheless, Samuels was the heavy favorite.

It looked like the 1974 gubernatorial primary would be the end of the line for Carey's political career. A seven-term congressman, his advancement in the US House had been blocked by rivals. His dream of being mayor of New York likewise ran aground. He was at risk of becoming one of the many perennial, also-ran candidates for higher office.

Hugh Carey was born in Park Slope, Brooklyn, in 1919, one of six children, all boys, of second-generation Irish Americans, Denis and Margaret Carey. While not wealthy, the Careys were far from poor. During the 1920s, Denis owned a successful motor fuel distribution business, Eagle Petroleum, that delivered gasoline to filling stations serving the burgeoning automobile market. Although the company failed during the Great Depression, Denis Carey bounced back and started a second oil company in the 1940s, which became very profitable. In 1947, Hugh's older brother Edward struck out on his own in the oil business, forming New England Petroleum Corporation, which became wildly profitable supplying fuel oil to electric utilities, including Consolidated Edison Company and Long Island Lighting Company.

After graduating from St. Augustine's High School in Brooklyn, Hugh Carey enrolled in St. John's College, but his studies were interrupted by World War II. After serving in the infantry, Carey mustered out in 1945 and was at first drawn to politics. Carey worked for the New York State Democratic Party doing veterans outreach for two years. In 1947, he received his reward: he was offered a job as a truant officer in the Brooklyn Department of Education. Disappointed and insulted, Carey told the party officials where to stuff it and instead enrolled in

St, John's Law School. After graduation, he went to work with his brother at New England Petroleum Corporation. However, the tug of politics never lost its grip on Hugh.

In 1960, excited by John F. Kennedy's presidential campaign, Carey became annoyed that his congressman, Francis E. Dorn, a Republican, was bashing Kennedy, a fellow Irishman, and proudly predicting his Brooklyn district would go for Nixon three to one come November. While the Twelfth Congressional District was relatively well-to-do and conservative, it was also heavily Irish Catholic, and Carey thought Dorn was hurting himself politically with his overly enthusiastic support of Nixon. Carey wanted the Democrats to run someone against Dorn that year, and he and his brother Edward would help bankroll that candidate.

Carey brought his idea to his local Democratic leader, Al Hesterberg. Hesterberg, being a professional, thought running against Dorn, a popular incumbent, was a fool's errand, but, taking note of brother Edward's deep pockets, told Hugh that he had no candidate lined up and thought Hugh would make a fine candidate. Seeing that Hugh was both flattered and intrigued by the idea, Al Hesterberg did the only intelligent thing one could with a self-financed candidate willing to take on a lost cause: he immediately marched Hugh over to Brooklyn boss Joseph T. Sharkey's office before Hugh might change his mind. Sharkey, after satisfying himself that Edward Carey's millions of dollars were real and available to Hugh, was all smiles and Hugh was given the endorsement.

Dorn was right—Nixon easily carried the Twelfth Congressional District—but Hugh Carey was right too. The Irish resented the Irish Dorn badmouthing the first Irish American to win the presidency. Carey upset the heavily favored

Dorn by a whisker—only 1,097 votes separated them. Dorn ran again in 1962, and Carey won again, but by an even smaller margin—383 votes. But after that race, Carey never again faced a serious challenge for reelection.

In 1969, with John Lindsay vulnerable in his reelection campaign, Carey announced that he would be a candidate for mayor in the Democratic primary. Carey's hopes were dashed, however, when former Mayor Wagner announced that he was entering the race as well, as Wagner's base of support was needed if Carey was going to have a fighting chance. Wagner convinced Carey to run on his ticket for New York City Council president instead. In the June primary, Carey narrowly lost to Francis K. Smith by a mere 2,107 votes out of 322,000 cast. Wagner lost his primary too, to City Comptroller Mario Procaccino. Carey toyed with the idea or reentering the mayor's race as an independent, but ultimately decided against it.

Back in Washington, Carey continued to be an effective congressman, working his way into the leadership. Carey was considered to be the front-runner to be the Democratic Party whip in the House after John McCormick retired in 1971 and Carl Alpert and Hale Boggs each moved up a notch to speaker and majority leader, respectively. Both Alpert and Boggs favored Carey for whip initially, but two fellow Irish Catholic New York City Democratic congressmen felled Carey's chances. John Rooney and Jim Delaney, both jealous of Carey's success, high profile, and money, told Alpert and Boggs that if Carey was selected, they'd revolt. Not being supported by your state's delegation for a leadership role was extremely troubling, and Alpert decided that the whip position would go to his second choice, Congressman Thomas P. "Tip" O'Neill of Massachusetts, who had no enemies in the Democratic caucus.

O'Neill and Carey were good friends. O'Neill felt badly for Hugh—that he had been denied the whip post that was rightfully his and that he was stabbed in the back by his New York colleagues. O'Neill was very touched when Carey told him he was genuinely happy for O'Neill and that he held no resentment toward O'Neill for winning the whip position. As far as O'Neill was concerned, Carey was a stand-up guy, and O'Neill promised himself that, whenever he could, he would go to bat for his pal Carey.

In truth, Carey was extremely bitter over losing the whip contest. But the reality was that Carey had always rubbed certain people the wrong way. Part of it was his brooding nature. Part of it was his access to his brother's nearly limitless funds—by the early 1970s, Edward Carey's wealth was reported to be well over $1.5 billion—more than the personal wealth of all the Rockefeller brothers combined. But while fellow politicians seemed to tolerate the wealth-driven privileged attitudes of Kennedys and Rockefellers in politics, for some reason they did not give Hugh Carey a pass in that regard. Perhaps they didn't know Carey had the fuck-you money, which explained his sometimes fuck-you attitude. Perhaps it was because Carey didn't look or talk like other politicians thought a rich man should. Instead, they resented Carey's moodiness, money, and ambition.

Carey's ambition and money did not fail him in 1974, however. During that Watergate summer, being the establishment candidate and having a party endorsement were liabilities not assets. With Samuels carrying the party endorsement, Carey painted him as a tool of the bosses and ran as the independent man, the antiestablishment candidate. With his brother's money funding political consultant David Garth's brilliant television advertising campaign, Carey closed the gap by Labor Day and began to pull away. By primary day on September 10, it was no longer close. Carey received 580,733 votes to Samuels's 433,901. With the state's fiscal situation so dismal, and the bill for Nelson Rockefeller's fifteen-year borrowing and spending excesses having come due to Malcom Wilson, even in a good year for Republicans, Wilson's chances would not have been good, and 1974 was the worst year for Republicans since 1932. Carey clobbered Wilson in the November 5 general election, 58 percent to 42 percent.

As with Nelson Rockefeller, Thomas Dewey, Franklin Roosevelt, and Al Smith before him, soon after Carey was elected governor, the talk of Carey being "presidential timber" began. Having served in Congress for fourteen years, pulled off an upset in the Democratic primary and defeated a sitting governor in a landslide, the talk was not idle. From a career becalmed three years earlier after his humiliating loss in the whip race to a legitimate contender for the presidency—talked about in the same company with Teddy Kennedy, Henry "Scoop" Jackson, and Jerry Brown—Carey felt vindicated. But he had no time to bask in the glory. The state's financial position was worse than at any time since the Great Depression.

Carey was not so distracted by the state's budget problems that he neglected to reward his generous campaign donor, Anthony Scotto. On November 9, the Democratic State Committee met in Albany to do the new governor-elect's bidding. Carey directed the committee to replace the state chairman, Joseph F. Crangle, with his handpicked successor, Bronx boss Patrick Cunningham. The committee also elected delegates to the National Democratic Party off-year "mini-convention" to be held in Kansas City in December. The mini-conventions, now long discarded, were essentially boondoggles, where party insiders could drink and hang out for three days on the party's dime and, if they felt the urge, argue over the language of the party's platform for the upcoming presidential election that they were ostensibly there to craft. Delegate appointments to the mini-convention were a highly sought-after plumb perk awarded to loyalists. Carey made sure Anthony Scotto made the cut. Scotto avoided the drafting sessions in Kansas City and installed himself at a corner table at the Red Fox bar across from the convention hall where he held court with the new state chairman Cunningham, Frank Rossetti (the Manhattan boss), and Meade Esposito of Brooklyn.

Rather than using the distraction of the November election to quietly come clean on the extent of the city's fiscal problems, Beame and Goldin doubled down on denial. When it came to selling more New York City bonds, Beame and Goldin set aside their differences and suspicions. They wrote a joint letter to the *New York Times* on November 11 castigating its editorial board for spooking bondholders unnecessarily. Beame and Goldin repeated the often made but misleading claim that the city's bonds and notes had a first lien on all city revenues and that bondholders and noteholders were "investing in the world's wealthiest and soundest city as far as fiscal obligations are concerned."[9] That same day Goldin met with S&P, which to Goldin's relief agreed to not downgrade the city's debt at that time.[10] A similar meeting was held with Moody's, which also agreed to not downgrade the city's rating.

The business press also hammered away at the city's fiscal problems. On November 27, *The Daily Bond Buyer* published an article reporting that over $1 billion of municipal securities were unsold on the books of underwriter banks and that "there was simply no market for New York City's bonds at the original price levels."[11] Knowledgeable business reporters paid close attention to trading prices immediately after underwriters break syndicate on an offering. The syndicate breaks when all the bonds or notes underwritten by the banks have been sold and the underwriters stop stabilizing the price of the bonds or notes through buying bonds or notes from short-term speculators. Once the stabilizing bids stop, the bonds or notes trade without support from the underwriters in the aftermarket. When the syndicate broke for the city's October note offerings, the prices dropped dramatically. The yields on city short-term notes were soaring, even while the yields on the short-term notes of other cities were declining.[12]

On December 2, the city offered $400 million of RANs and $200 million of TANs for sale and was required to pay record-high interest rates averaging 9.5 percent. The high yields on those notes further drove down prices of the banks' growing inventory of other unsold city debt. Beame and Goldin were clearly failing in trying to convince the municipal bond market that concerns about the city's fiscal outlook were much ado about nothing.

On December 11, Mayor Beame finally changed tactics. If he couldn't bamboozle the market about the city's problems, he would have a try at phantom solutions. He held a press conference announcing that the city would eliminate 3,725 jobs and force the retirement of 2,700 other employees who had reached retirement age. Beame claimed this would save the city $100 million annually. Predictably, the heads of the city's public employee unions responded with performative outrage at the modest cuts.[13] "The Mayor is putting the economy completely on the backs of the workers," announced Victor Gotbaum, president of the 125,000-member District Council 37 of the American Federation of State, County and Municipal Employees, the city's largest public employees union. Albert Shanker, leader of the 80,000-member United Federation of Teachers, called the layoffs "intolerable." John DeLury, president of the 10,000-member Uniformed Sanitationmen's Association, said the cuts were "doing great damage." Richard Vizzini, president of the 10,000-member Uniformed Firefighters Association, said, "The City is proceeding headlong in the direction of potential loss of life and injuries from fire."[14]

The union leaders might have appeared to be perpetually angry and reflexively unreasonable, but that was posing to placate the real radicals in their union ranks that might challenge the serious men who made sure to deliver rich contracts. The serious work that the serious men relied on to get those contracts was, more often than not, done for them by Jack Bigel, America's preeminent union consultant. Bigel was a revolutionary figure in the American labor movement because he realized that success, particularly for public employee unions, was not to be had by crippling strikes but by data. Bringing a city to its knees might temporarily be satisfying and superficially empowering, but it did not put more money in rank-and-file pockets. As municipal labor unions met with one success after another in the three decades after World War II, they were able to secure the ability to resolve contract disputes by means of arbitration. Success in arbitration meant convincing well-educated arbitrators, typically lawyers, that the union position is more fair than the municipality's. What was fair? Fair started with what other comparable municipalities agreed to, as adjusted by the different circumstances at hand. Winning the "fair" argument was done with data and statistics, not picket lines and work stoppages.

Jack Bigel was born in Brooklyn in 1913, graduated from Boys High School, and then graduated from City College of New York in 1934. He helped organize the first major public employee union in New York City, United Public Workers, comprised of sanitation workers and hospital employees. In 1950, that union was expelled from the Congress of Industrial Organizations, a predecessor to the AFL/CIO, for alleged communist leanings. After that, Bigel founded Program Planners Inc., a consulting firm for organized labor organizations. His first major client was the Uniformed Sanitationmen's Association. John DeLury there made no move without consulting Jack Bigel. That was not based solely on Bigel's charm. Before Bigel arrived on the scene, sanitation men made 25 percent of what policemen made. By 1969, they were making 90 percent of what the cops made. In 1975, Bigel employed more than sixty statisticians and economists at Program Planners, and they would be indispensable in navigating the city's union leadership through the treacherous waters that lay ahead.

Bigel came up with a creative plan to avoid even the modest number of layoffs proposed by Beame. Bigel's proposal involved lowering the retirement age to sixty-two and forcing those affected to take buyouts.[15] Older workers howled, claiming the plan violated federal law, as it was age discrimination. Eleanor Holmes Norton, the chairwoman of the city's Commission on Human Rights—focused on the fact that those laid off would, under union work rules, be those with the least seniority, which would disproportionately hurt Blacks, Puerto Ricans, and women, but those forced to retire under Bigel's plan would be disproportionately older white males—declared Bigel's plan legal. But Peter Brennan, President Ford's secretary of labor and himself an old, white male, opined that Bigel's plan did violate federal law, so that was the end of that.[16]

The union leaders didn't worry too much, for they knew Beame was playing for the cameras, most specifically for Wall

Street and the municipal bond investors. For just as Jim Cavanagh could make budget numbers dance a jig, so too could he make job and layoff numbers dance. They knew Beame was playing for time. He'd toss some "austerity" red meat to Wall Street and the press, but behind the scenes he would work tirelessly to keep every city job possible.

It was impossible to track for certain how many of the 6,425 proposed layoffs and forced retirements actually resulted in real employees losing their jobs because in 1975, incredibly, the city had no central database of city employees. There was literally no way of knowing at any time how many people worked for the city. A good guess is that the number of actual job losses was closer to 2,000 than it was 6,425. Many of the "layoffs" were simply unfilled positions that the city eliminated—which resulted in no cost savings. Many others were part-time jobs and unpaid internships. Still more "layoffs" were workers shifted on the books from city-funded programs to state- or federal-funded ones—but those book entry shifts saved no money. And the city's governance in 1975 was such that the mayor had no authority to fire anyone at the Board of Education or the Health and Hospitals Corporation—he could only reduce their overall budgets. The Board of Education simply ignored Beame and kept as is its padded payroll on which 30 percent of teachers did not teach, but held down research and administrative jobs. While its budget was cut, the Board of Education simply defied the mayor, refused to fire teachers and cut special education and sports programs instead. Beame didn't make too much of an issue over it. Teachers were more important politically than special needs students anyway. Teachers voted.[17]

The municipal bond market was not impressed with Beame's layoffs or organized labor's response. On December 13, Donald

Platten, the chairman and chief executive officer of Chemical Bank, received a memorandum from his head of investment banking, which stated that the market for city securities was no longer viable despite the strength of the overall bond market because of the unsold inventory of city notes and bonds and concerns about the city's continuing budget deficits.[18]

The *New York Times* reported on December 16 that the city's underwriters were suffering enormous losses, and that $200 million of notes underwritten in October was still on the books of the underwriters, unsold. Unnamed municipal bond market participants were calling the situation a "disaster." At 5:00 p.m. that afternoon, the comptroller's Technical Debt Management Committee met at Goldin's office. Representatives of Merrill Lynch, Salomon Brothers, Morgan Stanley, Citibank, Chase Manhattan Bank, and other banks suggested to Goldin that the city's public employee pension funds buy city bonds and notes to provide relief to the supply-demand imbalance (Jack Bigel, always ahead of the game, already had a team of economists looking at that option). They also demanded that Goldin cancel the city's planned January notes offering (Goldin agreed).[19] The committee agreed to reconvene the following morning—at Gracie Mansion—so that Mayor Beame could hear directly from the bankers what they were telling Goldin.

Beame did not react as the bankers had hoped. After being told that institutional investors and out-of-state investors were no longer purchasing any city notes or bonds and that the banks had lost $50 million on the October offerings, Beame accused the bankers of not "selling the City."[20] He castigated the bankers for charging the city high interest rates on recent offerings. The problem, Beame said, was that the bankers were not doing their jobs well, not that Beame wasn't doing his well.[21] Hadn't they heard about the 6,425 layoffs?

What was actually galling Beame was the holier-than-thou attitude the bankers seemed to now be taking. Beame had lined their pockets for years as comptroller, doling out financing deals, underwriting fees, city deposits, and a hundred other goodies the banks got from the city. These bankers had no qualms about collecting fees from selling bonds supported by phony receivables—as long as the municipal bond investors bought them. But now that the city was going through a rough patch, they had the temerity to lecture him about fiscal responsibility. They had no loyalty, Beame concluded, about the worst character defect a man could have, as Beame saw it.

The substantive result of the committee's meetings with Beame and Goldin was that the city would publicly offer $1 billion less of notes in fiscal 1975 than previously planned, and that the city's public employee pension funds would be asked to purchase those notes instead of municipal bond market investors.

The large New York City banks were in a tough spot. Politicians, particularly clubhouse politicians from Brooklyn who were not obsessive about guarding the public treasury, could be enormously helpful to the banks. There were not only fees from note and bond issuances, mortgages, cash management, pension fund brokerage, and a myriad of other services the city paid banks for, the city had substantial deposits to place—or not—with banks. And a bank executive could never know when he might have a bad loan out to a bankrupt railroad and a helpful politician might have Bill Shea negotiate a way for the state's taxpayers to repay that loan. Never were all the deals squeaky-clean, even at white-shoe banks. Even John McCloy of the Milbank

Tweed firm, the so-called "chairman of the Establishment" and David Rockefeller's longtime counsel at Chase Manhattan Bank, was no stranger to the smoke-filled room. It was never good business to anger the politicians and always best to play along.

AS 1974 CAME TO A CLOSE, HUGH CAREY, THEN GOVERNOR-ELECT of New York, paid a visit to his old friend Abe Beame at Gracie Mansion. Beame had helped Carey sub rosa at the Democratic state convention back in the spring. With the bosses behind Howard Samuels, Beame had to be careful to avoid incurring their wrath, but he secretly encouraged delegates to vote for Carey so that he could reach the 25 percent threshold to be on the ballot in the September primary without the costly, time-consuming, and often futile task of gathering signatures to do so. Carey was grateful and he wanted Beame to know it. Seeing the trouble that lay ahead for the city in 1975, Beame's first order of business with Carey was to make plain to him that the city would be pressing him for emergency funding in the new year. "Both of us know the way to Washington," Carey replied with a fatalistic laugh.[22] The state, they both knew, had its own fiscal problems, and there were limits to Carey's gratitude.

Steven Clifford also knew the way to Washington, DC. Clifford was not the typical sort of employee working in the New York City comptroller's office. He was genuinely a counterculture sort, too radical in thought and appearance even for the long-haired Ivy League youngsters in the Lindsay administration. A 1968 Harvard Business School graduate, Clifford had worked for a while in the Lindsay administration, but he wasn't enamored with the nine-to-five life. He also eschewed suits and ties—and shoes at times. He wasn't much for collared shirts or haircuts either. He didn't just look like a hippie, he was one. But he was also a genius at municipal budgeting and, ironically, one of the most fiscally conservative employees in city government. His reputation for radical thinking did not come from any affinity for Che Guevara or Fidel, but because he adamantly believed that city budgets should be honest, honored, and balanced. And he was brilliant. Hearing much praise for this talented if quirky young man, Goldin had hired him as a consultant. Clifford sent a continuous stream of hilarious memos to Goldin during 1974, describing in colorful language the gimmicks and disasters in the city's accounting and budgeting functions and proposing possible solutions to the ever-growing fiscal black hole. In a December 14, 1974, memo to Goldin, Clifford concluded, starkly, that the city could not on its own stave off bankruptcy. Albany would not be able to solve the city's fiscal crisis either. The city would need to go to Washington and convince the Ford administration and Congress to allow the city to borrow approximately $3 billion from the US Treasury, which he hoped would charge the city no more than 8.5 percent interest and allow it to repay the loan over twenty years. Clifford knew that the feds would require real accounting and budgeting reform as a condition to such a loan, and that was the only way the city would ever clean up its act, Clifford concluded.[23]

Over the next year, there would be groundbreaking legislation creating a Municipal Assistance Corporation and an Emergency Financial Control Board, declaring a debt "moratorium," bankruptcy by another name, as well as a number of temporary rescue financings, near endless committee hearings and debates, and high-stakes litigation challenging all of that legislation, but it would all end just as Clifford, the hippie, had predicted.

CHAPTER FIVE

A CROWDED THEATRE ON FIRE

IF ON AUGUST 5, 1973, SOMEONE TOLD YOU THAT LESLIE L. KING JR. would be president of the United States a year later, you would have summoned a mental health professional. But on August 6, 1973, the *Wall Street Journal* broke the story that Vice President Spiro T. Agnew was under investigation by a federal prosecutor in Maryland for taking bribes while Agnew was Baltimore County executive and, later, as governor of Maryland. That prosecutor, George Beall, had the goods on Agnew and was proceeding full-speed ahead on an indictment. After failing to convince House Democrats to investigate the matter in order to stay Beall's prosecution (Tip O'Neill, then majority leader after Hale Boggs died in a plane crash, adamantly refused to go along despite Speaker Alpert's sympathy for Agnew's predicament), Agnew quit in the corner, agreeing to resign as vice president as part of a plea deal to avoid prison time.

This all went down at a very inconvenient time for President Nixon, as the nation was transfixed during the summer of 1973 by the daily, nationally televised hearings of Senator Sam Ervin's Watergate committee. Virtually every day that summer those hearings brought forth embarrassing revelations of 1972 campaign shenanigans by Nixon administration officials and in some cases, serious felonies. Many knowledgeable political observers on August 6, 1973, were convinced that Richard Nixon would not serve out his full second term as president. One of those was O'Neill, who was convinced that Agnew was hoping to delay his prosecution until Nixon resigned or was impeached, at which time Agnew could pardon himself as the new president.

Leslie L. King Jr. was better known by the name he took from his adoptive father, Gerald R. Ford Sr. In September 1973, after Agnew resigned, Ford, then the Republican minority leader of the House of Representatives, was on everyone's short list to replace Agnew as vice president, putting him one impeachment vote away from the presidency.

Despite the difficulties of his early childhood—his parents divorced in 1915 when Ford was two years old and his father was mostly absent from his life—Gerald R. Ford Jr. was as close as you could get to the all-American boy. His mother remarried when Ford was ten years old, and thereafter Ford had a relatively comfortable childhood in Grand Rapids, Michigan, even throughout the Great Depression. Ford was a high school football star and was recruited to play big-time college ball at the University of Michigan. In his first seasons playing varsity, Michigan won two national championships, going undefeated both years. After his senior year, Ford was recruited to play professionally by the Detroit Lions and the Green Bay Packers, but turned them both down to go to law school at Yale. After graduating from law school in 1941, Ford returned to Grand Rapids to practice law. His budding legal career had barely started when the Japanese attacked Pearl Harbor, and shortly thereafter Ford joined the Navy.

After the war, Ford returned to Grand Rapids and joined the prestigious law firm of Butterfield, Keeney & Amberg. In 1947, unmarried at age thirty-six, Ford met Betty Warren, a newly divorced fashion coordinator for a large department store. They married the following year.

The year 1948 was a banner one for Ford not only because of the marriage, but also because he decided to challenge his local congressman, Bartel J. "Barney" Jonkman, an isolationist, in the Republican primary at the suggestion of Michigan Senator Arthur Vandenberg, a leading internationalist. No one gave Jerry Ford much of a chance, and Jonkman barely campaigned. But everyone who met Ford liked him, and he was a tireless campaigner. Ford cleaned Jonkman's clock, out-polling him by nearly a two-to-one margin in the September primary. Ford cruised to victory in November with over 60 percent of the vote. For seven terms, Ford served as an effective congressman, popular with his colleagues on both sides of the aisle, and bided his time to move up in the Republican leadership.

Ford's chance came in 1962 after a lousy showing by the Republicans in that year's midterm election. A group of young congressmen—the Young Turks, as the press called them—which included Mel Laird of Wisconsin, Charles Goodell of New York, and Donald Rumsfeld of Illinois, challenged the Republican Minority Leader Charles Halleck by putting up Ford to run for the conference chairmanship, the third-ranking post in the House Republican leadership, then held by Charles Hoeven of Iowa. Ford won narrowly. After his defeat, Hoeven warned

Halleck that Ford would soon be after his job. After the disastrous 1964 election, Ford proved Hoeven right. The Young Turks ran Ford against Halleck for the minority leader position. After conservative Bob Dole of Kansas swung his delegation to Ford, Halleck was finished, losing to Ford seventy-three to sixty-seven.

By the summer of 1973, Ford had been minority leader for over eight years and it looked like that was where his political career would top out, his dream of being speaker of the House a practical impossibility. The Democrats had held the House since 1955, had a fifty-seat advantage after the 1972 election, and with Watergate savaging the Republican brand, the 1974 midterm would undoubtedly widen the Democrats' advantage (it did—the Democrats held a hundred-seat advantage after the midterm). On October 2, 1973, everything changed for Jerry Ford. Nixon invited Ford to the White House and asked him to be his nominee for vice president to replace Agnew.

Ford sailed through his confirmation hearings during November—one of the reasons Nixon selected him was his popularity with Democrats in both the Senate and the House (Ford's close relationship with the supremely partisan O'Neill annoyed many of Ford's partisan Republican allies). Another reason Nixon selected Ford was that Ford told Nixon he had no ambition to be president and would not be a candidate in 1976. Ford was sworn in as vice president on December 6, 1973. Chatting with O'Neill at the White House reception following his swearing in, Ford was bemoaning the logistics of moving from his longtime Washington, DC, home into the new vice presidential mansion at the Naval Observatory. "Why bother?" O'Neill asked Ford, "You'll be living upstairs by next summer." Ford thought O'Neill was kidding. O'Neill wasn't. He had been convinced for months that Nixon was finished.

Until very late in the game, Ford continued to buy Nixon's line that he knew nothing in advance of the Watergate burglary and had not participated in any cover-up. By the summer of 1974, White House Chief of Staff Alexander Haig insisted that Ford be briefed on all national security issues so that he would be prepared to take over for Nixon on short notice. By August, Republican Senators informed Nixon that he did not have the votes in the Senate to win acquittal when the inevitable House articles of impeachment were sent over. Nixon resigned on August 9.

Like most inhabitants of the White House, Gerald Ford decided that he rather liked living there and, accidental president or not and notwithstanding what he told Nixon, by the time 1975 rolled around, he had made the decision, which he kept to himself for many months, that he would be a candidate for president in 1976. His chances did not look very good. After the Nixon pardon, his approval numbers in the polls dipped below 50 percent. The economy had slipped into recession again. Inflation was running over 12 percent, and the unemployment rate was over 7 percent. His vice president, Nelson Rockefeller, was a potential rival for the nomination from his left flank and the popular former California Governor Ronald Reagan was preparing to challenge him from the right. And in New York, a fiscal time bomb ticked.

What the hippie Steven Clifford knew and Hugh Carey knew and Abe Beame knew as 1975 dawned—that a federal government bailout of New York City would be needed and would be obtained—was not a special knowledge known only by a select few. Surely Comptroller Goldin knew. In the boardrooms of the nation's great banks, all headquartered in New York City, this was certainly known—to Walter Wriston at Citibank,

Ellmore Patterson at Morgan Guaranty Trust Company, Billy Salomon at Salomon Brothers, Donald Regan at Merrill Lynch, Donald Patten of Chemical Bank, and David Rockefeller at Chase Manhattan Bank. David Rockefeller's brother, Nelson Rockefeller, undoubtedly knew without his brother telling him, because in his nearly fifteen years as governor of the State of New York, Nelson, as much as anyone, had laid the tracks for the train wreck that lay ahead. And since the vice president knew, it is safe to assume that President Ford knew as well, because even if his vice president did not tell him, his treasury secretary, William Simon, formerly head of the Salomon Brothers municipal bond department and senior member of the New York City Comptroller's Technical Debt Management Committee when Beame was city comptroller, assuredly would have clued him in.

So the great game in politics for 1975 was one whose end all the important players knew. What was not known, however, to the politicians, bankers, union leaders, and lawyers, was who the winners and losers of this game would be, so it mattered very much how they played the game. Careers and reputations would be made and lost that year, and not only in New York, for after 1975 came 1976, which was a presidential election year where New York's forty-one electoral votes (second in number only to California's forty-five) would be up for grabs, for New York was, in 1976, what was referred to then as a "swing state," meaning either party's nominee had a realistic chance of winning the state. In the prior six presidential elections, New York had gone for the Republican three times and the Democrat three times.

What was also not known was the precise form the bailout from the federal government would take. In Beame's dreams, it would take the form of more outright aid—maybe the federal government taking over all of the city's welfare costs. A loan from the US Treasury at a low interest rate and a long maturity date to refinance the city's sizable and troublesome short-term debt, allowing the city a fresh start, would also have been most agreeable to Beame, as long as the covenants contained in such a loan didn't permit federal bureaucrats in Republican presidential administrations to meddle too directly in city affairs. Less attractive would be a program whereby the feds doled out money on an as-needed basis for a short period of time and with many strings attached—like requesting an actually balanced budget, without Jim Cavanagh's gimmicks, monitored by an accounting system using accounting practices resembling GAAP, or other bells and whistles Clifford might approve of. Something like one of those options would hopefully keep the city out of the municipal bond market long enough for it to address the glut of city bonds and allow the city to borrow normally thereafter.

What was also unknown was what the federal government would require from the State of New York in order for New York City to get the money. President Ford would likely require Albany—the people of the State of New York—to kick in as much money as possible to keep afloat its profligate largest city. Ford would certainly require the public employee unions to take the same pain—perhaps contribute something to their pensions. It was quite possible that Ford would require the holders of the city's notes and bonds to kick something in as well, like lowering interest rates and extending maturities. And Ford would under no circumstances come through unless he was convinced there was no way the banks, the public employee pension funds, or the municipal bond market would provide the needed funds to the city.

None of these details were of any immediate concern yet to the deciders in Washington as 1975 dawned. Official Washington was mostly backward-looking that January. On New Year's Day, John Mitchell was convicted of conspiracy, obstruction of justice, and three counts of perjury for his role in the Watergate cover-up. The national security establishment was panicked over revelations in a December 22, 1974, *New York Times* article by Seymour Hersh of CIA assassination attempts of foreign leaders and covert actions to overthrow foreign governments. On January 27, the Senate established a select committee—the Church Committee—to investigate the goings-on over at Langley. And the daily dispatches from South Vietnam told of the latest military defeat at the hands of the advancing North Vietnam communist army.

Back in New York, it was abundantly clear that the city's ability to tap the municipal bond market, at any price, was coming to an end. On January 7, the city sold $620 million of RANs through an underwriting syndicate headed by Chase Manhattan Bank and Citibank at an interest rate of 9.4 percent. Beame called the interest rate "unfair, unwarranted and outrageously high."[1] He publicly blamed the underwriters, denouncing the "current treatment by lending institutions."[2] He told reporters that he would meet with leaders of the financial community that week.[3]

Beame's "outrage" was entirely for public consumption. As much as he resented the bankers for their cut-and-run disloyalty and holier-than-thou lectures about fiscal restraint, Beame knew that the underwriters didn't determine the interest rates on bond offerings—the investors did. Too much supply relative to demand meant the city had to pay more. And there was no need to publicly announce a meeting with the bank executives. Beame was in daily contact with the banks, with David Rockefeller regularly visiting him for early morning private breakfast meetings throughout this period.[4] But a big production had to be made of the mayor calling the bankers on the carpet, for the voters could not be allowed to believe that the mayor and the comptroller and the bank presidents were all quite chummy and feathered each other's nests with the voters' money.

So on January 9, the solemn-faced titans of banking filed into Gracie Mansion at precisely 8:00 a.m. past the gathered press gaggle—Rockefeller of Chase Manhattan Bank, Ellmore Patterson of Morgan Guaranty Trust Company, William Spencer of Citibank, Donald Patten of Chemical Bank, Charles Sanford of Bankers Trust Company, and John McGillicuddy of Manufacturers Hanover Trust Company. Once the meeting began, and after Beame again accused them all of bad-mouthing the city—which scolding was again promptly leaked to the reporters—there was very little to talk about, since the purpose of the meeting had then been fulfilled. Before leaving, they all agreed that they ought to meet again—for certainly it would be useful in the months ahead to demonstrate how tough Beame was being with the banks or how tough the banks were being with Beame, as the case may be. They even came up with a name for themselves: the Financial Community Liaison Group. Ellmore Patterson was given the honor of chairing it.

The following day, at the City Club of New York, David M. Breen, a respected municipal securities analyst from the Weeden & Co. investment bank, gave a speech on the city's fiscal problems. Unlike at the meeting the day before at Gracie Mansion, Breen discussed truths and realities, including that if the banks were unwilling to continuously roll over the city's short-term debt with massive loans, which he doubted the banks would do for very long, even if the city miraculously and immediately balanced its budget, the city would need to file bankruptcy. The city would always need short-term loans to smooth out the revenue-expense timing mismatch, Breen explained. But the city would have to refinance much of its wrongfully borrowed short-term debt—borrowed against Cavanagh's phony revenues and taxes to fund deficits—into long-term debt in order to be creditworthy for future, appropriate short-term borrowings. The city had to clean up its balance sheet. And since no one—not the municipal bond investors, not the banks, not the State of New York, not the public employee pension funds, and not the US Treasury—was likely to loan the city real cash dollars on a long-term basis for such a large refinancing, someone was going to have to force the short-term noteholders to swap their short-term notes for long-term bonds. The only way that could be accomplished was by means of a federal bankruptcy filing, Breen reasoned. On that last point, Breen was not entirely correct, as we shall see—it could only be done *legally* by means of a federal bankruptcy filing. It could be done illegally in Albany.[5]

Bankruptcy, said Breen, would solve the city's fiscal crisis by forced extension of the maturity of the short-term notes into long-term bonds and thereby guaranteeing the city future access to appropriate short-term seasonal borrowing by providing new short-term lenders with a super-priority lien on future city revenues, priming the existing city debt. This is common in corporate bankruptcies, called "debtor-in possession" (DIP) financing.

The mere mention of the *B* word sent shivers up the spines of mayors, governors, comptrollers, and politicians of both parties in Albany and New York City. Bankers and union leaders would get squeamish at the thought as well. This is so because in a bankruptcy, a federal judge decides who gets paid how much and when, and there can be no assurance as to how persuadable a random federal judge—not removable from office by the mayor, the governor, or Meade Esposito—might be. Federal judges do things, for example, like sending Anthony Scotto to prison. A federal judge, armed with the power of the Supremacy Clause of the United States Constitution, could override the New York State Constitution and reorder bond and note payment priorities. Such a judge can reduce union pension benefits. Clifford might be listened to by such a judge and budgets might actually be required to be balanced. Not even Bill Shea could guarantee a satisfactory outcome in a federal bankruptcy proceeding.

Word of Breen's speech quickly made its way back to Beame, who issued a scathing press release calling the speech irresponsible, akin to yelling fire in a crowded theatre,[6] which of course is not irresponsible at all when the theatre is in fact on fire. Beame couldn't bear the thought of being the first mayor since the Great Depression to enact mass layoffs or being the mayor to dismantle the city's hospital or university systems. Being the mayor to sign the bankruptcy petition for New York City? Never, Beame adamantly and conclusively told his cronies. He'd resign before he'd do that.

On January 14, Beame directed attention to where his solution lay and asked the New York Congressional delegation to support legislation creating a federal municipal financing agency that would buy municipal securities at low interest rates. Beame also proposed legislation that would require the federal government to pay the city its aid revenues in equal monthly installments, rather than sporadically, to ease the revenue-expense mismatch. He asked for a law to require the federal government to pay for all of the city's welfare contribution, reimburse New York City for the cost of the United Nations, and fund the cost of narcotics treatment in the city. Junkies, like foreign diplomats, it appeared, seemed to gather disproportionately in New York City.

It was an inopportune time for Beame's fate to be in the hands of Congress, for in 1975, the New York congressional delegation was perhaps at its weakest in over a century. There were no New Yorkers in positions of leadership in either the House or the Senate. The defenestration of Hugh Carey by his fellow New York congressmen highlighted the dysfunction of the delegation: Carey would have been majority leader then, had they held their tongues, and in a position to strong-arm aid legislation to bail the city out. Emanuel Celler of Brooklyn, the House Judiciary Committee chairman who served in Congress since 1923, was defeated by a progressive neophyte, Elizabeth Holtzman, in the 1972 primary. The delegation was short on seniority and long on unpopular members with difficult personalities, like Bella Abzug and Ed Koch. Beame's legislative wish list was dead on arrival.

The next day, to show Wall Street seriousness in cutting spending, Beame ordered more than 4,000 additional layoffs. Union leaders reacted with requisite shock and horror. By the end of the month, Beame would quietly cancel most of those proposed layoffs for token union concessions.

Meanwhile, fiscal trouble was boiling over in Albany just as Hugh Carey moved into the governor's mansion. The boiling pot was the UDC, the low-income housing agency former Governor Rockefeller rammed through the legislature in the wake of Martin Luther King Jr.'s assassination. Many of the same banks that underwrote the city's bonds also underwrote the UDC's "moral obligation" bonds, and the UDC's financial situation was even worse than the city's. The market was no longer buying UDC bonds, and the banks were no longer interested in loaning the insolvent agency any more money. Edward J. Logue, the president of the UDC, blasted the banks: "We cannot allow basic public policy of this importance to be made in corporate board rooms and issued to the public by means of fiat."[7] Carey, knowing the UDC was a lost cause and eager to blame its woes on his Republican predecessors, quickly leaked that the politically ambitious real estate developer Richard Ravitch would be named chairman of the UDC, and Logue fired. That helped to solve Carey's immediate political problem at the UDC, but its financial mess remained. On January 21, Carey submitted emergency legislation seeking a $178 million loan from the state to the UDC to keep it afloat through March—the UDC had a $100 million BANs issue maturing on February 24 and a $78 million operating deficit through March 31.[8] John Mitchell's moral obligation was coming due. This UDC bailout was a cost Carey could have lived without. On January 30, he announced his fiscal 1976 budget of $10.69 billion, which included $806 million of new taxes, including a wildly unpopular $0.10 per gallon gasoline tax.[9] Mayor Beame's fiscal woes were even worse. Despite a record real estate tax increase, the city's fiscal 1975 $12 billion budget was already $883.9 million in the red by January.

On January 6, Carey and Beame went to Washington to meet with Vice President Rockefeller and beg for more federal aid. For Nelson Rockefeller, the meeting was a wonderful opportunity to separate himself from the mess he'd helped create. He would gladly serve as President Ford's heavy in bringing New York to heel. Rocky made it very clear to Beame and Carey that he was now on Team USA not Team New York: "The interesting thing to me is that Hugh and I have reversed roles," he quipped to the press. "The last time I came to Washington, I was Governor, Beame was Mayor, and we went to see Hugh Carey who was on the Ways and Means Committee. Hugh Carey's arguments today are the ones I used to use, and his arguments are the ones I'm using today."[10] It was far too early. Things would have to get much worse for Beame and Carey before Ford would do what all three of them knew he must ultimately do.

Carey came home to a worsening crisis at the UDC. He had hoped submitting legislation to pay for the February 24 BANs maturity and operating expenses through March would buy time for his team to prepare a permanent plan to stabilize the agency, which had 184 pending construction projects requiring billions to complete. But his plan, which contemplated that the state would provide an additional $270 million and the New York banks would buy $200 million of new bonds, was facing resistance in both the legislature and at the banks.

After a week of nearly continuous negotiations, neither the banks nor the legislature would budge. On the morning of February 24, Carey reached out to the Federal Reserve Bank of New York, hoping it might grant an emergency loan to stave off a UDC default.[11] It demurred. At 1:00 p.m., Robert P. Adelman, treasurer of the UDC, called Chase Manhattan Bank, the trustee for the BANs noteholders, and informed it that the UDC would default in repaying the BANs. That which Governor Rockefeller and John Mitchell had promised would never happen did. As it turned out, the moral obligation was not worth the paper it was printed on.[12]

The UDC default would have broad implications for the other New York State and New York City agencies that had issued billions in moral obligation bonds. Now that one norm had been violated, would "full faith and credit" bonds and notes be sacrosanct? If the state would turn its back on the UDC, would it cut New York City loose too? The fine print and web of laws and constitutional provisions that defined the legal rights of holders of the numerous debt instruments of New York City and its agencies took on a new-found importance.

On February 19, Comptroller Goldin announced that the city had negotiated a sale of $260 million of TANs, $100 million to be purchased by a syndicate led by Bankers Trust Company and $160 million by a syndicate led by Chase Manhattan Bank, at an average interest rate of 7.6 percent, the best rate the city had received in eight months.[13] It was structured as a "bought offering," meaning that the underwriters agreed to purchase the notes before they had tried to line up buyers for the notes. Many market observers believed the banks purposely underpriced the interest rate and took a loss as an accommodation to the city and possibly to signal optimism to the municipal bond market as to the city's prospects, which in turn might increase the value of the hundreds of millions of unsold city bonds on the banks' books. It didn't work.

In addition to the UDC default, municipal bond investors were concerned about the issues raised in a lawsuit brought by a Brooklyn Law School professor and gadfly named Leon Wein, challenging the legality of the SRC and the validity of any bonds that the SRC might issue. The underwriters wanted every *i* dotted and *t* crossed for the bought TANs offering—and all city offerings going forward. Bankers Trust Company, not comfortable relying on the advice of the legal counsel usually representing the underwriters of city securities, brought in its own counsel, the law firm of White & Case, to advise it on the pending TANs offering.

The White & Case partner overseeing the offering was Marion J. Epley III. Epley was very motivated to be extremely diligent in advising Bankers Trust on this high-profile matter because Epley himself was under a cloud of controversy as a result of the Securities and Exchange Commission (SEC) having brought a complaint against White & Case in 1972 alleging that

Epley's representation of a client, National Student Marketing Corporation, that issued phony financial statements violated the antifraud provisions of the federal securities laws. (In 1977, White & Case would settle the matter with the SEC, and Epley would be barred from practicing before the SEC for six months.) Epley, leaving no stone unturned, soon identified a fundamental flaw in the proposed TANs issuance—the city could not prove it had sufficient real estate tax receivables to support $260 million of TANs.

The city had provided White & Case documentation for the amount of real estate tax receivables as of January 30, 1975, which showed sufficient receivables of $408 million. The problem was that an enormous amount of real estate taxes was paid on January 31 of each year, the last day of the thirty-day grace period for the payment of real estate taxes due on January 1. Before the UDC failure, before the Wein lawsuit, underwriters would have taken the city's word for it, but no longer. If the TANs were found to not be validly issued, they might be subordinated in right of payment in a bankruptcy proceeding to all city debt that was validly issued, guaranteeing the underwriters would face a lawsuit from investors. It was at this point that the city's antiquated accounting system came back to bite it. There was simply no way to produce accurate records of any payments of real estate taxes subsequent to January 30. White & Case refused to issue its legal opinion, a condition to the closing of the bought offering, and the underwriters cancelled the deal.[14] Comptroller Goldin blamed the underwriters for "a sudden demand . . . unprecedented in the history of the city, for data that could not physically be computed, checked and verified in the short time available."[15]

It would turn out that Marion Epley was right to withhold White & Case's legal opinion. A later audit revealed that there were only $86 million valid real estate tax receivables on February 28.[16]

CHAPTER SIX

THE NUMBERS WERE JUST TOO BIG

EVERY YEAR IN NEW YORK CITY, A LOOSELY ORGANIZED, UNOFFI-
cial guild of the political writers, past and present, of New York
calling itself the "Inner Circle" puts on a lampoon show, and it
was in the 1970s (and remains today) a must-attend event for the
insiders of New York politics. The 1975 show, held on March 1 at
the New York Hilton, was entitled "Abie's Irish Woes (or Cash 'n'
Carey)." Over 1,500 pols, businessmen, media types, and labor
leaders paid $100 to attend. The highlight of the first act of the
show was a song about a laid-off zookeeper to the tune of "Bad,
Bad Leroy Brown":

> *Now baby, little Abie only*
> *Stands about five feet two*
> *But every inch would make a grown man*
> *Flinch and lose a job or two*
> *It transpired that I was fired*

Me and several thousand more
Me and cops and sanitation men
And firemen were going out that door
But it's funny that the money
That they took from our backs
Went right down to the clubhouse
As a raise for all the party hacks

The most laughs of the night came during a number performed by a reporter playing First Deputy Mayor Cavanagh to the tune of "Million Dollar Baby":

I got an office next to Abie
He's always knocking on my door
We run a billion-dollar city
Like a corner candy store

Anthony Scotto was particularly jovial that night, for the *New York Times* had just put to bed a story to be published the following day regarding a $400 million New York City– and State-funded redevelopment project to build a container port on the docks in Red Hook, Brooklyn. Despite the city's financial woes, despite the cancelled TANs offering, the city somehow came up with the money, and the *New York Times* piece would give all the credit to him: "The man who has been a prime mover for the container port is Anthony Scotto, the 40-year-old president of Local 1814 of the International Longshoremen's Association."[1]

The media attention that came with the cancelled TANs offering highlighted the city's inability to produce basic financial information. It also raised a troubling question: If Beame, Cavanagh, and Goldin were perfectly comfortable selling millions of dollars of city notes with no basis upon which to conclude the notes were validly issued, what else had they been comfortable doing? The Wein litigation, combined with the UDC default, had the banks that underwrote the city's debt deeply concerned about the legal enforceability of the notes and bonds they held in their growing inventories, as well as their liability to investors to whom they sold city notes and bonds. All of these concerns begged the question of what disclosure obligations the underwriters had to investors, given the city's precarious fiscal state.

The immediate task at hand, however, was arranging a temporary fix to the city's liquidity crisis created by the funding gap left in the wake of the cancelled TANs offering. To shore up the city's dwindling cash reserves, the large New York City banks agreed to provide the city a two-week bridge loan.[2] The city also proposed that the banks underwrite a $537 million BANs offering the following week.[3] The initial problem the banks had with the proposed bridge loan and BANs offering was that the take out financing for the bridge loan and proposed BANs were bonds to be issued by the SRC, the agency whose legality was being challenged in the Wein litigation. If the SRC were found to be illegal, would BANs issued in anticipation of SRC long-term bonds be legally enforceable? How would the city take out the BANs if the SRC were unable to issue bonds? What were the underwriters' obligations regarding the disclosure of these legal risks to prospective investors? All these questions landed in the lap of Marion Epley at White & Case.

As Marion Epley mulled over these questions, their answers only led to more difficult questions. If the SRC were found to be illegal, might other city bond issuing agencies like the Education Construction Fund, the Housing Development Corporation, and the Transit Construction Fund be found to be illegal as well, and, if they were illegal, might all of that "off balance" sheet debt then be "on balance sheet" for the purposes of the constitutional general debt limit? If all of the city agencies' debt were included in the constitutional general debt limit, would that limit be exceeded? The good news was that the city would still be within the constitutional general debt limit. The bad news was that it was not by much—and even the limited headroom the city had depended upon the assumption that the numbers Cavanagh pulled out of the pockets of his baggy brown suits bore some semblance to reality.

When the implications of the issues raised by Marion Epley percolated their way up the management chains of command of the city's underwriters, one by one, each of the banks decided they wanted to be represented by separate counsel. Epley was soon joined by Richard Eide of Davis Polk & Wardwell, brought in by Morgan Guaranty Trust Company. Soon thereafter, Chemical Bank brought in its outside counsel, Richard Simmons of Cravath, Swaine & Moore. Chase Manhattan Bank brought in James O'Sullivan, John McCloy's partner at Milbank Tweed Hadley & McCloy. Citibank had Joseph Doyle of Sherman & Sterling join the working group, which was rounded out when Salomon Brothers brought in Cleary, Gottlieb, Steen, and Hamilton.[4]

On March 6, advised by the best legal minds a great deal of money could buy, the banks agreed to provide the bridge loan and underwrite the BANs offering, but subject to a number of unusual conditions. The underwriters required a legal opinion from the city's Corporation Counsel that the Wein lawsuit was without merit and an opinion from the New York attorney general as to the legality of the BANs. Additionally, the city would have to issue a press release at the time of the announcement of the offering describing the risks relating to the BANs, to be followed by a more detailed disclosure document that the underwriters could deliver to prospective investors when they resold the BANs. The principal of federalism created a loophole in the federal securities laws—cities and states have no disclosure obligations under those laws when selling their securities. Underwriters of those securities, however, had liability to investors if they failed to disclose the risks of investing in those securities. In the good times, when the banks were lining up to collect fees from underwriting New York City securities, to suggest the comptroller prepare a lengthy disclosure document that protects you (but not him) from potential investor suits would quickly get you thrown out of the underwriting syndicate. So investors were historically told next to nothing about the city's financial condition.[5]

On March 7, the Financial Community Liaison Group met at the offices of Chase Manhattan Bank to discuss the city's near-term cash flow situation. No one could say for sure how much cash the city actually had. There were hundreds of bank accounts in dozens of city agencies and departments and no up-to-date centralized system of aggregating the balances. There were self-insurance accounts and bond sinking fund accounts with a substantial amount of cash in them, but no one knew for sure whether that cash could be loaned to the city or who had the authority to do so.

On the heels of the $537 million BANs offering announcement, Goldin asked the banks to underwrite $275 million of RANs on March 13.[6] The banks had concluded that the proposed RANs offering would provide the city with the cash it needed through mid-April, but that it would need an additional

$1.5 billion to get through the end of the fiscal year on June 30. Even if the banks were willing then to agree to underwrite that amount, which they weren't—at some amount, much less than an additional $1.5 billion, the unsold notes on the banks' balance sheets would draw critical attention from regulators and shareholders—that amount of borrowing would exceed the city's available tax and aid revenue receivables to borrow against. One thing all the lawyers agreed on was that the city would need to finalize its disclosure document in advance of them even considering bidding on the RANs on March 13. While the bankers were concerned that such disclosure might be so ugly so as to render the notes unsalable for an extended period of time, the army of lawyers worried about the banks' liability if the disclosure document wasn't ugly enough.

Four days later, the members of the Financial Community Liaison Group and their attorneys met with Beame and Goldin. It was the banks' turn to do the lecturing this time. The banks held over $1 billion of unsold city securities on their balance sheets, and they had no desire to increase that exposure. Only half of the $527 million BANs issue had been sold, and most of that amount was sold to investors who did not traditionally buy municipal notes and likely had little appetite for more city notes. The banks told Beame and Goldin that the city's legal capacity to issue more TANs and RANs was nearly exhausted, and the constitutional general debt limit would be reached that year at the rate the city's deficit spending was growing. The only solution the bankers could think of was the creation of an entity similar to the SRC, but with more credit support, that would refinance the city's short-term debt with long-term debt. That credit support would have to come from the State of New York.[7]

On March 12, the day before the scheduled $275 million RANs offering was to be bid on, the city finally produced its disclosure document entitled the "Statement of Essential Facts." There was more good news that day. Word came that the judge in the Wein lawsuit would uphold the legality of the SRC. A Citibank-led syndicate underwrote the RANs at an interest rate of 8 percent.[8] It would be the last underwritten offering the city would complete for four years.

The next key date for the city's liquidity was April 14. By that day, the city would need to raise $500 million, the biggest use of which would be to pay off $400 million of TANs coming due that day. The bankers were quite adamant to Goldin that they had no interest in underwriting any more city debt. Goldin thought the bankers needed to deliver this message directly to the mayor.[9] In the early morning hours of St. Patrick's Day, David Rockefeller, Ellmore Patterson, and William Spencer quietly gathered at Gracie Mansion to personally inform Beame that the fiscal crisis had entered a new phase. The large New York City banks had between 20 percent and 25 percent of their capital invested in New York City securities. Any higher percentage would get the federal bank regulators antsy. They were no longer willing to provide any more funds. It was time to look elsewhere, to Albany, to the public employee pension funds, and, ultimately, to Washington, DC.[10] As this was a serious meeting, what was said was not leaked to the press.

And so the first act of the drama was over. The city's financing needs were too large for the private sector to absorb, so center stage would move elsewhere. In Beame's dreams, it would move straight to Washington, but, with a Republican in the White House, that was not going to happen. But Beame tried.

Testifying before the US Senate Budget Committee on President Ford's budget, Beame proposed that the US Treasury provide interim term loans to the city to enable it to reduce reliance on short-term borrowing in the municipal bond market. Treasury Secretary Simon responded, dismissively, that "we're looking at it."[11] Of course, they weren't looking at it, not seriously anyway, for it was still far too early in the game for the federal bailout. Long before the Ford administration would come to the rescue, many other pieces would have to be in place.

The first of those pieces was for Beame to assemble. He would need to convince the holders of the federal purse strings that the city had done all it could on its own to straighten out its fiscal mess. Bill Simon was looking for Beame to raise taxes to the highest level such that going any higher would do more harm than good. Bill Simon was looking for painful austerity cuts to be made to the budget. That meant layoffs—real ones, not the next creative scheme Jack Bigel cooked up. Of course, those measures, in and of themselves, would not be sufficient to get the dough from the Ford administration. It would further need to be demonstrated that New York State had provided the city with all the aid that it could. That too would not be sufficient. Washington would need to be convinced that the municipal bond market and the banks had been fully tapped out, although there was pretty convincing evidence of this by mid-March. Jac Friedgut, a Citibank executive, gave a confidential briefing to the New York congressional delegation in Washington on March 18, telling them that Citibank would no longer underwrite New York City securities. Like most confidential briefings in Congress, Friedgut's remarks were leaked to the *New York Times*. Finally, the unions would have to kick in their share, loaning their pension fund money to the city in sufficiently large amounts to repent for the largesse the unions extracted from the city over nearly two decades.

The means by which Beame would need to do this convincing was the city's fiscal 1976 expense budget. On March 26, Beame called a rare Sunday press conference to announce plans to address the fiscal crisis and to set the tone of the budget he would soon propose. He opened his remarks by "calling on the State and Federal governments, on the banking community, on the business community, on organized labor and on the general public for cooperation and support of the program I am announcing today." Beame claimed he had bought a substantial amount of city notes a few weeks earlier and had to buy them at a premium to par (a preposterous assertion), which led him to believe the alleged lack of market demand for city debt was being overstated (an equally preposterous assertion). Beame promised to reduce short-term borrowing in fiscal 1976. He asked Albany to pay state aid to the city more frequently to reduce the need for RANs offerings. He promised to eliminate the gimmicks in the city's accounting and budgeting practices. He promised to cut the budget by an additional $135 million, which when combined with a full-year run rate for the earlier cuts of $478.6 million he made in fiscal 1975, would yield $663.6 million in savings. That savings would be accomplished through the elimination of 10,000 jobs, approximately 3 percent of the city payroll. He referenced unspecified tax increases and "developing a national coalition of labor leaders and businessmen, who, along with the country's mayors, will press the federal government for emergency assistance programs for local governments, welfare reform, welfare takeover, a loan fund for municipalities, and massive public works and public employment programs to relieve the country of its severe unemployment problem."[12]

Beame then announced he would go on retreat that week to work on the budget and asked that the City Council give him an additional thirty days past the legal deadline—until May 15—to formally submit his expense budget.[13]

While Beame was away on his "budget retreat," a delegation of city and state officials, including Goldin, Cavanagh, Arthur Levitt (New York State comptroller), and Peter Goldmark (Governor Carey's budget director), and members of the financial community met in Washington with the undersecretary of the Treasury, John Bennett, and representatives of the Federal Reserve Bank of New York. Bennett asked Arthur Levitt whether the state could loan the city money to solve its outstanding short-term debt issues. Levitt said he was pessimistic about that happening. Bennett asked Richard Debs of the Federal Reserve whether it could loan the city money. Debs advised him that the Federal Reserve lacked the statutory authority to do that (a not precisely accurate summary of the Federal Reserve Act because the Federal Reserve Banks could, in fact, make short-term loans of up to six months to municipalities). The members of the financial community indicated they had no solutions to offer. Bennett told the group that he had no solutions either, so they all went home.[14] It was still much too early.

As the April 14 maturity date for the $400 million TANs issue approached, with no solution in sight, the banks, desperate to unload the unsold city notes they had underwritten in the prior months, became concerned that the city's disclosure document—the "Statement of Essential Facts"—did not contain comprehensive, up-to-date disclosure regarding the city's financial condition that would protect them against liability when they used the document to confirm sales of unsold notes. They asked Marion Epley to consider revisions to the document. Epley's proposed revisions read like a death warrant. For years, the city had included in offering announcements that TANs, RANs, and BANs had a "first lien" on all city revenues. In truth, the New York State Constitution gave short-term city notes a first lien on city revenues only with respect to accrued interest. As to the principal amount of those notes, the "first lien" didn't arise until five years after the original date of issuance of the applicable notes.[15] If the city were to file bankruptcy, the principal amount of all outstanding RANs, TANs, and BANs would likely be subordinated to all other "full faith and credit" debt of the city. This important detail had never been disclosed, because, until very recently, no one thought the city might file for bankruptcy. Epley also told the bankers that the disclosure document needed to disclose what a "first lien" actually meant. Any noteholder who thought he would get paid before other claimants was likely to be sadly mistaken. Beyond the legal niceties of state constitutional payment priorities, would a bankruptcy judge really pay noteholders before handicapped or indigent New Yorkers got their welfare payments? Would any judge not pay the police, fire, or sanitation workers and risk mayhem in the streets in order to pay noteholders first? Epley doubted such a judge existed. The required disclosures made additional sales of city notes impossible unless a steep distressed debt discount was offered. Different banks had different risk tolerances—which unironically seemed to correlate with the sizes of their unsold inventory of city debt—some wanting more detailed risk disclosures and some less. At the end of the day, the banks could not agree on disclosure, so it was decided that each bank would disclose what it saw fit to disclose in offloading the notes it owned.

On April 2, S&P announced that it had suspended the city's A rating on its general obligation bonds. This, together with the earlier Fitch downgrade, meant that many large institutional municipal bond investors would be severely limited in their ability to buy city debt. While the ratings downgrade should have come as no surprise to anyone given the litany of fiscal woes that had preceded it—the sorry state of the city's budgeting and accounting functions, its budget deficit, its liquidity issues, the Fitch ratings downgrade, the high interest rates on recent note issues, the UDC default, and the cancelled TANs offering—it nonetheless stunned the public. New Yorkers had grown accustomed to mayors and comptrollers crying wolf about budget deficits and cash flow crises and never knew what to actually believe when banks warned of dire consequences from city fiscal misfeasance. But, more than two years before the scathing SEC report on the conduct of the ratings agencies leading up to the fiscal crisis (and three decades before the subprime mortgage crisis), the ratings agencies still had enormous credibility with the public. "We watched the animosity, distrust and suspicion building between the banks and the city, and the numbers were just too big," recalled Brenton Harries, president of S&P, years later. The S&P rating suspension marked the beginning of the fiscal crisis for most of the public, even though one ratings agency, Moody's, announced that, for the time being, it would maintain its A rating on city debt.[16]

The New York voters, awakened to the possibility that the city might, in fact, default on its obligations on April 14, demanded that something beyond talk and empty gestures be done to address the fiscal crisis. For Beame, still knee-deep in producing a budget, the downgrade hit like a torpedo below the waterline. Token job cuts and cosmetic cost savings measures while biding for time for Albany and Washington to deliver more aid would no longer be acceptable to the anxious public. Beame would have to be what he never wanted to be: a mayor who inflicted pain on the city.

The S&P downgrade convinced a reluctant Hugh Carey that Beame would not be able to manage the crisis without state assistance. But once Carey crossed that Rubicon, once he stroked that first check to bail out the city, he would bear responsibility for it thereafter. But not writing that check also had risks. If the city defaulted on its debt, the amount of the check that he might have to write then might have another zero on the end. The following day, Carey announced that the state would advance the $400 million of aid to the city that would have otherwise been paid months later to allow the city to make the April 14 TANs maturity payment.[17] To come up with these funds, the state borrowed $400 million, effectively incurring interest expense on behalf of the city, to the chagrin of State Comptroller Arthur Levitt. The $400 million in aid advanced by the state had been borrowed against by the city to issue RANs back in March. Those RANs were coming due in June. The legality of using funds backing an outstanding RANs issue to pay off an unrelated TANs issue was in substantial doubt. But those were legal niceties the city did not concern itself with in April 1975. The TANs were repaid. June seemed a long way off.

CHAPTER SEVEN

CAREY'S FIXER

WITH THAT $400 MILLION CHECK SENT TO THE CITY, GOVERNOR Carey realized that the city's fiscal crisis had become the state's as well, and therefore his crisis. This, on top of the UDC insolvency and the state's budget deficit, was very bad news for Carey's young administration, but Carey was no stranger to bad news.

On July 4, 1969, New Yorkers awoke to the news that two of then-Congressman Carey's sons had died in a car crash near Carey's summer home on Shelter Island. Ten years before, Carey had lost a brother in a plane crash. On March 8, 1974, Carey's wife Helen died of cancer at age forty-nine. They had fourteen children, including a daughter from Mrs. Carey's first marriage to a Navy officer who died in the Pacific in 1945, later adopted by Carey. Carey was devastated by his wife's death. It took over a year before he could bear to have a picture of her in his office. Thereafter, he would frequently move the picture to where he thought she looked best. He rarely spoke of his losses in public or to the press. Unlike the politicians of today, who shamelessly exploit every family tragedy, real or imagined, for political advantage, reminding voters at every campaign stop of their private pain, Carey never did anything of that sort. He would have much preferred to lose an election than to stoop to that. Whatever criticism is rightfully leveled at Carey for his easy associations with shady Brooklyn union bosses and the like, one must be awed by how Carey performed his duties in 1975 under the tremendous pressure of the multiple crises while at the same time carrying almost unimaginable personal grief and family responsibilities.

Carey's most pressing objective in April 1975 was to take the offensive on solving the New York City fiscal crisis, now his crisis, without taking responsibility for the consequences of the solution. It would be Abe Beame and Gerald Ford who would take that blame, if Carey achieved that objective well. To do so would require Carey to traverse a very treacherous tightrope.

Carey's first decision after he intervened in the fiscal crisis was to go to Washington and assess the mood of Congress and the Ford administration. The mood was somber. On April 30, Saigon fell, ending the Vietnam War. The images of the American evacuation of the city—Operation Frequent Wind—of helicopters leaving rooftops, landing on aircraft carriers, and, their jobs done, bulldozed into the sea, was a metaphor for the incompetence, futility, and absurdity of the entire American involvement in the conflict. That day marked the nadir of the 1970s, America's decade of humiliations—Watergate, gas lines, overrun embassies, seized hostages, leisure suits, and disco. America's largest city going bust at that moment seemed fitting.

While in Washington, Carey met with Treasury Secretary Simon and testified before a Senate subcommittee, seeking more federal assistance. At his meeting with Simon, Carey brought along Mayor Beame, David Rockefeller, Ellmore Patterson, and William Spencer. The city needed $1.5 billion to pay its debts in June, Carey told Simon, and the bankers with him could confirm that private-sector financing would not be available to the city to do so.[1] Simon said he would look into the possibility of speeding up payment of already approved federal aid to the city, but as for additional assistance, congressional approval would be needed and, even if approved by Congress, support from Ford was unlikely.[2] Later that day, Carey testified before Senator Edmund Muskie's subcommittee on intergovernmental relations and requested that Congress approve a $4 billion aid package to state and local governments, with the lion's share going to New York City.[3] Before returning to New York, Carey requested that Simon arrange a meeting with President Ford on May 13 for Carey to plead his case for aid directly to the president. Simon passed along the request, and Ford agreed to meet with Carey.

Three days before the meeting, Simon publicly announced that the Ford administration would not support any additional financial assistance to New York City at that time, thus blunting any fallout from Carey's meeting with Ford, the results of which were preordained. "Based upon these meetings and our own internal evaluation, we have concluded that not only is the federal government's legal authority to provide financial assistance limited, but also that such assistance would not be appropriate," Simon told the press.[4] Beame quickly put out a statement attacking the decision: "The federal government has not hesitated to rush in and assist banks with cash flow problems, or to provide emergency funds to Lockheed or the Penn Central. But when the City of New York, the second largest government in the U.S., asks for help, we are given legal double talk and specious arguments about appropriateness."[5]

The Federal Reserve, in theory politically independent of the president, was also actively dismissing hopes that it would come to the city's aid with a loan. When a financial historian unearthed that in 1915, in the early days of the Federal Reserve, it invested excess funds in short-term New York City notes, a reporter asked John E. Sheehan, a member of the Federal Reserve Board, what he thought of the idea that the Fed do so again. "This is a swamp in which the Federal Reserve does not want to go—it is filled with quicksand," Sheehan said.[6]

Despite knowing that the meeting would be fruitless, Carey kept the date. It would be the first time all the principal elected officials—Beame, Carey, Rockefeller, and Ford—would be in the same room together to discuss the fiscal crisis. With the exception of Beame and Ford, all the men knew one another very well, so there would be no need to take the measure of one another. And they all knew the political theatre of the event: Beame and Carey would need to supplicate themselves, and Ford and Rockefeller would need to deny them. But Carey knew there might be clues as to the path forward. Perhaps it might be the Federal Reserve after all that would come up with a loan. Perhaps the money might be buried in a dozen aid bills. Perhaps Ford would betray nothing at this meeting, which in and of itself would be valuable information. The clues as to how Ford would play it were what Carey was after in this meeting.

They met for over two hours in the Cabinet Meeting Room in the White House. That Ford even kept the meeting in the first instance was useful information to Carey. The day before, the SS *Mayaguez*, a US merchant vessel, was shot at, boarded, and seized in international waters by a Cambodian gunboat manned by Khmer Rouge forces, setting off a confrontation that risked dragging America back into the conflict in Southeast Asia. This told Carey that the Ford administration was deeply concerned about the domestic political consequences of the New York City fiscal crisis. This also told Carey that Ford was almost certainly running for president in 1976. For various parts of the meeting, Treasury Secretary Simon, Alan Greenspan (chairman of the Council of Economic Advisers), and L. William Seidman (Ford's economic advisor), joined,[7] further evidence of Ford's concern over the New York City situation. Ford listened politely and promised Carey and Beame a formal response to their aid request within twenty four hours.

Carey and Beame then made their way on the muggy and rainy afternoon to Capitol Hill where they met with House Majority Leader Tip O'Neill to recap the meeting with Ford and to discuss a strategy going forward.[8] O'Neill had already thought through the realities of New York City's predicament and the path forward, and O'Neill had a plan. To formulate his plan, O'Neill did not consult the world's leading economists, many of whom were in residence at the Massachusetts Institute of Technology, located in O'Neill's district. He did not consult with experts in municipal finance at Harvard Business School or the experts in the law of municipal finance at Harvard Law School, even though Harvard too was in his district. No, O'Neill consulted with Leo Diehl, who held no advanced degree except from the school of political hardball.

O'Neill met Diehl in 1936 when both were freshman legislators in the Massachusetts House of Representatives, and each of them developed an intense respect for the other's political skills. When O'Neill became the US House majority whip, he hired Diehl to be his top political staffer. O'Neill brought Diehl into the New York City fiscal problem because Diehl had seen it all in politics, and because of that, in the unlikely event that

O'Neill missed something, it was extremely likely Diehl would not miss it as well. They were quite a duo, Tip and Leo. After late-night legislative sessions (and a few scotches), they could be heard skipping arm-in-arm along the marble floors on the House side of Capitol Hill, singing old Irish songs known only to them, the time kept by the bottom of the metal leg braces Diehl had worn since childhood polio that he had learned to tap dance a beat with.

Like Carey, O'Neill had concluded that Gerald Ford would be a candidate for president in 1976. Armed with that knowledge, O'Neill asked Diehl to prepare a detailed timeline of the 1976 Republican presidential primary season. When O'Neill and Diehl sat down to go over that, one date stuck out to O'Neill—January 6.

January 6, 1976, was the date of the New York State Republican convention, where 37 of New York's 154 delegates to the Republican Convention in Kansas City would be elected (the remaining 117 would be chosen in New York's June primary). It was the first major event of the 1976 Republican primary season. Those New York Republicans would just be back from their Christmas vacations, thought O'Neill, assuming they could get away at all. With New York City teetering on the cusp of default, many of them wouldn't be able to take a Christmas vacation—they'd be dealing with the planning for a city bankruptcy. Their wives would be stuck in their houses with antsy children on school breaks with nowhere to go. Christmas Day for those New York Republicans might not be much fun either, with the phones ringing off their hooks. And the parties leading up to Christmas, all they'd be talking about is what's going to happen when the city defaults. Thanksgiving dinner might be ruined too. Diehl had checked the New York Giants schedule for 1975. The Giants would be playing the Dallas Cowboys on Thanksgiving weekend. Those New York Republicans were sure going to be sore at not being able to see much of that game, with the phones ringing off the hook and whatnot. Ford was going to want this mess settled before Thanksgiving, O'Neill concluded. Diehl concurred. That made O'Neill certain, as on a matter of politics such as this, the possibility that O'Neill and Diehl could both be wrong was zero. If Ford loyalists got throttled at that January 6 convention, it would be big news that could turn the tide at the all-important Iowa caucuses two weeks later. And if Ford lost Iowa to Reagan, he might lose New Hampshire, and then it would be over for him.

Carey listened carefully, nodding knowingly throughout, as O'Neill went through his analysis. O'Neill said that if Carey could get New York City enough money to make it through Thanksgiving, Ford would agree to bail out the city on favorable terms shortly thereafter because he could not risk the wrath of those New York Republican delegates come January 6. If Carey could not do so, it would be most unfortunate for him as Ford would hold the better hand and would require the city to default and seek bankruptcy protection before providing federal money. There would not be the votes in Congress to override a Ford veto, so there was little that could be done without Ford being on board. Up until the moment Ford provided the federal money, he would play tough, to placate the conservative base of the Republican party, to fend off a Reagan insurgency. Since he was in a very tight spot—he risked displeasing those all-important New York Republican convention delegates if he was perceived as being too harsh on New York, and he risked displeasing the conservative Republican base nationwide if he was perceived as being too soft on New York—Ford was going to want to keep the

New York City fiscal crisis out of the national headlines. O'Neill told Carey his job was twofold—keep the crisis in the headlines and, most importantly, find the money to get New York City through Thanksgiving.

O'Neill worried that the weakness of the New York congressional delegation would make his job difficult in getting any bailout legislation, in whatever form it ultimately took, through a Democratic caucus that had no love for New York City. But he told Carey not to worry about that. That was O'Neill's problem, and he would not let his old pal down.

True to his word, President Ford's response came the next day by way of a brief statement to the press: "I believe that the proper place for any requests for backing and guarantee is to the State of New York."[9] Beame was at a Democratic Party fundraiser at the Waldorf Astoria Hotel in Manhattan when Ford's press release came out. Beame called an impromptu press conference there and attacked Ford: "It is incredible to me that the President of the United States thinks more about the stockholders of Lockheed or Penn Central than the eight million people of our City."[10] In response to Beame, the Ford administration trotted out Bill Simon again. Simon told reporters that a New York City default would have a "negligible"[11] effect on the national economy. Simon proposed that New York City hike tuition at City University, place tolls on the East River bridges, and increase transit fares.[12] As for Lockheed and Penn Central, Simon, struggling to differentiate them from the current crisis, said those bailouts were "smaller."[13] "We do not think it is the responsibility of the Federal Government until New York City does everything legally possible and everything fiscally possible—which they have not done—to put the City on a sound fiscal footing," Simon responded.[14]

O'Neill was going to do everything within his power to help his old pal Carey. This meant hurting his other old pal Ford. But that's how the game was played. All 282 pounds of O'Neill was old-school, partisan Democrat. He looked like North Cambridge's answer to Jim Cavanagh, redoubled. Thick, white hair, red face, ever-present cigar, accent unmistakably Boston Irish, O'Neill was a proud backroom politician, and he was at the peak of his powers in 1975, getting much of the credit for pushing through the articles of impeachment on Nixon ten months earlier. After Ford's rejection, O'Neill had Congressman Henry S. Reuss, chairman of the House Banking, Currency and Housing Committee, quickly introduce legislation providing for a federally guaranteed loan program to help New York City.[15] "If Mr. Ford shares any kind of solicitude for our declining cities as he has shown for victims and refugees [of Vietnam] tonight, he will go along with the resolution," Reuss said.[16]

And so, on the national political stage, the battle lines had been drawn predictably, with Ford and most of the Republicans in Congress insisting that New York City and Albany do more, and the Democratic leaders in Congress castigating Ford and the Republicans for heartlessness when it came to urban suffering but compassion when corporations need bailing out. The conservative Democratic members of Congress, however, did not share the willingness of their party's leadership to provide assistance. Representative Charles Rose, Democrat of North Carolina, spoke for the Blue Dog Democrats: "It takes a great deal of arrogance or insensitivity, maybe even that New York quality of chutzpah, to vote against helping the nation's farmers and then ask those of us who represent rural areas to subsidize the subway riders in New York City."[17] Senator Joe Biden of Delaware echoed that sentiment: "Cities are viewed as seeds of corruption and duplicity, and New York is the biggest city."[18]

New York City has never been popular in the heartland of America, and it was considered a downright scary and hopelessly decadent place in 1975. Many people west of the Hudson derived their impressions of New York from what they saw on television and in the movies. Ten years earlier, Americans saw a pleasant New York City with attractive, clean-cut couples like Rob and Laura Petrie (Dick Van Dyke and Mary Tyler Moore) on *The Dick Van Dyke Show* or Paul and Corey Bratter (Robert Redford and Jane Fonda) in *Barefoot in the Park*. In 1975, they saw Archie Bunker (Carroll O'Connor) getting mugged in a cab on *All in the Family* or Sonny Wortzik (Al Pacino) in *Dog Day Afternoon* being cheered on by a misanthropic crowd of bystanders after he takes hostages while robbing a bank in Brooklyn so he can pay for his lover's gender reassignment surgery.

There was much more work to do in Albany before there was any hope of a payday in Washington, and Albany would be center stage in the fiscal drama for the succeeding four months. The main protagonists there would be Governor Carey and Senator Warren M. Anderson, the Republican majority leader from Binghamton, and both men would play their roles extremely effectively.

Warren Anderson had served in the New York Senate for twenty-two years before the arrival of Carey in Albany. *Competent, responsible, quiet, reserved,* and *dignified* were the adjectives most associated with Anderson in the Senate. Born in 1915 in Bainbridge, New York, the son of a New York State senator and Supreme Court judge, Anderson attended public schools in Broome County and graduated from Colgate University and the Albany Law School. After serving in the Army Judge Advocate

General's Corps during World War II, he served as an assistant
county attorney and then joined the firm of Hinman, Howard
& Kattell. He was elected to the State Senate seat held by his
father in 1952. Anderson was named chairman of the powerful Senate Finance Committee in 1965 by his mentor, Senate
Majority Leader Earl Brydges, and when Brydges retired in 1972,
Anderson was elected majority leader. Slow to anger, Anderson
would be patiently amused by the histrionics of many of the
opposing party's downstate senators, but those wise among
such attention seekers knew not to push Anderson too far: he
would quietly, eventually exact his revenge on those who abused
his deep reserves of fair play. His only personal flamboyance
came on the last day of the legislative session each year when
he donned a garish plaid sports coat to signal the end of the
year's work.

At first, Anderson took a hard line with Beame—no new
taxes, no more state aid, and certainly no state borrowing to
solve the city's $1.5 billion June cash deficit or its $650 million
estimated fiscal 1976 expense budget deficit. For the upcoming
1976 fiscal year, Beame was asking for $430 million in new city
taxes and an additional $220 million of state aid. Anderson's
line was that the deficit spending and Cavanagh's budget and
accounting gimmickry had cost the city its credibility with
municipal bond investors and that Beame needed to stop the
gimmickry and balance his budget without more taxes or state
aid. With that accomplished, said Anderson, the municipal bond
market would reopen for the city. "I can only liken it to someone
addicted to heroin," Anderson told the *New York Times*, "Do you
really help him by giving him more?"[19] Anderson was well aware
that those solutions would certainly not come in time for the city
to pay its June bills. With a thirty-six to twenty-four Republican

majority in the Senate, Anderson held a strong hand, but not a lay-down hand, as seven of those Republican senators were from New York City and, as Tip O'Neill famously put it, "All politics is local." Anderson knew that there was a limit to the pain that could be inflicted upon the city beyond which those seven senators would cross the aisle and vote with the Democrats.

On May 17, Anderson offered Beame a deal: cut $640 million out of the fiscal 1976 expense budget and the state would loan the city $1 billion for ninety days—to tide the city over until it could reenter the municipal bond market (even though Anderson knew it would take much longer than ninety days for the city to do so).[20] Governor Carey, meanwhile, remained uncommitted on state aid to the city. His only public announcement in May was that he would veto any new state spending for the city until the state closed its own $500 million budget gap.[21] At the end of May, Carey and Anderson decided to continue the Band-Aid approach. They agreed to advance the city another $200 million, representing welfare funds scheduled to be paid to the city in January and March of 1976.[22]

The State came up with the $200 million after a two-week failed loan negotiation—played out in the newspapers—between the city and the Financial Community Liaison Group. Goldin at first asked the banks to attempt an underwriting of BANs to raise $280 million. Given the disclosure issues involved with selling city securities at this point and the state of the municipal bond market for New York City debt, the bankers thought Goldin had taken leave of his senses. It was actually quite shrewd of Goldin after S&P's rating suspension. The game was now as much one of political perception and public relations as it was one of finance. The more times the city could get the bankers to publicly rebuff the city, the more convincing its argument that state and federal government interventions were necessary and appropriate. Of course, blaming the bankers also played well to poor and working-class voters. Rebuffed on the BANs offering, Goldin pivoted and asked the banks for an outright loan of $200 million. That too was summarily rejected. The Financial Community Liaison Group sent a letter to Goldin stating that the city's financing requirements were beyond the ability of the New York financial community by itself to provide.[23] Beame enlisted Victor Gotbaum to further pressure the banks. Gotbaum publicly labelled Citibank "Public Enemy No. 1," mostly because of the publicity in the wake of the leaking to the press of Jac Friedgut's confidential briefing of the New York congressional delegation regarding Citigroup's unwillingness to underwrite any more city notes. Gotbaum called for a boycott of the bank by the municipal unions, their members, and the city, and he scheduled a mass protest outside the bank's headquarters at 111 Wall Street for June 4.[24] Two days later, Beame told reporters the banks were "the Tories of our times" who sought to "dictate our destiny from bank boardrooms."[25]

With his state aid and tax proposals languishing in Albany, it was clear to Beame that the delivery of his fiscal 1976 expense budget was a critical bargaining chip in his negotiations with Anderson. If Beame delivered a budget with cuts that did not include all of the $650 million of new taxes and aid he requested, Beame could be held to that, and that budget would be the starting point from which more concessions would ultimately have to be made. Anderson, of course, viewed things in a completely opposite manner. Any state aid conceded and put into the city's budget would be long forgotten by the Ford administration when the time came months later for the state to demonstrate to Washington that Albany had done its part in bailing out the city. As the extended May 15 deadline for delivery of the budget approached, neither side was prepared to give in. So Beame requested a second extension for an additional week.[26] Beame wanted this time to show what horrors would befall the city if he did not get his $650 million of new taxes and aid from Albany.

Beame brought in all of the city government department heads, told them the amount their budgets would need to be cut. Taking their cue, those department heads would select the most critical aspects of city services they provided to satisfy those cuts in hopes of generating maximum outrage from the public. Beame would highlight layoffs—for up to 20 percent of the city payroll. The unions knew the game. Their leaders would run to the press, feigning outrage. "There's now a feeling that the only ones really asked to sacrifice are unions," said Victor Gotbaum. "I'm not going to stand still and let anybody cut the city unions up in pieces," said John J. Delury, president of the Uniformed Sanitationmen's Association. Barry Feinstein, president of Local 237 of the Teamsters Union, blamed the banks for "squeezing us to death" with high interest rates. "The banks could hold some of the paper," Feinstein said. "They could pitch in and hold some 6 percent or 5 percent paper."[27] Feinstein, a sophisticated union leader, knew, of course, that the banks were already choking on unsold city securities that were dropping in value precipitously and that responsible risk management at the banks required them to reduce exposure to New York City debt, not increase it.

Cuts that would hurt middle-class New Yorkers, particularly those who lived in the districts of the seven New York City Republican senators, were highlighted: a 25 percent reduction in police street patrols, elimination of sixty-six fire department units, elimination of kindergarten classes, elimination of 16,000 teaching jobs, and a one-third reduction in garbage collections.[28] When Anderson wouldn't budge,[29] Beame sought and received a third extension to deliver the budget, until May 29, allowing the pressure to build on the seven Republican senators.[30]

When Beame finally delivered his budget, it came with a gimmick novel even by the outlandish standards of New York City budgets. He delivered two budgets: one assuming he received $641 million of new taxes and state aid, his "austerity budget," and another assuming no such taxes or aid, his "crisis budget." Despite all the alleged catastrophes that would ensue if the crisis budget were to come to pass, that budget provided for 10 percent *more* spending in fiscal 1976 as compared to fiscal 1975.[31] And the assumptions underlying both budgets were laughably optimistic. Beame projected sales tax receipts of $862 million, even though less than $800 million was to be collected during fiscal 1975.[32] He budgeted for personal income tax receipts of nearly $600 million when only $564 million was to be collected during the 1975 fiscal year.[33] Beame projected that 10 percent more in real estate taxes would be collected.[34] And Cavanagh's gimmicks continued: $535 million of expenses were shifted to the capital budget.[35]

Beame, during his "budget retreat," decided he was going to come out swinging. He would blame Wall Street. He would blame the Republicans in Albany. He would play dirty. Anderson would have to come up with the money or his Republican senators in New York would feel the heat. The more intransigent Beame remained, the better the city would come out, Beame concluded. That was the frame of mind of Beame as he approached the microphones at City Hall.

In his budget address, Beame blamed the banks for the city's woes: "And what is ironic, puzzling and astonishing about this situation is that instead of being encouraged by my administration to move the city to a sounder financial position, the financial community instituted its bank embargo. Why is this taking place? Why has the financial community created an atmosphere of doubt and uncertainty about New York City securities at this point in time? Who started the whispering campaign to denigrate our fiscal integrity? A whispering campaign that has manifested itself in roaring headlines and hand-wringing editorials. I believe the people of this city deserve some answers to what is being done to them."[36] Beame's answer was a congressional investigation. "I am therefore asking for an immediate congressional inquiry into the entire matter which has cost the American public hundreds of millions of dollars in exorbitant interest rates, the depreciation of New York City notes and bonds, and has done irreparable damage to the fiscal integrity of this city."[37]

Beame's wild talk of congressional investigations and a crisis budget that nonetheless contained double-digit spending growth unsettled Carey. What unsettled Carey more was the reality that there was only so much aid the state could advance to the city, and that amount was nowhere near enough to fill the city's $1.5 billon funding gap through the end of fiscal 1975. And the city's short-term funding needs for fiscal 1976 were even larger. Carey knew that until Washington came to the rescue, the State of New York would be the city's lender of last resort. Carey needed a plan to spread that credit burden, a way to get the banks back to lending to the city and the unions to share the financial risk as well. The more militant Beame got, the more difficult Carey's job would become in dealing with Anderson. Carey admired the fight in old Beame and he had not forgotten what Beame had done for him at the Democratic State Convention the prior year, but this was now Carey's crisis. Hugh remembered

Tip O'Neill's fixation on January 6—and that Ford needed this over by Thanksgiving. Like it or not, Carey had to finance New York City until then, and he was going to make sure Beame didn't run up his tab.

Every political instinct Carey had told him to put as much distance between himself and the crisis as he could, while still controlling the financial risk. Distance from a political mess, as every seasoned politician knows, is best accomplished by assembling a committee of "independent experts" to recommend sound policy to navigate the crisis, and then following the recommendations of the "independent experts." And if those recommendations bring disaster, or even just mild disappointment, it is the experts who must be blamed. And also, as every politician knows, the key to the success of this strategy is finding experts who are not in the least independent and will do precisely what the politician asks of them. In this regard, Hugh Carey chose most wisely.

In early May, Felix Rohatyn, the star mergers and acquisitions investment banker and Lazard Frères partner, was having breakfast with National Democratic Party Chairman Robert Strauss to discuss plans to hold the 1976 Democratic National Convention in New York City. Given the city's fiscal woes, Strauss and Rohatyn both agreed that hosting the convention in a bankrupt, Democrat-run New York City would be a disaster for the party's brand.[38] Rohatyn's involvement in Democratic Party politics, primarily as a major fundraiser, was motivated not simply by the business imperative of being close to political power; he thought of himself as a statesman-financier, and when he looked in the mirror, he saw a future secretary of the Treasury, or at least a chairman of the Board of Governors of the Federal Reserve.

Rohatyn was born in Vienna in 1928 to a prosperous Jewish family that owned a number of breweries in Europe. To put some distance between themselves and Nazi Germany, the family moved to France in 1935. After Hitler invaded France in 1940, they fled first to Casablanca, then to Rio de Janeiro and finally settling in New York City. After graduating from the McBurney School in New York, Rohatyn attended Middlebury College, where he obtained a physics degree in 1949. After serving in the Army for two years during the Korean War, Rohatyn returned to a position at the Lazard Frères investment bank where he quickly became a favorite of the legendary investment banker Andre Meyer and made partner in 1961. Rohatyn had first made a national name for himself representing the conglomerate ITT Corporation in front of the House Judiciary Committee during its antitrust hearings in 1969. His effective testimony there brought him to the attention of the leadership of the New York Stock Exchange, which in 1970 was desperate to arrange a tax payer–funded bailout of the failing investment banking industry whose solvency it was supposed to regulate, but didn't. Charming, erudite Rohatyn, the master of public relations, was the public face the New York Stock Exchange wanted to show as it went hat in hand to Washington, DC. Rohatyn delivered.

Two years later, ITT again found itself in hot water with the Antitrust Division of the Nixon Department of Justice. ITT's chairman, Harold Geneen, sent his boy Rohatyn down to Washington and again Rohatyn delivered—perhaps too well. A bribery investigation followed. Rohatyn, in the crosshairs, was no longer portrayed as the crisis solver, but something akin to a well-dressed, well-paid bagman. Nothing came of the criminal investigation for Rohatyn except a nickname: "Felix the Fixer."

At his breakfast with Strauss, a great vision of the future came to Rohatyn. He too knew that ultimately Ford would bail out the city. But since Rohatyn was a banker and not a professional politician like Tip O'Neill, he did not have an accurate sense of timing as to when that bailout might take place. Rohatyn feared it might take place after the Democratic National Convention in 1976. But when Ford did bail out the city, there would be much credit to be taken. The person anointed as the architect of the city's rescue would be a civic hero. That person could very well be a banker—the one advising Governor Carey. Rohatyn, a banker and a prominent one, an equally prominent Democrat, and a prominent Democratic banker who coaxed an unlikely bailout of Wall Street from Washington less than five years earlier, was the perfect candidate to be that civic hero, thought Rohatyn. If he played his cards right with the press—and no one played the press better than Rohatyn—when the inevitable bailout came, it might be Rohatyn who would be bathed in glory. It would expunge the stain of the ITT scandal and catapult Rohatyn into a higher realm of investment banker. Not just corporate moguls and takeover artists, but presidents, prime ministers, and heads of state would brag of having him on retainer.

Rohatyn told Strauss that he would be happy to assist New York City any way he could. Strauss passed this on to Carey who, in mid-May, reached out to Rohatyn and asked if he would serve as a special advisor to him on the New York City fiscal mess and possibly join a "blue ribbon panel" of experts. Rohatyn, still transfixed by his breakfast vision, hesitated not at all in acceding to Carey's request.

On May 21, Carey told the press that he would be appointing a four-member panel of experts to consider solutions to New York City's fiscal crisis. In addition to Rohatyn, Carey appointed Simon H. Rifkind, a former federal judge and a partner at the corporate law firm Paul, Weiss, Rifkind, Wharton & Garrison with a colorful past that went all the way back to Tammany

Hall of the roaring twenties. Rounding out Carey's panel were Richard R. Shinn (the chief executive officer of the Metropolitan Life Insurance Company) and Donald B. Smiley (the chairman of R.H. Macy & Co., the department store company).[39] "First, I seek their advice on the steps necessary to assure that New York City does not go into default," Carey told the press when introducing the new panel in Albany on May 22.[40] "Second, I seek their advice on how New York City can best return to a healthy status in the money market."[41]

Carey's panel worked over the Memorial Day weekend to come up with a plan acceptable to the governor to address the city's $1.5 billion June cash needs and its estimated $650 million fiscal 1976 expense budget deficit. Joining the panel at Richard Shinn's home in Greenwich, Connecticut, on Memorial Day were representatives from the Financial Community Liaison Group.[42] Out of this Memorial Day meeting came the blueprint for the state's response to the crisis. It was the same plan the Financial Community Liaison Group laid out for Beame and Goldin at their meeting on March 11, now purloined by Rohatyn. First, a new funding vehicle for the city would be set up. The SRC was supposed to be such a vehicle, but it had failed in this role because it lacked credit support from New York State (it only had certain revenues owing from the state to the city as credit support). The new vehicle had to have the state's "moral obligation" behind it. There was no time for a statewide referendum to obtain approval of the state providing "full faith and credit" support for the new vehicle's debt, and it was highly doubtful such approval would have been obtained in any event. This funding vehicle was supposed to serve the purpose of not only providing for the city's short-term cash needs, but also refinancing the city's excessive short-term debt with long-term debt. Second, this vehicle would be given fiscal oversight authority over the city by means of its conditioning delivery of its bond proceeds to the city on the city balancing its budget and making progress toward eliminating the accounting gimmicks. On paper, it was a sound plan. It would, in practice, fail miserably at its stated objectives. Its failure, however, would prove critical in achieving ultimate success in Washington, DC.[43] But first, Carey needed to get it through the Republican-controlled State Senate, and he needed to get Beame to go along with it.

CHAPTER EIGHT

WELCOME TO FEAR CITY

ON JUNE 2, CAREY UNVEILED TO THE LEGISLATIVE LEADERS IN Albany his draft legislation creating the state agency to refinance the city's short-term debt into long-term debt. "Call it the Municipal Assistance Corporation—the 'Big Mac,'" Carcy joked with reporters.[1] Cary provided very few other details to the press at the time, except that the state would control the MAC board and that the agency would be empowered to impose a new accounting system on the city and eliminate the budget gimmicks. The MAC would issue long-term bonds backed by the city sales tax and stock transfer tax and by the state's "moral obligation" to repay the bonds in the event those taxes were insufficient to do so.

After being briefed on the legislation, Beame vowed to fight it. Carey and his Big Mac were going to steal the city's sales tax and stock transfer tax receipts—and what was the city going to get in return? Beame publicly criticized the plan, saying that if the state was going to usurp the city taxing authority, it should take over city functions that properly rest with the state—the court and prison systems, welfare, and the City University.[2] If Beame decided to go to war with Carey over the MAC, he had an ally in City Council President Paul O'Dwyer, the Irish-born younger brother of former New York City Mayor William O'Dwyer, who relished a fight, so long as he was the underdog and faced long odds.

Born in County Mayo, Ireland, Paul O'Dwyer emigrated to Brooklyn as a seventeen-year-old in 1925. Paul graduated from Fordham University and St. John's Law School thereafter. He was his brother Bill's closest confidante. Bill O'Dwyer, born in 1890 in County Mayo, thought he wanted to become a priest and studied at a Jesuit seminary in Spain. He changed his mind and came to America where he got a job on the New York City police force and went to law school at night at Fordham University. He got involved in Brooklyn politics and got a county judgeship in the 1930s. He ran for Brooklyn District Attorney in 1939 and won. In 1941, he ran against Fiorello La Guardia for mayor and lost. After serving as a brigadier general in World War II, he was selected by the bosses to run for mayor again in 1945, winning that time.

All seemed rosy for Mayor O'Dwyer until his reelection campaign in 1949. There were whisperings of illegal campaign contributions and of O'Dwyer's political patronage dispenser, a former policeman named James Moran, in particular Moran's relationship with Harry Gross, New York City's biggest bookie with over thirty-five illegal gambling dens and three hundred employees. After the 1949 campaign, which O'Dwyer won, Brooklyn District Attorney Miles McDonald and Manhattan District Attorney Frank Hogan impanelled grand juries. Scores

President Gerald Ford *(center)* with **Governor Hugh Carey** *(left)* and **Mayor Abe Beame** *(right)*. By early 1975, Ford, the accidental president, was determined to run for president in 1976. To win the Republican nomination and the election, he needed to win New York—and in 1975, New York City needed a bailout. (GERALD FORD PRESIDENTIAL LIBRARY/NARA.)

Tip O'Neill, the Democratic majority leader of the US House of Representatives, was an old friend of Ford's, but politics came first for O'Neill. He would mastermind the strategy to get New York its bailout from Washington. (LIBRARY OF CONGRESS, U.S. NEWS & WORLD REPORT COLLECTION.)

Despite two failed attempts, **Nelson Rockefeller**'s lifelong ambition to be president was resurrected when Ford selected him to be his vice president. The fallout of New York City's fiscal crisis would finally extinguish Rockefeller's aspirations. (LIBRARY OF CONGRESS/WARREN K. LEFFLER, U.S. NEWS & WORLD REPORT COLLECTION.)

James Cavanagh *(right)*, with **Abe Beame** and **David Dinkins**) was a wizard when it came to manipulating budget numbers to make the New York City expense budget appear balanced. By 1975, Cavanagh's gimmicks had caught up with him. (AP PHOTO/SUZANNE VLAMIS.)

Before Ford agreed to bail out New York City, he required New York State to contribute significantly to cleaning up the city's financial mess. Republican State Senate Majority Leader **Warren Anderson** (seen here shaking hands with **Governor Carey**), an experienced and wily legislator, held the purse strings in Albany. (NEW YORK STATE ARCHIVES, GOVERNOR PUBLIC INFORMATION PHOTOGRAPHS.)

Fiscal irresponsibility was a bipartisan affair among New York politicians. One notable exception was State Comptroller **Arthur Levitt**, who opposed Nelson Rockefeller's "moral obligation" bonds and resisted investing in Hugh Carey's Municipal Assistance Corporation bonds. (MOSHE PRIDAN/PD ISRAEL & BRITISH MANDATE.)

New York City Comptroller **Harrison Goldin** ran as a reformer, an antagonist of the clubhouse bosses who put Mayor Beame in City Hall. However, as a result of the fiscal crisis, his fate would be tied to Beame's. Goldin survived the crisis but would not attain an office higher than city comptroller. (AP PHOTO/BOB DAUGHERTY.)

City Council President **Paul O'Dwyer** was an unreconstructed political maverick and old-school liberal who relished representing the underdog and fighting long odds. He was willing to lock arms with Beame and defy Wall Street and the Republicans in Albany and Washington by defaulting on New York City bonds rather than subject the city's poor to painful austerity measures. Beame took a different path. (AP PHOTO/FILE.)

Carmine DeSapio *(wearing dark sunglasses)* was the powerful boss of the Manhattan clubhouse Democrats, the system that produced the last of the clubhouse mayors, Abe Beame, who desperately wanted to show the city that the clubhouse system could still manage the "Ungovernable City." (THE DAILY NEWS ARCHIVE/ GETTY IMAGES.)

Meade Esposito was the Democratic boss of Brooklyn, running the most powerful political organization in the nation in the mid-1970s. The famed Madison Democratic Club was among the party organizations that reported to Meade. Mayor Beame and Governor Carey both came out of the Brooklyn organization run by Esposito. (© KEN REGAN/CAMERA 5.)

When the New York City fiscal crisis spun out of control and became New York State's problem, Governor Carey assembled a team of experts led by Lazard Frères investment banker **Felix Rohatyn** *(in the foreground)*, with labor consultant **Jack Bigel** *(behind him)*. Although Rohatyn's plan for the Municipal Acceptance Corporation to reopen the municipal bond market for New York City by September 1975 failed miserably, Rohatyn's masterful handling of the press deflected blame to Mayor Beame and President Ford. (NEW YORK DAILY NEWS ARCHIVE/GETTY IMAGES.)

Governor Carey's other expert advisor during the fiscal crisis was lawyer **Simon Rifkind** (seen here with **President Kennedy**). Rifkind, an eminence in the New York bar, was a longtime Tammany Hall presence going back to the days of Governor Al Smith. Rifkind's brilliant scheme would keep New York City out of federal bankruptcy court but give the power brokers all the benefits of bankruptcy without the drawbacks. (ABBIE ROWE. WHITE HOUSE PHOTOGRAPHS. JOHN F. KENNEDY PRESIDENTIAL LIBRARY AND MUSEUM, BOSTON.)

Albert Shanker *(left)* and **Victor Gotbaum** *(right)* were the two most powerful labor officials in New York in the 1970s. While of similar backgrounds and philosophies, they were rivals and personally antagonistic to each other. (AMERICAN FEDERATION OF TEACHERS COLLECTION/WALTER P. REUTHER LIBRARY, ARCHIVES OF LABOR AND URBAN AFFAIRS, WAYNE STATE UNIVERSITY.)

Roy Cohn (pictured with **Ronald Reagan**, President Ford's rival for the Republican nomination in 1976) rivaled Bill Shea and Simon Rifkind when it came to political influence in New York in the 1970s. Cohn's controversial past—prosecuting the Rosenbergs, acting as Joe McCarthy's chief counsel, and his own criminal difficulties—was overlooked by the New York establishment, who knew Cohn would do whatever it took to win. Whenever a judge or politician got into legal difficulties during the 1970s, Cohn, Shea, or Rifkind (and sometimes all of them) would offer their services, usually pro bono. It turned out to be very good for business. (RONALD REAGAN PRESIDENTIAL LIBRARY/NARA.)

William Shea *(left)*, for whom Shea Stadium was named, came out of the same Brooklyn clubhouse politics as Abe Beame and Hugh Carey. Shea was the most politically powerful lawyer in New York City in the 1970s, and one of the most powerful in the nation. The cozy relationship among big business, the unions, and the government in New York was often facilitated by Bill Shea and his firm, Shea & Gould, which was very profitable for all involved, save the taxpayers who paid for it. (LIBRARY OF CONGRESS.)

Perhaps the most influential power broker in New York during the 1970s was **Jerry Finkelstein** *(right)*, publisher, political kingmaker, and confidant to governors, mayors, and presidents since the 1940s. (NEAL BOENZI/THE NEW YORK TIMES/REDUX.)

No real estate developer was better connected politically than **Fred Trump** (with son **Donald**). Fred Trump, a major contributor to both Beame and Carey, built his empire with the help of government contracts and subsidies—and with legal help from Roy Cohn, Bill Shea, and, most of all, Bunny Lindenbaum, Beame's best friend. (LIBRARY OF CONGRESS/BERNARD GOTFRYD.)

(*below*) **John Scanlon** was a former Roman Catholic monk turned public relations man whose first big client was Anthony Scotto. Carey and Rohatyn chose Scanlon to be the in-house public relations director for the Municipal Assistance Corporation (MAC). It was an inspired choice. Scanlon's brilliant manipulation of the press brought Carey and the MAC positive coverage that won the battle with President Ford over a favorable bailout for New York City. Scanlon's conflicts of interest would result in his resignation, under a cloud of scandal, from the MAC position months after the bailout. (CHARLIE ROSE INTERVIEW, "PRESIDENTIAL PRIMARIES '92," BROADCAST ON FEBRUARY 16, 1992, 11 MIN., 58 SEC.)

(*above*) **Anthony Scotto**, head of the Longshoremen's Union in New York, was movie-star handsome, politically powerful, and closely associated with the Gambino crime family. When Scotto was indicted for racketeering, Hugh Carey, the sitting governor of New York, was the star character witness for him at his trial. (MEYER LIEBOWITZ/THE NEW YORK TIMES/REDUX.)

(above) John Scanlon's handiwork. (AP PHOTO.)

(right) The 1975 Inner Circle Show, the annual lampooning of New York politicians by the New York press corps, took place just as the fiscal crisis was coming to a head and was perhaps the most memorable performance. (THE INNER CIRCLE SHOW [HTTPS://WWW.INNERCIRCLESHOW.COM], 1975, FRONT COVER; HENRY WALTER PAPERS [MS 3016], NEW-YORK HISTORICAL SOCIETY. ILLUSTRATION BY JOHN PIEROTTI.)

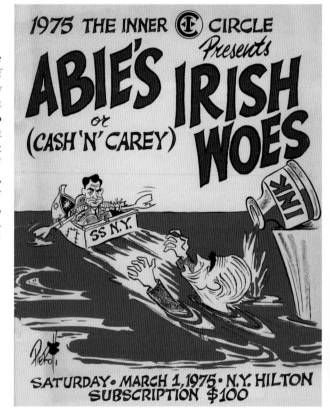

of policemen resigned from the police force rather than face the grand juries, and more than a dozen were indicted. An ambassadorship for Mayor O'Dwyer was arranged with President Truman, to Mexico, to get O'Dwyer out of town. In March 1951, Congress got interested, and Senator Estes Kefauver called some prominent New Yorkers to testify in front of his Crime Investigating Committee. One of them, John P. Crane, president of the Uniformed Firemen's Association, told the committee he had turned over an envelope to Mayor O'Dwyer with $10,000 in it (and one to James Moran with $55,000 in it). This was of great interest to Frank Hogan, who immediately marched John Crane in front of the Manhattan grand jury.

Crane's grand jury testimony brought joy to Hogan because Crane revealed that greatest of all circumstances to a prosecutor—the presence of corroborating witnesses. Crane claimed he approached O'Dwyer's mayoral campaign manager, Jerry Finkelstein, with the idea of the payoffs, showed Finkelstein the envelopes with the cash, and talked about the payoffs in the car with Crane's driver, Victor T. Wilder, present. Hogan was less joyful when it turned out Wilder was hard of hearing and wore hearing aids and claimed he did not hear what Crane and Finkelstein were discussing. But Hogan did not lose heart. He called Finkelstein in front of the grand jury.

Finkelstein, thirty-five years old at the time, was a politically connected lawyer and the owner of *The Civil Service Leader,* a newspaper for public employees. There was no way Finkelstein was going to lie to the grand jury or take the Fifth Amendment—he was a successful, on-the-rise businessman and respected confidante to high-ranking city politicians. But even the healthiest of thirty-five-year-olds sometimes forget the details of things that happened years earlier, don't they? Finkelstein answered,

"It could have happened, but I don't remember," "I couldn't say yes or no," "I have no recollection of that" or phrases of similar import so many times the jurors' eyes glazed over. Hogan went ballistic and moved to have Finkelstein held in contempt for refusing to answer questions. Judge Louis Valente told Hogan there was nothing that could be done. Finkelstein answered the questions, Hogan just didn't like the answers. To Hogan's fury, Bill O'Dwyer was never indicted (although the IRS did get him for failing to declare the $10,000 as income).

Finkelstein had demonstrated, like Bill Shea, that he knew how to keep his mouth shut, and Jerry went on to make many millions of dollars in business while at the same time becoming one of the most important power brokers in New York City during the second half of the twentieth century. When JFK needed to raise money in New York for his 1960 campaign, he went to see Finkelstein. LBJ selected Finkelstein to co-chair (with James Farley) his 1964 campaign in New York. When Bobby Kennedy was deciding whether to run for Senate in New York, he met with Finkelstein, who encouraged Bobby and raised millions for the campaign. Finkelstein was also a fundraiser and confidant for Republicans like John Lindsay and Nelson Rockefeller. A grateful Rockefeller appointed Finkelstein as commissioner of the Port Authority of New York and New Jersey. Finkelstein left his most enduring mark on the city during the time he served as chairman of the City Planning Commission. He was appointed by Mayor O'Dwyer over the objections of Robert Moses, who wanted a lackey as chairman, which Finkelstein most definitely was not. Finkelstein, in 1950, was the first city official to successfully oppose Moses's more outlandish plans for road building and neighborhood demolition, outfoxing Moses time and time again, and reducing him to tears of frustration and rage while preserving many of the city's architectural gems.

Paul O'Dwyer was never implicated in any of his brother's scandals. But the ordeal of it all soured Paul on the clubhouse politicians and their corrupt ways. He became a maverick and started his own law practice representing troublemakers of all stripes. O'Dwyer represented communists, Irish Republican Army gunrunners, Irgun and Stern Gang "terrorists" in Israel, Black civil rights workers in Alabama, striking Kentucky coal miners, and anti–Vietnam War protestors. O'Dwyer ran for many offices over the years, losing a close congressional race to Jacob Javits on the Upper West Side in 1948. He won a City Council seat in 1963, from which he ran for mayor in 1965, finishing fourth, well behind Beame in the Democratic primary. O'Dwyer was an early backer of Senator Eugene McCarthy's presidential run in 1968, and he ran for US Senate that year, and in a major upset won the Democratic primary. He lost decisively in the general election, again to Jacob Javits. He ran again for the Senate in 1970, finishing a close second to Richard Ottinger who would go on to lose to James Buckley, William F. Buckley's brother. In 1973, O'Dwyer won the election for New York City Council president.

Paul O'Dwyer echoed Beame's criticisms of the MAC plan: "We're back to the bankers' agreement of the nineteen thirties. Only worse. We'd be solving their default problems but not our own."[3] O'Dwyer thought defaulting on the short-term debt coming due on June 11 might be a preferable option to ceding too much control and tax revenue over to the MAC. "I'm just saying that it's not something to say never, never about. It's not a very desirable option, but I would not reject it [bankruptcy] out of hand. It's a hard decision for me to make. It depends how harsh the terms of the [MAC] corporation are. I want to check every word, every comma in that bill."[4]

Beame's first instinct was to lock arms with O'Dwyer and the unions and fight—striking out at the greedy Wall Street bankers, the heartless Republicans in Albany and Washington, and Governor Carey, who apparently was willing to throw the city overboard to placate the suburbs and the upstate voters. But that fight might mean default and bankruptcy. Chaos and lawlessness in the streets might result. And what if he failed? What if the bailout from Washington came with draconian conditions? What if he became the first mayor of New York City to preside over the city when it defaulted on its debt—when it filed bankruptcy—and the people blamed *him* for the chaos and the lawlessness? What if all the anger and defiance came to nothing but ruin—and Beame was remembered as the last of the old clubhouse politicians who was not up to running the ungovernable city? He would be blamed for reducing the clubhouse to a pile of rubble. O'Dwyer and the unions would abandon him if the wrong federal bankruptcy judge was drawn and injunctions issued. When imagining that possible future, Beame folded.

The climatic sit-down between Rohatyn, on behalf of Carey, and Beame and O'Dwyer was scheduled for June 4, at City Hall. Rohatyn had one trump card to play: Governor Carey promised to do whatever it took to prevent the city from having to default, from having to file bankruptcy. Beame would never have to face that historic indignity. The price for that promise was that Beame would need to go along with the subordination of the city's authority, the prerogatives of the mayor, to those of Governor Carey and New York State. Beame would have to agree to become Carey's junior partner. In the moment, Beame felt betrayed by Carey, but that was misplaced emotion. Beame played a much bigger role in putting the city in the hole it was in than Carey did. The city would be out of money soon even if it defaulted on all its upcoming maturing debt, Rohatyn reminded them, and the banks and the state would extract worse terms after a default than before one.[5] Perhaps Beame didn't think he could win the fight. Perhaps he was too old and too tired for the fight. But in the fateful decision that set the path for the remainder of his administration—and the end of his political career—Beame agreed to Carey's offer. And thus began a three-way negotiation of the fine print among Carey, Beame, and Anderson with shuttle-diplomacy between Albany, City Hall, and the offices of Paul, Weiss, Rifkind, Wharton & Garrison, Simon Rifkind's law firm and outside counsel to the MAC.

On June 6, Carey publicly released the draft of his bill creating the MAC. The other details included that up to $3 billion of MAC bonds would be authorized for issuance. The MAC board would have nine members, all appointed by the governor, four of whom would be appointed upon the written recommendation of the mayor of New York City. The city would be given ten years to adopt a state-approved accounting system and remove all expenses from the capital budget.

Anderson weighed in the next day. He insisted that the legislation include a hard cap on the amount of short-term debt the city would be allowed to incur and that four "ex officio" members of the MAC board be appointed by state legislative leaders.[6] Those modifications were agreed to by Carey and Beame. Paul O'Dwyer demanded that the city legislative leaders get to appoint two ex officio members of the MAC board as well.[7] This was agreed to. The parties also settled on a short-term debt cap of $8 billion.

In the early morning hours of June 10, the Senate passed the MAC legislation by a vote of fifty to six. The New York City Council approved the related home-rule message by a vote of twenty-eight to one. By dawn, the State Assembly approved the bill, which was thereafter immediately signed by Governor Carey.

Less than nine hours after Carey signed the bill into law, he and Beame jointly announced their appointments to the MAC board. The chairman of the board would be Thomas P. Flynn, a partner in the accounting firm of Arthur Young & Co. The governor's other appointees were Felix Rohatyn, Simon Rifkind, Donna Shalala (a Columbia University professor), and Robert Weaver (a former secretary of Housing and Urban Development). The Beame-recommended appointments were John A. Coleman (former chairman of the New York Stock Exchange), Francis T. Barry (president of the Circle Line Company), William Ellinghaus (president of New York Telephone Company), and George D. Gould (chairman of the board of the investment bank Donaldson, Lufkin & Jenrette Inc.).

Real estate baron Lew Rudin came up with an idea to help the city—and save some money at the same time. He had had many good ideas over the decades, as he and his brother Jack had built a modest family real estate company into a New York City colossus with over twenty-five buildings. Rudin's grandfather, Louis Rudinsky, came to America in 1883 and worked as a grocer. He started the family real estate empire when he bought an apartment house in 1920 on East 54th Street in Manhattan. John D. Rockefeller Jr.'s townhouse was on the block, and Rudinsky concluded that property there would hold its value. He was right. The family later built a thirty-two-story office tower there. Born in the Throggs Neck section of the Bronx in 1927, Lew graduated from DeWitt Clinton High

School and New York University and served as a sergeant in the Army during World War II. After the war, Lew and his brother Jack joined the family firm. Jack oversaw construction while Lew, a natural schmoozer, ran the sales and leasing office. Lew was also the greatest cheerleader New York City ever had, forming the Association for a Better New York with Preston Robert Tisch and Howard Rubenstein in 1971.

The genius of Lew Rudin's idea in May 1975 was that it would not only save him some money, but also help the city with its short-term borrowing needs. Rudin's plan was simple. The next city real estate tax payment was due on August 1. The city needed cash—$1.5 billion of it—by June or it would go bankrupt. And by late May, it looked like no one would lend the city any more money. Well, why couldn't the large real estate owners prepay their August 1 real estate tax bills, but discounted to reflect a market rate of interest on the "loan" of the funds to the city for two months, thought Rudin? The interest rate he proposed was 7.25 percent—less than the city's last short-term borrowing rate, but just above the current prime lending rate—a good deal for both the city and the real estate owners. Rudin quickly rounded up support for his plan from other large real estate tax payers—New York Telephone Company, Consolidated Edison Company, Lehman Brothers, and other major financial institutions. Beame was soon on board: "We think this a commendable example of the spirit of the City of New York and the people who make up business and the community and are proud to call themselves 'New Yorkers.'"[8] By the end of May, the City Council had approved the plan.[9]

With the public relations impresario Howard Rubenstein on retainer, Rudin's prepayment scheme was soon spun by Rubenstein into a selfless act of great philanthropy by the real estate moguls. They too could thereafter claim they saved the city in its darkest hour.

To raise the $792 million the city needed to refinance the obligations coming due in June, the Financial Community Liaison Group arranged a one-year bridge loan from the banks to refinance the $280 million of short-term notes that were coming due. The banks also provided the MAC with a $100 million bridge loan, to be taken out by the first MAC bond issuance. The state advanced another $200 million against future state aid for education, and $160 million was obtained from Rudin's plan for prepayment of real estate taxes and raiding a number of bond "sinking fund" accounts. And for the first time in the crisis, Victor Gotbaum and the other union leaders agreed to make available the city public employee pension fund money to provide financing to the city. Those pension funds purchased $52 million of the city's notes to complete the refinancing package.[10]

With the MAC's authorization to issue $3 billion of bonds, the city would be assured of its cash-flow needs through the end of September—assuming, that is, that the MAC could sell those $3 billion of bonds. The city's financing issues would not end there by any stretch of the imagination. The city would need to borrow $4 billion more to get through fiscal 1976.[11]

The official thesis behind the MAC was that by October 1975 the city would be able to again access the municipal bond market. The unofficial thesis was that, at a minimum, the MAC would buy time for a federal bailout and perhaps raise enough money to get the city through Thanksgiving. Anderson was blunt with the press regarding the likelihood that the city would be able to borrow in the municipal market come October: "It's very hard to say that they can. It's hard to say there's anything they can do."[12] Anderson urged the city to press the Federal Reserve for a loan but had little confidence in Beame or Cavanagh. "He's a delightful guy," said Anderson of Cavanagh. "He's had three shells out there and the pea in his pocket. Most of the occupations for which he is suited have been declared illegal."[13]

Rohatyn hedged his bets on his adopted brainchild from the beginning, telling the *New York Times*, "I want to emphasize again that the MAC is no guarantee. It can possibly, hopefully, get you over June 11. It can buy you a couple of months. It can take some short-term debt off the city and create a climate and a series of perceptions that might enable the city to get itself back into the market place, which is going to be the ultimate test of this thing."[14] While the MAC would fail, Rohatyn's invaluable success for Carey was in convincing Beame to go along, to not fight, to join Team Carey. Because if the showdown with Ford had taken place in May and not November, Ford would have had the stronger hand.

On the same day that the MAC was born, Donald J. Trump, son of Fred Trump and the new president of Trump Management Corporation, signed an agreement with the US Justice Department in which he promised that his company would not discriminate against Blacks, Puerto Ricans, and other racial minorities and that it would give the New York Urban League a list every month of all vacancies in Trump buildings and allow the Urban League to fill every fifth vacancy with a qualified Black applicant. The Justice Department had sued Trump in federal court in 1973 alleging racial discrimination, and this agreement settled that lawsuit. Trump claimed "full satisfaction" with the agreement because it did not contain "any requirement that would compel the Trump organization to accept leasees on welfare."[15]

The Trump organization did not hire Fred Trump's old friend, Bunny Lindenbaum, to handle this matter. Nor did it hire Bill Shea, who handled many of the Trump organization's corporate matters. For this matter, Donald Trump turned to the most infamous lawyer in America during the 1970s—the self-proclaimed legal executioner: Roy M. Cohn. "They all said, 'You have a good case, but it's a sticky thing,'" Trump said about the other lawyers he discussed the case with. When he first met with Cohn to discuss the case, Cohn told Trump, "You'll win hands down," Trump recalled to journalist Ken Auletta during an interview for *Esquire* magazine.[16]

Today, in New York City, Cohn is remembered as a pariah, a right-wing Republican zealot who prosecuted the Rosenbergs, served as Joe McCarthy's chief inquisitor, and, worst of all, represented Donald J. Trump. But in truth, in the 1970s, Cohn was a member in good standing of the New York City establishment, a registered Democrat, and a trusted ally of the Brooklyn Democratic clubhouse politicians who ran the city and the state. For example, Cohn was one of the eight members of the New York City Democratic Party Finance Committee. "I used to be wary of Roy, but then I went to one of his parties, and the people I saw there were all respected," said Lew Rudin.[17] Howard Rubenstein said of Cohn, "I know if I was in a fight, I'd want Roy Cohn in my corner."[18] At Governor Carey's inauguration gala at the Waldorf Astoria, Cohn was in attendance, working the room, seen chatting with Anthony Scotto, Howard Rubenstein, Lew Rudin, Paul O'Dwyer, Jerry Finkelstein, Mayor Beame, and, of course, his good friend the governor.[19]

Cohn's parties were must-attend events in the 1970s for those in, or aspiring to enter, the New York political, social, and business elite. A young, ambitious first-term assemblyman from Brooklyn named Chuck Schumer wrangled a coveted invitation to one of Cohn's birthday parties. Regulars at those parties included Mayor Beame; Carmine DeSapio, the former Manhattan Democratic leader; Frank Rossetti, the current Manhattan Democratic leader; Donald Manes, the Queens Democratic leader; Jerry Finkelstein, who often arrived with his sons Andrew, a state assemblyman and future City Council president, and James, publisher of the *New York Law Journal*; Cardinal Cooke who came with his personal assistant, the yet-to-be defrocked Monsignor Theodore E. McCarrick; Andy Warhol; William F. Buckley Jr. and his socialite wife Pat; *New York Times* journalists William Safire, Abe Rosenthal, and Sidney Zion; magazine mogul Si Newhouse; Fred and Donald Trump; and a kick line of New York Supreme Court justices, including John M. Murtagh, Hyman Korn, Thomas Hughes, Alvin F. Klein, Joseph Marro, Alfred M. Ascione, and Manuel Gomez. The State Appellate Court judges were not left out—Vito Titone nearly always came—nor were the federal judges—US District Court Judge David Edelstein was another habitual attendee.

Roy Cohn always looked after the judges. Cohn, along with Bill Shea and Simon Rifkind, were the go-to lawyers whenever a judge found himself in trouble, and they often represented those judges pro bono. Their respective firms were also chock-full of retired judges and children of judges. Throughout 1975, Cohn was representing one of those judges in trouble, US Customs Court Judge Paul P. Rao Sr. of Brooklyn, in the highest-profile public corruption case of the year.

In June 1974, Rao had found himself ensnared in a trap laid for him by a special prosecutor named Maurice H. Nadjari. Nadjari had been appointed the special prosecutor for public corruption in New York City by Governor Rockefeller in 1972, after the Knapp Commission, formed to investigate New York City police corruption (memorialized in the movie *Serpico*), recommended the position be created to root out corrupt public officials in New York City in all branches of government. Nadjari used unorthodox and very aggressive tactics to obtain indictments. In Rao's case, he manufactured a phony robbery and had an undercover agent indicted by a real Brooklyn grand jury for the fictitious crime. He then had another undercover agent, posing as the girlfriend of the defendant, wear a wire while meeting with Rao in Brooklyn to try and catch Rao in accepting a bribe to agree to use his influence with the judge assigned to the phony case to reduce the bail requested. Rao advised the woman undercover agent to hire his son—who knew the judge—to handle the case. That was enough for Nadjari, who proceeded to indict Rao, whose first call was to Cohn.

Cohn's defense strategy was bold and brilliant. He would put Nadjari on trial. It was Nadjari, Cohn would tell the court, who was the real criminal here: Nadjari lied to the grand jury, he filed a false police report, he committed fraud upon the Brooklyn courts. Cohn accused Nadjari of twelve separate crimes. In December 1975, Cohn succeeded in having Rao's indictment dismissed by the New York Supreme Court. The judge who dismissed the indictment? Judge John M. Murtagh, one of the regulars at Cohn's parties.

Shortly after Cohn won Rao's case, Governor Carey petitioned New York State Attorney General Louis Lefkowitz to have Nadjari dismissed as special prosecutor. Nadjari claimed Carey was trying to get rid of him because he was about to indict Patrick J. Cunningham, Carey's handpicked chairman of the New York State Democratic Party, for selling judgeships. Carey claimed that not only were Nadjari's methods unsound, but his record was terrible. After nearly four years and with 160 investigators and an $11 million budget, Nadjari had yet to win a major corruption case. Only 80 of his 300 indictments resulted in convictions, and all of those were minor charges against low-level civil servants. Nadjari actually tried a City Housing Department official for taking a $30 bribe. Carey had a point. Spending nearly four years following around New York City political figures in the 1970s and not being able to make a major corruption case was like following the Grateful Dead around for four years and not being able to make a narcotics case. Lefkowitz decided to give Nadjari six months to make a case against Cunningham. He did bring charges against Cunningham—they were all dismissed before trial. The legal woes took a toll on Cunningham and his relationship with Carey, however, leading to Cunningham's resignation. Cohn was not discouraged at all by Cunningham's resignation. His successor? Stanley Friedman, Cohn's law partner. (Friedman would go on to have his own legal problems culminating in his conviction in a high-profile public corruption trial. Among his misdeeds were doing favors he shouldn't have for Cohn on behalf of a client while Friedman was deputy mayor, before he joined Cohn's firm. That client? Donald J. Trump. The prosecutor who convicted Friedman? Rudy Giuliani, future lawyer of Donald J. Trump.)

The elites of New York in the 1970s were not unaware of Cohn's character when they embraced him. New York City, then, was a place where the Mafia controlled entire industries and labor unions. Cops and judges were on the take. Licensing requirements and similar ordinances only applied to those who didn't "know someone" downtown. In that environment, Cohn's character attracted clients rather than repelled them. Those at the top of the heap in New York knew the game was rigged and that, for certain matters, it was best to have a lawyer willing and able to rig the game in your favor. Cohn was not unique among lawyers of the day in his utter lack of scruples in getting what he wanted, he was just the most successful at it. The roster of those who paid homage to Cohn at his well-publicized parties provides a blinding glimpse into the culture in which budget gimmickry and fiscal chicanery thrived.

For two weeks, the MAC staff and the lawyers at Paul, Weiss prepared the bond prospectus for the first MAC bond offering. On June 26, the details of the $1 billion offering were announced. The press was told that more than half of the offering had been presold to local financial institutions. What was not said was that the funds those financial institutions would use to purchase those MAC bonds would be the cash they received from the redemption of city short-term notes they held that would be repaid with the proceeds of the MAC bonds—a roundtrip—hardly a new financial commitment endorsing the MAC's creditworthiness.

As the largest municipal bond offering in history, fourteen managing underwriters were named.[20] The bonds received good ratings from both Moody's and S&P, A and A+, respectively.[21] With those ratings, the managing underwriters began the largest nationwide "road show" for any securities offering in history. A syndicate of 365 financial institutions scoured the country, meeting with virtually every significant municipal bond investor.[22] The underwriters highlighted the security for the bonds—the sales taxes and stock transfer taxes covered debt service requirements on $3 billion of bonds at a 9 percent interest rate by 2.55 times. The New York State moral obligation was also mentioned, although the debacle of the UDC lessened the benefit of that credit support. In short, the objective was to convince investors that MAC bonds were not New York City bonds, but bonds nearly as secure as the "full faith and credit" bonds of the State of New York.

On June 30, the managing underwriters priced the offering, which was tranched with staggered maturities ranging from two years to fifteen years. The weighted average interest rate of the bonds was slightly over 9.1 percent, just higher than the rate the underwriters first offered to investors in price negotiations.[23] The bad news: $200 million of the $500 million of bonds offered to investors could not be sold.[24] Worse, despite the unprecedented road show, virtually none of the bonds were sold to investors outside of New York State.[25]

One task for which the junior partner Beame was indispensable to the senior partner Carey was in putting pressure on Anderson to cough up more dough for the city. With his two expense budgets, and a $641 million funding gap between the austerity budget and the crisis budget, Beame had made clear the amount of additional aid and taxing authority he was asking from Albany. He had only come down $9 million from the $650 million he was originally asking for. If it were up to Carey or Assembly Speaker Stanley Steingut, Democrat of Brooklyn, Beame would get all $641 million he was seeking. Anderson, however, had other ideas. But Anderson had that weak flank—the seven Republican senators from New York City who would suffer a political cost for voting against additional aid to the city. With his thirty-four to twenty-six majority, Anderson could not afford to lose the votes of even four of the seven.

All the Republican senators represented white, middle-class or upper-middle-class neighborhoods for whom clean and safe streets were of paramount importance. Accordingly, Beame had a very straightforward strategy: show how New York City, if forced to adopt the crisis budget, would have unclean and unsafe streets. This meant cuts to the sanitation, police, and fire departments. According to Beame, under his austerity budget, 30,000 positions would be eliminated (although, as we know, there is a big difference between eliminating positions, often unfilled or reclassified with no cash savings, and firing flesh-and-blood employees). Under his crisis budget, 67,300 positions would be eliminated. Those extra 37,300 layoffs would deeply affect police, fire, and sanitation workers, Beame would make clear. The city's municipal labor unions were allies of Beame in pursuing this strategy, for virtually all the dollars of new taxes or aid Beame might coax from Anderson would find their way into the pockets of union members.

The first union labor action of significance during the crisis was a rally at Citibank's office at 111 Wall Street on June 4. Victor Gotbaum, in his capacity as chairman of the city's Municipal Labor Committee, which was comprised of the heads of the unions representing employees of agencies whose expenditures the mayor controlled, organized the rally, which drew 10,000 city employees.[26] Barry Feinstein, president of Teamsters Local 237, and Richard Vizzini, president of the Uniformed Firefighters Association, were among the labor leaders joining Gotbaum at the rally. Citibank continued to be singled out because Jac Friedgut, a Citibank vice president, had the temerity to honestly brief the New York congressional delegation regarding the city's inability to access the municipal bond market. Gotbaum knew it was nonsense to blame Citibank for the city's fiscal mess, but banks had clout in Albany so keeping the heat on them while Mayor Beame squeezed Anderson for more cash made all the sense in the world.

Four days later, Albert Shanker led over 25,000 demonstrators against proposed cuts to the education budget. "We want them to hear us in Washington and in Albany," roared Shanker to the crowd. "Brothers and sisters, we can get the money. It is in the banks and there is no question that your fight tomorrow is in Albany. That's why you've got to go."[27]

Albert Shanker was a forty-six-year-old former mathematics teacher, born and raised in New York City, a child of socialists. He graduated from the University of Illinois with a degree in philosophy and later received a master's in mathematics from Columbia University. He took a job thereafter as a public school teacher, joined the United Federation of Teachers, and worked his way up the ladder, becoming the secretary of his local in 1960 and its president in 1964. By 1973, he became president of the national union. A favorite of George Meany, president of the AFL-CIO, Shanker was considered a possible future president of that labor organization, the nation's largest. Like Meany, Shanker was a political moderate, refusing to speak out against the Vietnam War and a vocal opponent of affirmative action in hiring: "Quotas are authoritarian and essentially discriminatory," he told the *New York Times* in 1975. "Because you are saying that those less professionally qualified are equal to those who have met professional standards . . . Why not just convey an M.A. at birth on Blacks and minorities?"[28] Shanker's UFT represented approximately 80,000 teachers and other school employees making him the representative of the second largest number of city employees, behind his bitter rival Gotbaum's 125,000-member District Council 37 of AFSCME. Since the UFT workers were under the Board of Education, not subject to the direct hiring and firing discretion of the mayor, the UFT was not a member of Gotbaum's Municipal Labor Committee, naturally positioning

Shanker as Gotbaum's rival. The rivalry became bitter in 1969 when both District Council 37 and the UFT sought to organize the school paraprofessionals. Shanker prevailed, and the bad blood between him and Gotbaum resulting from that battle continued into 1975.

Victor Gotbaum was seven years older than Shanker. He too held a master's degree from Columbia (in industrial labor). Born in Brooklyn, Gotbaum was a highly decorated soldier in World War II. After working for the federal government briefly, he joined the labor movement, first with the meatcutters union in Chicago. He moved back to New York, taking a job with AFSCME and worked his way up to the presidency of District Council 37. Gotbaum's was a mostly blue collar union, representing employees of a wide range of city agencies and services. "There are things we can do that make the police and firemen look like nothing," Gotbaum bragged to reporters. "We could stop the collection of millions of dollars a day, turn off the water supply, pull out the ambulance drivers, leave Coney Island without lifeguards."[29] Despite the trash talk, Gotbaum, like Shanker, was a political moderate and even more cautious than Shanker, who led a number of New York City teachers strikes, even going to jail once for violating injunctions. Generally allied with Gotbaum were John D. DeLury, president of the 10,000-member Uniformed Sanitationmen's Association, and Barry L. Feinstein, president of the 15,000-member Teamsters Local 237. All three of them followed the counsel of Jack Bigel.[30]

The most aggressive union leader was Ken McFeeley, president of the Patrolmen's Benevolent Association (PBA), the largest police union with 24,000 members. Unlike Shanker, Gotbaum, DeLury, and Feinstein, McFeeley was not a professional labor organizer. He was a rank-and-file police officer. Under Beame's crisis budget, the Police Department budget would be cut 13 percent with layoffs of 6,000 from the 71,000-member police force.[31] Allied with McFeeley was Richard J. Vizzini, president of the 10,000-member Uniformed Firefighters Association. Like McFeeley, Vizzini was not a professional labor union man. He was a firefighter by profession.

The police and fire unions took Beame's cue to highlight public safety concerns to pressure the seven New York Republican senators a bit further than perhaps Beame imagined. Their members printed thousands of copies of a four-page booklet entitled *Welcome to Fear City: A Survival Guide to Visitors to the City of New York* and began distributing the leaflets during the second week of June at LaGuardia and JFK airports, at the Port Authority Bus Terminal and at midtown Manhattan hotels.[32] Purportedly to stop the distribution of the leaflets, but more likely to bring more attention to them, the Beame administration got a restraining order to prevent further distribution of the leaflets. Beame held a press conference, angrily waiving the leaflet, which had a skull on the cover, for all the cameras to see, calling it "a new low in irresponsibility," thereby guaranteeing the *Fear City* stunt would become national news.[33]

The *Fear City* leaflet proclaimed that: "By the time you read this, the number of public safety personnel available to protect residents and visitors may already have been further reduced. Under those circumstances, the best advice we can give you is this: Until things change, stay away from New York City if you possibly can." The PBA publicly defended the leaflet and vowed to appeal the injunction, calling it a "flagrant violation of First Amendment rights,"[34] which, of course, it was. "It seems to me a plainly unconstitutional limitation on the right of policemen and firemen to say whatever they want to say," said noted First

Amendment lawyer Floyd Abrams at the time.[35] On June 16, the New York Appellate Division unanimously ruled that the leaflet ban violated the First Amendment.[36] Despite vindication as to their constitutional rights, the unions stopped the *Fear City* campaign as a result of negative public response to it.

By mid-July, after 3,000 police officers had been laid off, the PBA was at it again, however, with two new leaflets: *If You Haven't Been Mugged Yet* and *Who's Next?*, blanketing high-crime neighborhoods.[37] That time, Mayor Beame had no comment.[38] Because, by then, his battle with Anderson for more money was over.

By the time the City Council and the Board of Estimate were required to vote on the fiscal 1976 expense budget, Beame had managed to wrangle a promise of $150 million more of taxing authority for the city from Anderson as well as an additional $46 million in federal aid; narrowing the $641 million gap between the austerity budget and the crisis budget to $445 million. The expense budget approved by the Board of Estimate and the City Council on June 19 of $12.087 billion reflected the additional taxing authority and aid.[39] To finance the budget, the City Council approved an 11.3 percent increase in the real estate tax—to $8.187 for each $100 of assessed value, the highest in the city's history.[40] That budget became the city's official expense budget on June 30, although Beame's efforts to secure more taxing authority from Albany would continue through the first week of July.

The expense budget contemplated the layoff of 2,934 sanitation workers. Their union contract, however, guaranteed the members' jobs through the end of the 1976 fiscal year, when the contract expired. On June 27, the Uniformed Sanitationmen's Association obtained an injunction barring the layoffs.[41] Four days later, the Appellate Division overturned the injunction by a three to two vote, and Beame announced that layoffs would commence the next day.[42] John J. DeLury, president of the Uniformed Sanitationmen's Association, upped the ante: "There will be wildcats. There is nothing I can do, there is nothing the court can do, there is nothing the Mayor can do to head it off. I, the Mayor or Christ Almighty is not going to stop this."[43] Ten thousand sanitation workers began a walkout on July 1, the first day of the 1976 fiscal year, "the best organized wildcat strike I've ever seen," said Sanitation Commissioner Robert T Groh.[44]

The day after the wildcat strike began, Beame took to the airwaves, asking the sanitation workers to honor their contract and return to work. Beame announced that he had obtained an injunction declaring the strike illegal and fining striking workers twice their daily pay.[45] Beame put the blame for the strike right in Anderson's lap: "I have spent as much time in Albany this past week as at City Hall, fighting for the right for the city to take action that would avert many of these dismissals. It should be clear that we are not seeking extra money from Albany. We are asking the legislature to allow us to tax ourselves."[46]

After the fire department closed 26 of its 360 fire companies on July 1 and laid off 1,650 firemen, Richard J Vizzini, president of the Uniformed Firefighters Association, told his men "to work at a pace conducive to safety," interpreted by all, particularly his union's members, as a call for a work slowdown.[47] The slowdown was immediately felt by the city, as garbage fires proliferated given the uncollected refuse.[48] The highway workers called a wildcat strike on July 2, protesting 570 layoffs, snarling rush hour traffic.[49]

By July 3, Anderson decided it was time to cut a deal. The agreement provided the city with an additional $180 million in new taxing authority, $330 million of new taxing authority in the aggregate for fiscal 1976—$147 million of additional corporate taxes, $80 million in additional bank taxes, $50 million in increased stock transfer taxes, $28 million in new taxes on services like haircuts, and $25 million in a new bond tax.[50] With that accomplished, Beame agreed to rehire over half of the laid off sanitation men in exchange for a $1.6 million cash contribution from union dues to pay a portion of the cost in a deal worked out by Jack Bigel.[51] By July 5, all the uncollected garbage—an estimated 58,000 tons—had been picked up, and the other work stoppages had been halted.[52] Over half the police officers and firemen given layoff notices were rehired that day as well, and eighteen of the twenty-six closed firehouses were reopened.[53] At the Board of Education and the Health and Hospitals Corporation, layoffs were resisted entirely. They indicated that they would implement efficiencies in their operations to live within their reduced budgets without any employees being laid off.[54]

On July 14, Anderson donned the plaid jacket, and the 1975 state legislative session in Albany concluded. The final measure passed was an amendment called up by Anderson at the end of the nineteen-hour marathon session. It was an appropriation of funds to a medical center run by Local 1814 of the International Longshoremen's Association, Anthony Scotto's local, introduced at Scotto's behest. It was passed unanimously. Earlier in the day, another bill pressed by Scotto, one more controversial, also passed. That one curtailed the power of the Waterfront Commission of New York and New Jersey to suspend waterfront workers accused of crimes. It was an impressive flexing of political muscle by Scotto, evidenced by a story in the next day's *New York Times* touting his legislative successes.

All things considered, Beame had performed admirably in his battle with Anderson during the legislative session. Seeking

$641 million in new aid and taxing authority, Beame got $330 million, better than a fifty-fifty compromise. Of the approximately 37,000 "layoffs" contemplated by Beame's crisis budget, only about 20,000 people were actually laid off. About 18,000 jobs were saved by the $330 million in new taxing authority. The rest were mostly unfilled positions that were eliminated on paper, provisional employees not permanently hired, or forced retirements of those already over the retirement age. With a workforce of approximately 340,000 employees, only approximately 6 percent were to be laid off. (Of the announced 31,000 layoffs in the 1975 fiscal year, only 2,000 people actually lost their jobs.)

But if Beame expected praise from Carey and the MAC directors for his success in getting Anderson to come up with the money, he would be sadly disappointed. When there is praise to go around, it is the privilege of the senior partner to take that praise and, conversely, when there is blame to be had, it is the job of the junior partner to fall on his sword and take that blame. The unfortunate reality for Beame was that MAC bonds were not trading well. If, as it appeared likely, the additional $2 billion of MAC bonds yet to be sold couldn't be sold, then Carey might be blamed. This the senior partner could not countenance. Carey and his allies weren't just going to concede that the MAC was flawed from conception. They were not going to admit that it was foolish to believe that the municipal bond market would view the MAC bonds as a fundamentally different credit risk than city bonds. So Carey flipped the script: Maybe the MAC bonds were more or less city bonds, but their failure to sell was a result of Beame's continuing profligacy and failure to implement genuine budget reforms.

CHAPTER NINE

HAWKS AND CHICKENS

ON FRIDAY JULY 11, MAC CHAIRMAN THOMAS FLYNN AND TWO other members of the MAC board, Donna Shalala and George Gould, met with Mayor Beame and First Deputy Mayor Cavanagh and informed them that the prospects for the planned additional offerings of MAC bonds were bleak. The only hope for success of future offerings, they said, was a comprehensive fiscal reform program that would convince the municipal bond market that New York City was serious about change, and that program, Beame and Cavanagh were told, would be prepared by the MAC board and presented to them for implementation. Beame and Cavanagh looked at each other with incredulity. Come up with a program of fiscal reform? What did these MAC people think they had been doing for the past four months?

Over the course of the following week, the MAC board members and staff met with bankers and city officials to develop proposals to present to Beame for a reform program. These included: a wage freeze for fiscal 1976 notwithstanding the union contracts that provided for 6 percent wage increases; an additional 27,500 layoffs; an across-the-board 10 percent salary cut for non-union management personnel; transit fare increases; and tuition increases at City University. This program was presented to Beame at a July 17 meeting of the MAC board at the offices of Paul, Weiss on the twenty-eighth-floor office of 345 Park Avenue. These measures were needed, the MAC officials told Beame, because the municipal bond market investors—particularly investors west of the Hudson—purportedly had "lost faith" in Beame.

All of those measures may well have been appropriate for Beame to implement, but the notion that taking those measures would reopen the municipal bond market to MAC and the city in August or September was ludicrous. The MAC bonds were unsalable because they were essentially New York City bonds and no one was buying the sales pitch that the New York State moral obligation—tarnished by the UDC default—made the MAC bonds fundamentally different and better. The MAC had only been in existence for five weeks, and Beame hadn't done anything in that time to fundamentally and negatively change the municipal bond market's view of New York City debt. Just like five weeks earlier, the market was saturated with New York City bonds and notes—and that included MAC bonds, as far as investors were concerned.

MAC officials gave no explanation to Beame as to what he had done in the previous five weeks to cripple the Big MAC. That was, of course, because Beame had done nothing during that time to injure the MAC. The MAC was stillborn. One anonymous MAC director admitted as much to the *New York Times* at the time: "We called it Big MAC, but everyone thought it was the same old hamburger meat. It was New York's, and it didn't smell good to them."[1] Rather than admitting that the MAC wouldn't work, a group of four directors, the "Hawks," as they were called, emerged, arguing that MAC should "go for broke," pushing as hard and as fast as possible for fiscal austerity so that even if MAC failed to sell the bonds, which they knew was the almost certain outcome, they wouldn't be blamed for the failure. The Hawks were Felix Rohatyn, Simon Rifkind, William Ellinghaus, and John A. Coleman.[2] Governor Carey was completely aligned with the Hawks: when the MAC failed, the failure must be blamed on Beame, not on those who told the public the Big MAC was the solution. For Carey, politically, the Big MAC was too big to fail.

Rohatyn, speaking for the Hawks at the July 17 MAC board meeting, told Beame that even if the MAC reform program were fully adopted, and then some, there was way "less than a fifty-fifty chance" that anything the city could do would help sell the bonds.[3] Rather than questioning why he should implement a program whose stated objectives were unlikely to be obtained, rather than setting some boundaries with Carey as to how far he would subordinate himself, Beame went along with the Hawks' plan.

On July 19, Beame proposed to the city's legislative leadership and the heads of major city public employee unions the reform program put to him by the Hawks. Following Beame's lead, the city legislative leaders endorsed the proposals. The union leaders did not. All the union leaders ruled out a wage freeze. Most vocal in opposition was Albert Shanker. "If we don't get a wage increase, our members have to vote on a new contract. They expect a salary increase and they have a right to it." When asked if that meant the teachers would go on a strike, Shanker said, "Sure."[4] Shanker said that he would ask for a 20 percent raise when contract negotiations began on July 23.[5] "We would rather see the city default," Shanker said. "That way everybody would be affected, bankers, utilities, oil companies, and not workers alone."[6]

On July 20, the Hawks began to exert themselves even more aggressively. They, along with Governor Carey, decided to remove Thomas Flynn as chairman of the MAC board and replace him with William Ellinghaus, a Hawk. It was also assumed that Simon Rifkind would resign from the board—not because he wasn't Hawkish enough, but because he wanted to continue to have his law firm bill the MAC as its outside counsel, and his remaining on the board and acting as outside counsel was viewed as a potential conflict of interest.[7] Rifkind was replaced by Dick Netzer, a professor of New York University's School of Public Administration. Rohatyn, thought by many to have been behind Flynn's ouster, denied involvement. "I'm not a hawk. But then I'm not a chicken or an ostrich either," Rohatyn told the press.[8]

There was one Hawk who did not get much press, and that's the way he liked it. John A. Coleman, a longtime governor of the New York Stock Exchange and its former chairman, for decades was the behind-the-scenes power at the Exchange, ruling the institution from "Post 13" on the floor of the Exchange where he ran the specialist business of Adler, Coleman & Company. Coleman was also a major donor to Democratic politicians, going all the way back to Al Smith. He was also the single largest fundraiser for the Archdiocese of New York. It was said during the 1950s and 1960s that three men ruled New York City: Mayor Robert Wagner, Cardinal Spellman, and John A. Coleman, and not necessarily in that order. When the investment banks began failing in large numbers in 1970, Coleman gave the nod for Rohatyn to be the chairman of the Exchange's

"Crisis Committee." Rohatyn, being a master of public relations and political maneuvering, succeeded in getting himself praised by the press as the savior of Wall Street. Coleman was perfectly happy for Rohatyn to get all the press he wanted, so long as Coleman got none. Coleman said little, on the record anyway, at the MAC board meetings, for Coleman knew that what was said mattered little and what would be done was decided in advance, in quick conversations with Governor Carey or his emissaries. There can be little doubt that the efforts of the Hawks to protect the MAC's and its board members' reputations were heavily influenced by Coleman, and that Coleman would leave no fingerprints in exerting that influence.

On July 21, the underwriters broke syndicate on the first offering of MAC bonds. When that happened, the prices of the MAC bonds plummeted 10 percent, a disastrous outcome for long-term investors.[9]

Later that same week, the MAC board appointed its permanent senior staff. Carey's candidate for executive director was Herbert Elish, a former corporate trust officer at Citibank and former director of the New York City Environmental Protection Agency and former sanitation commissioner. One MAC board member deigned to question Elish's qualifications, but was immediately put straight by David Burke, Carey's administrative secretary. Elish was unanimously elected. The next senior staff appointee was John Scanlon, the "Monk," as public relations director, also a Carey choice.[10]

Scanlon's first public relations objective was to convince the public that the failure of the MAC was a failure of Beame, and not of Carey or the MAC directors. In this effort, he found willing allies at the banks that underwrote the city's debt offerings. The banks knew they would be blamed as well for the failure to sell more MAC bonds. On July 24, Scanlon released a letter from David Rockefeller to the MAC board warning of the peril to the city if it did not fully adopt the MAC reform program: "A definitive program, strongly endorsed by the Governor, the legislature, the Mayor and the MAC board, must not only be announced in full detail, but agreed to and acted upon by all parties with no further delay."[11] Also relayed that day was a letter signed by William Sellers of Merrill Lynch and Thomas Labrecque of Chase, the two managing underwriters of the doomed second MAC bond offering, which concluded, "The city is in a fight for its life. Its chances are slim and mere words will not suffice."[12]

With more MAC bonds not salable in the municipal bond market, the banks not likely to put many more MAC bonds on their balance sheets, the Federal Reserve unwilling to lend, and the Ford administration still not ready to approve federal assistance, Governor Carey was running out of deep pockets to dip into to meet the city's funding needs through November. If Carey couldn't hold out that long, if the city were to run out of money before then, Ford would have him over a barrel, and Ford would insist on a bankruptcy filing by the city. If that were in the cards, if Carey couldn't prevent that, Beame might go rogue, co-opt the unions, really fight austerity measures, become obstructionist, and drag the state's finances right down the drain along with the city's. Carey had to find the money. The city's public employee pension funds had stepped up in June to buy city notes—and they would be asked to invest much more in the months ahead. One other possible source of funds was the state's public employee pension funds. But there was an immovable object preventing Carey's access to those funds—state Comptroller Arthur Levitt, the sole trustee of the state's public employee pension funds and a ceaseless critic of moral obligation bonds.

Levitt had led a one-man crusade against moral obligation bonds since Nelson Rockefeller first issued them at the HFA in 1959. Rockefeller at first tried to win Levitt over to the use of that financing tool, brokering a meeting between Levitt and John Mitchell at the Bankers Club in 1960. Levitt listened politely as owl-faced Mitchell, between puffs on his pipe, explained the ins-and-outs of moral obligation bonds and the benefits thereof. After the meeting, more convinced than ever of his reservations, Levitt continued his attacks on moral obligation bonds even more aggressively, calling them a "betrayal of the taxpayer." Levitt believed in the wisdom of the people—if you couldn't convince them of the value of a project by seeking their approval in a bond issue referendum vote, you shouldn't borrow the money. In July 1975, with the UDC debacle still unresolved and the city's credit destroyed from too much borrowing, it took all of Levitt's great stores of self-discipline to not take on an attitude of "I told you so."

Levitt was seventy-five years old at the time (but still worked out five days a week at the YMCA) and had served as state comptroller for twenty-one years. He was born in Williamsburg, Brooklyn, the son of a Russian-born dentist. He graduated from Columbia College and thereafter the Columbia University Law School. He served as an Army colonel in World War II. After the war, he returned to Brooklyn and became active in Democratic clubhouse politics. He was elected state comptroller in 1954. In 1961, he was Carmine DeSapio's candidate for mayor after Robert Wagner had his falling out with DeSapio and the other bosses. Wagner won the primary handily, and Levitt went back to being state comptroller. By 1975, he was an institution in New York State politics, winning reelection by the largest margins of any statewide candidate. There were a number of reasons for this: Levitt was very good at his job and, despite his club-house origins, was honest and incorruptible. He didn't need money—his son, Arthur Levitt Jr., had made a fortune as a founder of the investment bank Cogan, Berlind, Weill & Levitt.

When overtures by MAC officials were made to Levitt regarding what he thought about buying MAC bonds in late July, Levitt smelled trouble and preempted being put on the hot seat by publicly announcing, prior to even being officially asked, that it would be "inappropriate" for the $6.3 billion state public employee pension funds to buy MAC bonds. His reasons, he said, were that the pension funds were already fully invested, and as tax-exempt entities, tax-free bonds were not an attractive investment. Levitt also cleverly highlighted a conflict of interest in his authorizing a purchase of MAC bonds: he would be obligated to seek the highest interest rate on any MAC bonds he purchased on behalf of the pension funds, but he was also obligated to seek the lowest rate for the MAC to minimize the state's exposure to its "moral obligation" on the MAC bonds.[13] "The New York City pension funds should have the first chance to buy," Levitt coyly told reporters, "It's really a question to ask New York City, not us."[14] When asked to reply to Levitt's comments, William T. Scott, the city deputy controller with oversight of the city pension funds, also demurred on buying MAC bonds, explaining that the city's public employee pension funds already had 11 percent of their assets invested in New York City bonds and that standard practices called for pension funds to hold no more than 10 percent of their assets in any one issuer.[15] There was no longer any pretense, even, that MAC credit risk was different than city credit risk.

Having no luck with public employee pension funds, Carey sent Rohatyn back to Washington to meet with Treasury

Secretary Simon on July 25. Carey was implementing O'Neill's strategy with Ford—keep the crisis in the headlines, making it politically damaging for Ford among New York Republican delegates to continue a hard line against the city. The day before the meeting, Carey spoke to the convention of State Building and Construction Trades Council. "I want your pressure," Carey told the union officials. "I want it delivered to those high thrones in Washington, where Mr. Simon sits on one throne and Mr. Burns sits on another and we sit in between and pay and pay."[16] Rohatyn met with Simon at his office where he was joined by Arthur Burns, L. William Seidman, and Gerald Parsky, an assistant Treasury secretary. William Ellinghaus, Thomas Flynn, and Peter Goldmark accompanied Rohatyn. After the nearly two-hour meeting, Rohatyn briefed the press: "There was nothing that was discussed that gave us any feeling that we could look for help from the Federal government. Their view of fiscal discipline is 'God helps those who help themselves.'"[17] Simon commented later that while the Ford administration was not prepared to offer financial assistance, it did support the MAC reform program: "That's exactly the lead the City should be following."[18] Ford's strategy was simple too: keep the crisis out of the headlines, wait for the city to run out of money before Thanksgiving, and then dictate terms of the bailout to a desperate Carey, terms that would be harsh enough to keep Republicans from jumping ship to Reagan, but not so harsh that the New York Republicans gathering at the convention on January 6 would want to knife him.

With help from Washington not forthcoming anytime soon, the Hawks continued to pound on Beame. On July 31, John Scanlon issued a public statement from the MAC calling on the mayor to place a three-year ceiling on the city expense budget along with a limit on tax increases during that period.[19] It also called for an "independent management apparatus" to oversee the city's budgeting and auditing functions—a direct shot across Cavanagh's bow.[20] On the same day, Victor Gotbaum and most of the city's other public employee union leaders surprisingly agreed to Beame's wage freeze. Beame was not pleased that the MAC Hawks were undercutting his success by requesting even more austerity even as Beame was winning major concessions from the unions. (The police, fire, and teachers' unions did not agree to the freeze,[21] but Beame promised those unions that he would use emergency powers to be granted to him by the City Council to impose a wage freeze on them as well, whether or not they voluntarily agreed.[22] By the end of the month, the Uniformed Firefighters Association would agree to the wage freeze.)

Despite his displeasure, Beame continued to comply with the Hawks' requests. He agreed to form an independent management committee to oversee budgeting and auditing functions. On August 2, Beame announced that Richard R. Shinn, the president of the Metropolitan Life Insurance Company who served on Carey's four-person, blue-ribbon committee that recommended the creation of the MAC, would serve as chairman of an eight-member management committee with those powers. Four days later, Beame acquiesced again to the Hawks—agreeing to a three-year ceiling on the expense budget.[23] Beame also announced the co–executive directors of the new independent management committee: Herbert Elish, the executive director of the MAC, and John Zuccotti, chairman of the City Planning Commission, both of whom were preapproved by the Hawks.[24] If there was any doubt that Beame's independent management committee was a Hawk operation, it was dispelled when William

Ellinghaus was also named to the independent management committee.[25]

On August 7, the MAC's $960 million August financing package for the city was finalized. The banks agreed to purchase $350 million of MAC bonds. The New York City public employee pension funds agreed to purchase $165 million of MAC bonds. Arthur Levitt, under tremendous pressure from Governor Carey, agreed to a modest investment of $25 million from the New York State teachers' pension fund and $25 million from the New York State public employee pension fund.[26] The balance of the $960 million took the form of a $120 million advance payment of state aid to the city and a proposed offering of $275 million of MAC bonds to be marketed to municipal bond investors. Even that $275 million headline amount was misleading: $150 million had been presold to New York savings banks and insurance companies.[27] Out of the $960 million, only $125 million of MAC bonds was even attempted to be sold to the traditional municipal bond market. Even with price talk at a rich 9.5 percent to 10.25 percent for the tranches, that small quantum of bonds could not be sold. After a week of sales efforts, only $25 million had been sold. The offering was priced on August 14 with interest rates ranging from 10 percent to 11 percent, depending on the tranche maturity dates. By then, only $30 million of the bonds had been sold despite those high interest rates.[28] The Big MAC was an abject failure, and, after the dismal results of the second bond offering, there was no way of hiding that reality.

While the second MAC offering was floundering in the market, Rohatyn again went to Washington, meeting with Treasury and Federal Reserve officials, keeping the crisis in the news: "If it turns out we can't sell [the bonds], I'll go back, I'll go back

every hour on the hour."[29] Rohatyn proposed a federal assumption of all the city's welfare costs: "If a Federal take-over would
be accomplished. I know damn well we would have a viable city
financially."[30] He also proposed a US Treasury guarantee of
MAC bonds. The Ford administration and the Federal Reserve
continued to applaud the city's belt-tightening, but offered no
promise of aid.[31] Carey then went to Washington to meet with
Treasury officials.[32] He got the same response that Rohatyn did,
but that didn't matter. The reporters covered the meeting. He
told them that unless the federal government intervened, the city
had a 50 percent chance of defaulting on its obligations within
weeks, and the Ford administration was not budging on its "no
aid" stance.[33] Carey kept the headlines coming, and Ford kept
waiting for Carey to get more desperate. It was a game of chicken
with the clock ticking down, except neither one of them knew
for sure when time would run out for the city.

Complicating matters for Jerry Ford was the fact that he had
run afoul of his conservative base, requiring him, politically, to
continue to take a very hard line with New York City. The proximate cause of his latest issue with the base was Mrs. Ford, who
agreed to an interview with CBS journalist Morley Safer for the
60 Minutes television news program, which aired on August 10.
Betty was extremely candid with Safer, telling him she wouldn't
be surprised or angry if her daughter had an extramarital affair.
She also said all four of her children probably had used illegal
drugs, and she herself would probably have smoked a little reefer,
if she was younger. She said she had no problem with couples
living together before marriage. Most controversially, she called
the *Roe v. Wade* Supreme Court abortion decision "a great, great
decision." Needless to say, the conservatives were singing the
praises of Nancy Reagan. Washington insiders gossiped about

Betty's drinking, speculating that she must have had a few pops before sitting down with Safer.

The day after the Betty Ford interview aired, the SEC, which had never taken an enforcement action against a municipality, announced that it was considering opening an investigation of New York City officials and the underwriters of the city's debt for fraud as a result of their failure to disclose the city's budget gimmicks. "It amazes me that no suits have been brought," said A. A. Sommer Jr., SEC commissioner.[34] Three days later, Manhattan attorney Burton M. Abrams brought a billion-dollar class action lawsuit against Beame, Goldin, and the city's underwriters, claiming federal securities fraud.[35]

The SEC announcement and the Abrams lawsuit were manna from heaven for the Hawks. John Scanlon released a statement announcing that the city's accumulated deficit was $2.8 billion (later revised upward, multiple times, to $5.1 billion), with an $800 million deficit projected for the fiscal 1976 expense budget that Beame claimed was balanced.[36] The City Board of Estimate, chock-full of mayoral aspirants, used Scanlon's announcement of the city's eye-popping cumulative deficit as an excuse to further diminish Beame, holding meetings without him.[37] On August 20, Scanlon put out a MAC press release requesting that Governor Carey submit to the state legislature a plan for the creation of a state board to exercise direct control of the city's fiscal affairs.[38] Beame, hoping that cooperation with the MAC and Carey might blunt the authority of the proposed control board, continued to agree to virtually everything the Hawks asked of him. On August 21, Beame agreed to another demand of the Hawks: a three-year no-tax increase pledge.[39]

Beame committed an unforced error when he failed to deliver to the MAC board the city's three-year financial plan by the deadline mandated in the MAC legislation.[40] The day after the missed deadline, Beame appeared, chastened, at a late-night press conference along with Carey in the governor's suite at the Waldorf Astoria Hotel, where he announced his agreement to the creation to the proposed state control board. Carey told the gathered press that he intended to call the legislature into special session after the long Labor Day weekend to pass the necessary legislation.[41]

Carey also laid out the highlights of a $2 billion financing package to get the city through November, to the finish line in the game of chicken with Ford. The lynchpin of the package was a purchase by the state of $1 billion of short-term MAC notes, an unusual move since the principal purpose of the MAC was to convert the city's short-term debt into MAC long-term debt. The problem was that the state could not borrow on a long-term basis absent voter approval in a referendum, which, even if time permitted, would almost certainly not be approved. Borrowing on a short-term basis did not require voter approval. So Carey proposed that the state issue short-term notes, buy short-term MAC notes with the proceeds of those state notes, and then have the banks commit to underwrite long-term MAC bonds to take out those short-term MAC notes, allowing the state to repay its short-term notes.

A rather significant problem with Carey's plan was that the banks had not agreed to underwrite those MAC bonds. After the disastrous second MAC bond offering, there wasn't a snowball's chance in hell that the banks were going to commit to a billion-dollar MAC offering, even on a best-efforts basis. And they were furious with Carey for publicly announcing a plan that assumed they would. The day after Carey's press conference, Chase Manhattan Bank, Morgan Guaranty Trust Company, and

Citibank jointly announced that they would not commit to the take-out financing.[42]

With the city set to run out of money during the first week of September, and Carey's financing package dead on arrival, serious talk of default was heard at City Hall, at the State Capitol in Albany, and at the MAC offices. During the ill-fated second MAC offering roadshow, the underwriters were peppered with questions as to whether the MAC's right to the city sales tax and stock transfer tax receipts could be challenged in a bankruptcy under a "fraudulent conveyance" theory. The underwriters tried to convince accounts that the MAC's right to those tax receipts would stand up in court, but nobody knew for certain if that would be the case.[43]

A bankruptcy filing by the city was, practically speaking, impossible under then-existing federal law because of Chapter IX of the bankruptcy code, which governed municipal bankruptcies. Under the law then in effect, a bankruptcy filing required the approval of creditors holding a majority of the city's debt—an impossible task, given the tens of thousands of holders of the city's bonds and notes. New York Congressman Herman Badillo announced on August 21 that his House Judiciary Subcommittee on the Courts would hold hearings in October to amend Chapter IX to allow New York City to file bankruptcy without prior approval of creditors.[44] On August 24, Rohatyn told the press: "Default is a very real possibility next week."[45] The following day, New York City Corporation Counsel Bernard Richland announced that if the city defaulted, holders of the city's debt would have to wait for payment—measures to keep vital city services functioning would be funded first.[46] Prices of city and MAC bonds traded at record lows after Richland's announcement.[47] State Budget Director Peter Goldmark made a bad situation worse when he told the press that if the city were to default, the State of New York would likely default within thirty days thereafter.[48]

Late August was a brooding time for Carey. It looked like Ford might win the game of chicken. If a default was inevitable, he would have to agree to Ford's terms and have the city file for bankruptcy. If that happened, his own budget mess in Albany would become much worse. But Carey had a couple more tricks up his sleeve. Over the Labor Day weekend, he announced that he was calling the state legislature into session on Thursday, September 4, to consider legislation to create the control board and approve new financial aid to the city. As a contingency plan, Carey would also ask for a new state law to provide for some state court process to deal with creditors if default became unavoidable, given the unavailability of a federal bankruptcy pending Badillo's legislation being enacted by Congress. And he had the crafty, old bird Simon Rifkind thinking of ways to keep the city's creditors at bay outside of bankruptcy.[49]

Carey's last official act before the Labor Day weekend was his creation of the New York Economic Development Board, which he announced with great fanfare. The Economic Development Board would have the mandate of attracting businesses and jobs to the state. Carey stacked the board with heavy-hitter business leaders, including Leonard Lauder, Steven Ross, Howard Stein, and Muriel Siebert. To the prestigious board he also named the president of Local 1814 of the International Longshoremen's Association, Anthony Scotto.

CHAPTER TEN

PROBLEMATIC AT THIS POINT

WHILE THE BANKS HAD REJECTED CAREY'S REQUEST THAT THEY agree to underwrite $1 billion of MAC bonds, there was an amount they would agree to underwrite to stave off default: $250 million. On September 2, the MAC rolled out Carey's revised rescue financing plan, which provided for $2.3 billion of financing to fund the city through the end of November. The plan was complicated, with money coming from many and varied sources, and the keystone of which was a $750 million contribution from the State of New York.

The state was to fund its $750 million contribution by issuing notes in three installments of $250 million and using $500 million of the proceeds to purchase MAC bonds and $250 million to buy city notes secured by Mitchell-Lama mortgages on housing projects. The New York State public employee pension funds would be mandated by a new state law to buy $225 million of MAC bonds (the legal mandate prevented any objection by Arthur Levitt). Likewise, the city's public employee pension funds would be mandated by law to buy $500 million of MAC bonds. That law also required the state to indemnify Levitt and the city pension fund trustees from any liability if they were sued by retirees for investing in MAC or city securities. The New York banks would underwrite $250 million of MAC bonds and roll over another $156 million of New York City notes. Various city and state debt sinking funds would invest $180 million in MAC bonds, and a state insurance fund would purchase $100 million of MAC bonds. Finally, the Rudins and the other large New York City real estate owners would prepay another $150 million in real estate taxes.[1]

The rescue financing plan was conditioned on the creation of the new control board—named the Emergency Financial Control Board—comprised of the governor, the mayor, the state comptroller, the city comptroller, and a fifth member appointed by the governor. The Emergency Financial Control Board would be legally empowered to oversee city budgetary and finance functions, including approving all major expenditures and contracts.[2] The plan also called for the creation of a position of deputy state controller for New York City, with power to audit all city operations, but with the purpose of defenestrating Jim Cavanagh. The mayor would be required to submit to the Emergency Financial Control Board by October 15 a three-year plan to balance the city expense budget. Finally, Carey's legislative package included a state law delaying the ability of city creditors to sue for collection of their debts if New York City were to default, and it authorized the city and the Emergency Financial Control Board to file for bankruptcy in federal court, if necessary.[3]

In a letter to Carey formally proposing the rescue financial plan and related actions—a surrender letter, really—the MAC board was surprisingly candid, even as it placed blame squarely with Beame:

> When MAC came into being, it had been hoped that the financing mechanism provided by it would enable the city to take drastic and perceived remedial action during the period of July 1–September 30, 1975. During this period, MAC would raise $3 billion in long-term debt with which to refund a portion of the city's short-term debt, and at October 1, 1975, the city, as a result of its reforms, would be back in the markets itself. This hope did not materialize, chiefly as a result of the lack of credibility of the city's management and the clouded perception as to its actions.[4]

Carey was in Washington on September 2, keeping the spotlight on President Ford. He and Ford met for forty-five minutes in the Oval Office, where Carey made the case that the implementation of the Emergency Financial Control Board and the state's new $750 million financial commitment to the city demonstrated the aggressive state action that warranted federal intervention to help the city. To no avail, of course. "There was no change in the Administration's position," Ford's press secretary Ron Nessen told reporters after the meeting. "Federal assistance is not the solution to New York City's problem [and] it should not be the job of the Federal Government to manage the finances of the state and local government."[5] Carey also met with Arthur Burns for two hours that day, also without success—except for the headlines.[6]

On September 5, Carey called the state legislature into session in Albany and introduced the legislation to enact the plan. In his opening message to the legislature, Carey emphasized that the plan only financed the city until December and that financing for the rest of the city's fiscal year ending June 30, 1976, would still need to be obtained: "If all elements of the MAC-proposed plan were enacted, they would produce financing to New York City for the next three months. We have no assurances that at the end of this period the capital markets will be open again to New York City or to MAC. Should that be the case, the continuing inability of the city and MAC to obtain financing for New York City's debt and municipal services would impair the soundness of the financial plan and, in consequence, at a measurable level, the credit of the state."[7] Carey noted the "resources of the magnitude required for such financing are not available or known to us at this time, other than from the Federal Government"[8] and that "[t]he President and other Federal officials were understanding and sympathetic, but offered no commitments."[9]

That morning, President Ford was in Sacramento, California, to meet with Governor Jerry Brown. As he walked from his suite at the Senator Hotel across Capitol Park to the State Capitol, a woman dressed in a red robe pulled a Colt .45 pistol from her leg holster and raised the gun toward Ford and pulled the trigger. The gun did not go off. Before she could pull the trigger a second time, Secret Service Agent Larry Buendorf wrested the gun from her while other agents dragged the woman away. Ford, unhurt, continued into the State Capitol and had his meeting with Brown as scheduled. His assailant was Lynette "Squeaky" Fromme, a member of the Manson Family cult. Fromme claimed she planned to kill President Ford to bring attention to the need to preserve California's redwood forests.

The following day, while the New York State legislature was considering the MAC plan legislation, Warren Anderson met privately with Vice President Nelson Rockefeller and David

Rockefeller at the family compound at Pocantico Hills to discuss the growing fiscal crisis. Also in attendance were Bill Simon,
Arthur Burns, and L. William Seidman.[10] Anderson told the
group that New York City's crisis was now threatening New York
State's fiscal stability and that the state itself might soon be frozen
out of the credit markets. If the federal government failed to prevent a New York City default, New York State would default within
months. Anderson told them that New Yorkers would blame
President Ford for this, and Ford would lose New York State in
the 1976 general election and probably lose the election itself.

As Nelson Rockefeller listened to Anderson, he was less
focused on New Yorkers blaming Ford for this mess and much
more focused on the fact Ford would blame him for it. After
Ford decided to run in 1976, Nelson focused on 1980. He'd
be seventy-two years old, but long felt younger than his years.
Thanks to the Twenty-Fifth Amendment to the US Constitution,
Ford would be ineligible to run for reelection in 1980. Nelson
still had a chance to fulfill his destiny. But if Ford's game of
chicken with Carey went on too long and New York State's financial stability was brought down along with the city, Nelson would
be history. Ford would be forced to bail out both the city and the
state, and even moderates in the Republican Party would view
Rockefeller's presence on the ticket as a tacit endorsement of
fiscal irresponsibility and federal government bailouts. Nelson
could forget the presidency in 1980—he'd be jettisoned like yesterday's trash in 1975. The Rockefeller brothers told Anderson
that he should go to Washington with Bill Simon that week to
begin work on an administration proposal to assist the city, a
suggestion Anderson accepted.[11]

On September 8, the State Assembly passed Carey's rescue plan legislation by a vote of eighty to seventy—with one

substantive change insisted on by Anderson: the Emergency Financial Control Board was expanded from five members to seven to allow for upstate representation.[12] In the early morning hours of September 9, the Senate passed the legislation by a vote of thirty-three to twenty-six, with Carey signing it into law by daybreak.[13]

On September 10, New York State issued notes to provide for the first $250 million of its $750 million total contribution to the new relief package. The $250 million was included in a $755 million offering that also included $505 million to provide funds for other state purposes and was priced at the highest interest rates in New York State history—from 6.75 percent to 8.70 percent, depending on the maturity date of the applicable tranche.[14] Equally troubling, only one syndicate of underwriters, David Rockefeller's Chase Manhattan Bank, bid on the offering, as there was not enough interest among the banks to have competing syndicates bid on the offering.

Albert Shanker was in the middle of contract negotiations with the Board of Education at the Plaza Hotel when the state legislature was convened, and as soon as he read about the new Emergency Financial Control Board, he knew he would now be negotiating with Carey as well as Beame's Board of Education. Whatever deal he struck with the Board of Education could be renegotiated by the Emergency Financial Control Board. Even without this complication, the negotiations were not going well. The issues in contention were those one would expect: salaries, class size, and layoffs.[15] School opened as scheduled on September 8, without a contract, and with a strike vote looming later that day. The union delegates met at Town Hall on West 43rd Street and unanimously recommended a strike. Nearly 25,000 teachers jammed into Madison Square Garden to vote on the recommendation. The vote in favor of striking was overwhelming—22,870 to 900.[16]

The strike lasted nine days. On September 16, a tentative agreement was negotiated whereby the maximum class sizes would be reinstated as in the expired contract, and teachers would be given an annual cost of living adjustment of $300 and annual longevity raises, beginning at $750 for those with ten years of service and up to $1,500 annually for those with over fifteen years of service.[17] Shanker had originally sought a 25 percent across-the-board salary increase. His executive board approved the pact by 49 to 13 with the delegates approving by a vote of 662 to 359. The vote among the rank-and-file teachers was relatively close: 10,651 in favor and 6,645 opposed.[18] The pact was sent to the Emergency Financial Control Board for approval—the first test of the new entity.

On September 11, Carey appointed the three non-officeholder members of the Emergency Financial Control Board. Carey decided to move William Ellinghaus, chairman of the MAC, to the new entity and have Rohatyn succeed Ellinghaus as MAC chairman. Carey also appointed Albert Vincent Casey, chairman of American Airlines, and David I. Margolis, president of Colt Industries Inc.[19] Two days later, Mayor Beame appointed Kenneth S. Axelson, a senior vice president of J. C. Penney, as the city's newly created deputy mayor for finance, yet another move to limit the power of Cavanagh in order to placate the MAC Hawks, who were whispering to the press for Cavanagh's ouster.[20] Five days later, State Comptroller Arthur Levitt appointed Sidney Schwartz to fill the newly created position of deputy state controller for New York City.

Just as soon as the new personnel were settling in, the $2.3 billion rescue financing plan began to crumble. On

September 15, S&P issued an advisory warning that New York State's AA credit rating could be downgraded if the state's financial assistance went beyond the $750 million it had already committed to get New York City through to November.[21] On September 24, the New York City Educational Construction Fund, one of the city's "moral obligation" funding entities, faced default on $81 million of its maturing notes. With no other option to prevent the default, the Emergency Financial Control Board approved the borrowing by the city of the $81 million from the MAC for the refinancing, further worsening the city's funding crisis.[22]

The MAC was also struggling to raise the $250 million in new-money bonds that the banks agreed to underwrite as part of the $2.3 billion rescue financing plan. By late September, only $100 million had been sold. The MAC expanded its sales efforts toward large nonfinancial companies headquartered in New York. It was able to cobble together another $64 million in sales to retailers such as Federated Department stores, R.H. Macy, J. C. Penney, Gimbels, and Lord & Taylor, as well as Union Carbide Corporation, IBM, Bristol-Meyers Corporation, and the New York Times Corporation.[23] By the end of September, the offering was still more than $80 million undersubscribed. This was the fiscal equivalent of searching under the sofa cushions for quarters, and there were no more cushions to peek under.

On September 22, President Ford was back in California, speaking to the World Affairs Council at the St. Francis Hotel in San Francisco. As he was leaving the hotel and about to enter his limousine, two shots rang out. One missed Ford's head by five inches. The other struck John Ludwig, a taxi driver, who survived the gunshot. A San Francisco police officer, Timothy Hettrich, pulled the gun away from the shooter, a forty-five-year-old, five-time divorcee named Sara Jane Moore. Moore had developed an obsession with Patty Hearst, the kidnapped heiress and alleged member of the far-left terrorist organization, the Symbionese Liberation Army. Moore volunteered as a book-keeper for a Hearst family charity, People in Need. Moore was also an FBI informant. Four days before the assassination attempt, Patty Hearst had been arrested. Moore never linked the assassination attempt to the Patty Hearst arrest and never gave any motive for her actions, except to say, "It seemed a correct expression of my anger."[24]

Until late September, the large New York banks had avoided any direct lobbying of President Ford for financial assistance for New York City. It was thought to be counterproductive, as such efforts would be portrayed by the media and those opposed to assistance (or those opposed to the strings that would be attached to assistance) as a federal bailout of the banks from their bad investments in New York City debt. The meeting with Anderson at Pocantico Hills changed the calculus for David Rockefeller, however. New York State's solvency was now at risk. Equally as important, brother Nelson's future was also at risk. So on September 23, David Rockefeller made a call to Ford in the Oval Office and warned him of dire consequences to the markets and the economy if New York City were to default.[25] On September 27, Dennis Longwell, a Chase Manhattan Bank executive, submitted a letter to the Congressional Joint Economic Committee stating that: "We believe from both a local and national perspective that temporary Federal support for New York City is of the highest priority."[26] The letter continued: "What we believe to be the only viable alternative is a temporary substitution of Federal credit for the city's in order to insure the marketability of city debt until investor confidence is restored by a year or two of demonstrated performance in meeting the targets which have been set forth."[27]

Just when the stars seemed to be aligning for Carey, when the leverage seemed to be shifting in his favor against Ford, catastrophe struck. Carey's $2.3 billion rescue financing plan was dealt a fatal blow on September 29 when the New York Court of Appeals, in a six-to-one decision, struck down the provision of the emergency legislation that mandated that Levitt invest $225 million of the state's public employee pension funds in MAC bonds. The State Civil Service Employee Association, whose 240,000 members included teachers with pensions from the New York State Teachers' Pension Fund, which was mandated to purchase $100 million in MAC bonds, and the Police Conference of New York, Inc., which had 45,000 upstate law enforcement workers who participated in the New York State policemen's and firemen's pension fund, which was mandated to purchase $125 million of MAC bonds, brought suit challenging the mandate, claiming it violated Article 5, Section 7, of the New York State Constitution, which provided that state pension benefits cannot be diminished or impaired.[28] The court of appeals agreed, finding that eliminating Levitt's investment discretion impaired pension benefits.[29]

This decision was fatal for the $2.3 billion rescue financing plan for two reasons: First, Levitt, citing diversification concerns and his well-known objection to "moral obligation" bonds, publicly stated that he would not voluntarily buy any more MAC bonds with pension money. Second, the reasoning behind the court of appeals decision called in question the $500 million in mandated New York City public employee pension fund purchases of MAC bonds that were part of the rescue financing plan. The New York City Teachers Retirement System was to provide $200 million of that $500 million. A majority of the votes of the trustees of that pension fund were controlled by Albert Shanker, and he had a contract approval pending before the new Emergency Financial Control Board.

The same day the court of appeals decision came down, Shanker got word that the Emergency Financial Control Board was not going to approve the tentative agreement that ended the teachers' strike. An analysis of the contract indicated that it would cost the city $80 million more than was budgeted for the 1976 fiscal year. Governor Carey announced that if those numbers were correct, the proposed contract would violate the control board's budgeting guidelines.[30] Upon hearing this, Shanker responded that any attempt to abrogate the agreement would "constitute a declaration of war on teachers, children, parents, community school boards and the whole educational community."[31]

On September 30, the New York commercial banks and investment banks that underwrote the State of New York's notes and bonds had all refused to participate in a syndicate to underwrite the second $250 million tranche of state notes required to fund the rescue financing plan. This news came as a shock to Governor Carey and Rohatyn. They were well aware of the risk of contagion, that the city's fiscal crisis would infect the state's credit, but they never thought it would happen so abruptly. But markets are not always rational. If all at once the large municipal bond buyers are convinced the state will have to pay 200 basis points more on its short-term debt very shortly, they will sit out the offering today and wait for the repricing of the notes down the road. If those buyers are convinced the state may have a difficult time refinancing those notes when due in eleven months, that alone would be enough to pass on the offering, as a short-term investment might turn out to be long-term. If it looked like President Ford wouldn't blink, that he would succeed in requiring New York City to default before he bailed it out, he might take an equally hard line with an insolvent New York State. Pretty soon, a financial market can convince itself of some very dark ideas. "The marketability of that state paper is problematic at this point," Rohatyn told the press, with unusual understatement.[32]

Carey issued no public statement. The following morning, he flew to Washington to brief members of the New York congressional delegation.[33] What was needed immediately was some action by Congress to calm the municipal bond market, to convince its buyers that the money would come from Washington, DC—and soon. At this critical juncture, if Carey couldn't convince the municipal bond market that New York State would avoid default, how could he convince Beame that he could prevent a New York City default? It could all unravel very quickly. As Carey flew down the East Coast that morning, he knew that center stage for the city's crisis had moved from Albany to Washington. Luckily, he had a good friend in Washington who happened to be the House majority leader.

CHAPTER ELEVEN

DROP DEAD

THE FINANCIAL PICTURE LOOKED BLEAK. OF THE $755 MILLION of State of New York notes underwritten by the banks on September 10 to fund the state's first $250 million contribution to the rescue financing plan, $300 million remained on the books of the banks, unsold at the end of September. The notes that were sold were trading at an enormous discount, yielding 21 percent.[1] Carey's $2.3 billion rescue financing plan now had a $375 million hole. The $250 million more the State of New York had agreed to fund with an additional notes issuance was off the table, with the state frozen out of the municipal bond market. That hole would have been $500 million, but Arthur Levitt on October 2 agreed to use the state's public employee pension funds to buy $250 million of state notes. But what Levitt gave he also took away. The state law mandate requiring Levitt to have the state's public employee pension funds buy $125 million of MAC bonds had been thrown out by the court of appeals, and

Levitt was standing firm on not having those pension funds buy any more MAC bonds. To make matters worse, Moody's withdrew its ratings on the state's short-term notes.

Rohatyn was floating the idea of having the city's public employee pension funds loan the city $4 billion to finance it through June 30, 1976.[2] The city's five public employee pension systems had assets aggregating approximately $8.5 billion ($3.8 billion was in the New York City Employee Retirement System, $2.8 billion in the teachers' pension fund, $1.3 billion in the New York City Police pension fund, $500 million in the New York City Fire Department pension fund, and $125 million in the Board of Education pension fund).[3] Over $1 billion of those pension funds had already been invested in city and MAC securities.[4] Rohatyn's new proposal would result in nearly 60 percent of all the pension assets invested in city-related securities.

The unions in October were not in a generous mood. Back in July, most of them had agreed to a wage freeze that, it was promised, would prevent future layoffs. That promise was broken. Levitt had refused to invest more than 10 percent of the state public employee pension assets in MAC securities—Rohatyn was asking the city unions to invest 60 percent of their employees' pension assets in city and MAC securities. For years, the city had underfunded its employee pension plans and used the pension funds' income as a piggy bank. The question for Victor Gotbaum, Albert Shanker, Jack Bigel, and the rest of the city union leadership was how to maximize their newfound leverage. In truth, there was limited risk to the city employees' pensions if the pension fund assets were invested unwisely: the city was still legally obligated to pay the employees' pensions even if the pension fund assets were completely whittled away. Time was on the unions' side, for they now held leverage not only over the city but the state as well. Early in the state's next fiscal year beginning April 1, 1976, it would need to borrow $4 billion in anticipation notes to fund its expenses, almost all of which was passed on to cities and towns as aid. With the state then shut out of the short-term municipal bond market, a solution to New York City's fiscal crisis was necessary to avoid a statewide fiscal crisis.[5]

Down in Washington, Carey was looking to Tip O'Neill to introduce a bill his team had drafted in order to soothe the municipal bond market. Carey's proposed federal legislation, the Municipal Emergency Act of 1975, provided for the creation of a Federal "MAC-like" entity backed by the US Treasury that would guarantee new taxable bonds to be issued by municipalities and agencies like the MAC. The municipality at issue would need to demonstrate that the financial markets were closed to it, that it would balance its budget within three years, and that it would avoid accounting gimmicks.[6] The decision to make the new federally guaranteed municipal bonds taxable addressed the concern at the root of the New York City fiscal crisis: the municipal bond market was comprised mainly of tax-paying institutions buying tax-exempt debt securities, and it was oversaturated with New York City–related paper. Broadening the potential investor base to attract tax-exempt buyers—like public- and private-sector pension funds and university endowments that invested in taxable debt securities—would alleviate the oversaturation.

Carey was told by O'Neill that the votes were not there for his bill, and when that became apparent to the municipal bond market, Carey's problems might get worse.[7] Instead, O'Neill decided to accelerate and enlarge the legislation he had Congressman Reuss introduce back in May providing for a US Treasury guarantee of New York City notes and bonds in order to calm the markets. Reuss introduced a revised bill providing for $7 billion of guarantees on October 7.[8] The following day, Senator William Proxmire, chairman of the Senate Banking Committee, announced he would hold hearings on guarantee legislation.[9] The congressional activity had its desired effect. The municipal bond market calmed down, and liquidity returned for New York State obligations.

The market break in New York State bonds spooked Ford almost as much as it did Carey, and Ford was nearly as happy as Carey when the market stabilized. There were limits to the game of chicken Ford was playing, and the end of the game was fast approaching. Ford still had to appear tough enough on New York City to placate his conservative base, while at the same time not spooking the municipal bond market to the point where it might think New York State might go under.

Despite the fact that Ford administration officials were meeting with Anderson to come up with legislation for the bailout of New York City, Ron Nessen, President Ford's press secretary, continued to insist that there had been no change in President Ford's position that no federal aid would be forthcoming.[10] Any premature leaks would only help the Reagan Republicans in organizing opposition to federal aid. However, Bill Simon began making rather specific recommendations as to what New York City ought to do to resolve the crisis, which many interpreted, correctly it would turn out, as the prerequisite of a Ford administration bailout. On October 4, Simon told the *New York Times* that the banks that held city notes should declare a "moratorium" of some sort to defer the obligation to pay the notes for "two, three, or four years." He also said that taxes in New York City should be increased to pay down the deficit. Finally, he said that the city needed to produce a credible three-year plan to balance its expense budget.[11] Vice President Rockefeller followed on Simon's remarks by saying at a news conference in Portland, Oregon, that Congress should consider some form of aid to "bridge" the city's fiscal crisis.[12] Arthur Burns, testifying before the Joint Economic Committee of Congress on October 8, said that he was closer to considering approving legislation providing aid to the city.[13]

As the senior Ford administration officials dug in on coming up with the bailout program with Anderson, the more concerned they became. New York State was in worse financial condition than they thought, and its fiscal woes were not by any measure solely the result of New York City's problems. The state was running a $600 million deficit for fiscal 1976. And while they were aware of the problems at the UDC, they had not been aware that there were four other state agencies at risk of defaulting on their moral obligation bonds—the Housing Finance Agency, the Dormitory Authority, the Nursing Home Authority, and the Environmental Protection Authority. The worst problems were at the Housing Finance Agency, with borrowing needs at $100 million a month on average, with no credit source in sight.[14] Bill Simon, Arthur Burns, and L. William Seidman were growing concerned that, absent a federal bailout of New York City by year-end, the federal government might be bailing out both the city and New York State during the election year of 1976.

On October 7, Beame presented to the Emergency Financial Control Board his preliminary three-year plan to balance the city's expense budget and eliminate its cumulative deficit—then acknowledged to be $3.3 billion, but in truth was $5.1 billion. Without additional cuts, Beame told the board, expenses would exceed revenues over the next three years by $800 million in the aggregate.[15] His plan, deeply disappointing to Carey and the other members of the Emergency Financial Control Board, was a mere nine-page summary with no details on how the cost savings were to be obtained, other than extending the wage freeze through the end of the three-year period.[16] This wasn't making life any easier for Carey, as every bit of bad news about the city's fiscal situation or Beame's job of handling it risked a rebuke to the state's credit in the municipal bond market. But Beame's heart would never be in any fiscal austerity program. At the same meeting, the Emergency Financial Control Board officially rejected the accord reached between the Board of Education and Shanker that ended the nine-day teachers strike. The Emergency Financial Control Board directed the Board of Education to renegotiate the agreement with Shanker.[17]

The response of the city's union leadership to Beame's three-year plan of an extended wage freeze and inevitable lay-offs and the Emergency Financial Control Board's veto of the teachers' contract was to threaten a general strike, with Barry Feinstein and Ken McFeeley leading the charge. Shanker indicated that he was open to the idea. John DeLury was lukewarm to the idea. Only Victor Gotbaum expressed opposition, saying he was not open to a general strike.[18] The union leaders agreed that their support for any further investment in city-related securities would be conditioned on a "no layoffs" guarantee.[19]

On October 9, Senator Proxmire's Committee on Banking, Housing, and Urban Affairs began hearings on the New York City fiscal crisis and to consider a number of bills introduced to provide aid to the city. Now that a bailout was to be had, those who would benefit therefrom—a liberal senator from New York, for example, or contenders for the 1976 Democratic presidential nomination—tried to get in on the action. Senators Jacob Javits of New York, Hubert Humphrey of Minnesota, Lloyd Bentsen of Texas, and Henry "Scoop" Jackson of Washington had each submitted separate bills for consideration.[20] President

Ford, still playing chicken and not ready to go public with his plan to bail out the city, said at a news conference that he saw no reason for Congress to assist the city at that time, throwing cold water on the earlier statements by Secretary Simon, Vice President Rockefeller, and Federal Reserve Board Chairman Burns.[21]

Ford and the Democratic congressional leadership knew what the House and Senate hearings would be all about, and it was a rather simple show to follow: Should New York City be required to default and file bankruptcy as a condition to receiving federal financial aid? On the "No" side of that question were Beame, Carey, the unions (who did not want a federal bankruptcy judge reducing their pension benefits), and the municipal bond market (which did not want a federal bankruptcy judge reducing or extending their bond payments). On the "Yes" side? Conservative Republicans (who were in short supply in Washington after the disastrous 1974 midterm elections) and sophisticated thinkers (likewise in short supply) who could foresee that, absent pension reduction and debt forgiveness, New York City austerity would be taken out of the hides of the most needy (who paid no lobbyists in Washington).

The first witness was Secretary Simon who described the plan he laid out for the *New York Times* a few days earlier, except that he now believed that a voluntary moratorium would not be sufficient, as the banks and other large financial institutions did not own a large enough proportion of the city's short-term debt to generate enough short-term cash flow savings to keep the city solvent.[22] Simon said the city should file for federal bankruptcy and that Herman Badillo's bankruptcy legislation facilitating municipal filings pending in Congress should be passed forthwith to enable the city to do so.[23]

The following day, Proxmire's committee heard from Governor Carey, Felix Rohatyn; Simon Rifkind; Edward W. Kresky of Wertheim & Co., Inc.; Brenton W. Harries of S&P; Paul J. Markowski of Argus Research; Wallace O. Sellers of Merrill Lynch; William J. Solari of Donaldson, Lufkin & Jenrette; S. Grady Fullerton, auditor of Harris County, Texas; Joe E. Torrence, director of finance of Davidson County, Tennessee; John M. Urie, director of finance of Kansas City; and John Petersen of the Municipal Finance Officers Association. All the witnesses, except Solari, told of draconian consequences if New York City were to default and urged the Senate to approve some form of federal loan guarantees to prevent default.[24] Solari did not believe a New York City default would have a devastating impact on financial markets. Rather, he warned that a federal guarantee of municipal bonds would create distortions in the municipal bond market: the securities of the worst-run cities would be the safest because they would be the ones that benefited from the federal guarantee.[25]

On October 15, Beame submitted to the Emergency Financial Control Board his definitive three-year plan to eliminate the city's deficit and balance its expense budget. The plan included 8,000 more layoffs. Gotbaum called the plan "unconscionable." Shanker made no public comment that day. He was instead cooking up a plan of revenge.

Pursuant to Carey's September $2.3 billion rescue financing plan, the City Teachers Retirement System Pension Plan had committed to invest $200 million in MAC bonds. As of October 15, $150 million of that money had not been invested. Shanker was going to hold that money hostage. After the mandate for Levitt to invest $125 million of the state's public employee pension funds was thrown out by the New York State Court of Appeals, the city public employee pension fund trustees were free to reconsider their commitments and act as they believed their fiduciary duties directed them, Shanker reasoned. Shanker had voluntarily agreed to the teachers' pension fund purchasing the MAC bonds back in September and, unlike Levitt, had not insisted on being directed to do so by the state legislature. The city had $450 million of revenue anticipation notes maturing on October 17—and the teachers' pension fund money was needed to redeem them. At a meeting of the teachers' pension fund trustees on the evening of October 16, all three of the union representative trustees (Reuben Mitchell, Joseph Shannon, and Bernard Goldberg) voted to withhold the money.[26] No action could be taken by the teachers' pension board of trustees unless one of the union representatives agreed, and none agreed to anything unless Shanker gave the nod. Several hours later, at 1:30 a.m. on October 17, another vote was taken. Again, the union representative trustees voted no. It was agreed that the trustees would go home and reconvene at 7:00 a.m.[27]

After the first no vote was taken, MAC officials called Governor Carey, who was at the Waldorf Astoria Hotel for the annual Alfred E. Smith white-tie dinner, a marquis event on the New York political calendar. Carey and several top aides abruptly left the dinner and gathered back at the governor's Manhattan office, where Carey called legislative leaders in Albany and Ford administration officials in Washington to alert them that New York City might default the next morning.[28] Beame had called Ford at 12:25 a.m., but aides told Beame the president was sleeping and would not be disturbed.[29] L. William Seidman was briefed by Rohatyn, who in turn briefed Ford after he had breakfast. Ford decided to wait and see what the day brought in New York rather than immediately offer emergency aid.[30]

Shanker made his terms clear: a no-layoffs pledge and a reversal by the Emergency Financial Control Board of its rejection of the teachers' contract. Carey would not budge. He concluded that if he gave in to Shanker's hardball tactics, every other union would re-trade concessions as well.[31]

Richard Ravitch was not at the Al Smith dinner that night. He was at a dinner given by Gus Levy of Goldman Sachs for the trustees of the Federation of Jewish Philanthropies.[32] Ravitch left early, and went to bed around 9:00 p.m., because he was very tired from a day trip to Washington, DC, and back to meet with Henry Reuss, chairman of the House Banking, Currency and Housing Committee, at the behest of Governor Carey.[33] He was awakened from a brief sleep by a phone call from Carey summoning him to the governor's Manhattan office. Carey knew that Ravitch's wife was friendly with Shanker (she had conducted research and written on union issues and had pleasant dealings with Shanker) and thought that Ravitch would make an effective intermediary between Shanker and Carey. After meeting with Carey, Ravitch went to Shanker's apartment, arriving shortly after midnight, and spent five hours attempting to convince Shanker to change his mind, but to no avail.[34] After a few hours of fitful sleep, Ravitch returned to the governor's Manhattan office shortly after 9:00 a.m. About an hour later, Shanker, who was at Gracie Mansion with Beame and former Mayor Wagner, called Carey and suggested they all meet. It was agreed that Carey and Shanker would meet at Ravitch's apartment at Park Avenue and 88th Street. A large group convened at Ravitch's apartment: Carey and his counsel, Judah Gribetz, Simon Rifkind, and Ravitch; and with Shanker were former Mayor Wagner, Shanker's deputy Sandy Feldman, and labor leader Henry Van Arsdale.[35] For over two hours of discussion, it became clear that Carey would not budge, and Shanker blinked. At 1:00 p.m., Shanker instructed the union representative trustees to approve the $150 million purchase of MAC bonds.[36]

In truth, Shanker wildly overplayed his hand. After the second no vote, Beame had called John DeLury, president of the Sanitationmen's Union, and asked him if his pension fund would take up the $150 million of MAC bonds if Shanker didn't relent. DeLury promised that his pension fund would do so.[37] Gotbaum implied to Beame that he might be willing to do so as well.[38] And even in the unlikely event that Shanker's holdout forced the city to default, that may have resulted in the city filing for federal bankruptcy protection—Ford's preferred course—which would not only have put the teachers' contract at risk, but also risked a bankruptcy court reducing pension benefits for retirees. Shamelessly, Shanker and his public relations people would thereafter proclaim that Shanker saved New York City from bankruptcy, by reversing his ill-advised reneging on his September commitment.[39]

After Shanker finally came through with the funds he had promised, Carey sent a telegram to President Ford asking for him to reverse his objection to federal aid and informing him the city only had funds available to meet its obligations through mid-December: "We need not a handout, but recognition by the Federal government that we are part of this country."[40] Ron Nessen, the White House press secretary, responded that the latest crisis was a self-inflicted act by the people who have been running New York City.[41] Nessen compared New York to a "wayward daughter hooked on heroin. You don't give her $100 a day to support her habit, you make her go cold turkey to break the habit."[42]

Behind the scenes, however, Ford knew the time was fast approaching when he'd need to change course. Mid-December was after Thanksgiving, according to Ford's calendar. Carey had successfully waited him out. If he played the game of chicken too long, even if he "won" by requiring the city to default and file bankruptcy, he would lose if he was viewed as playing politics with the health and safety of the people of New York and the Republicans that would meet in Albany for the state convention on January 6 bolted and elected thirty-seven delegates for Reagan. He would need to put some proposal on the table for assistance to New York City, publicly, and soon.

The day after the "near-default" that was not quite as near as the mythmaking would have it, Senator Proxmire's committee resumed its hearings with Beame as the first witness. Beame told the committee that New York City would default by the end of the year without federal financial assistance.[43] He blamed the national recession for the city's fiscal woes. Joining Beame at the witness table were Kenneth Axelson, the city's deputy mayor for finance, and Ira Millstein, a partner of the law firm of Weil, Gotshal & Manges, the city's bankruptcy counsel. Later in the day, bankers David Rockefeller, Elmore Patterson, Walter Wriston, A. W. Clausen (president of Bank of America), Peter G. Peterson of Lehman Brothers, Morris Crawford Jr. (chairman of Bowery Savings Bank), Stewart Rauch Jr. (chairman of Philadelphia Savings Fund Society), and Harry W. Albright, Jr. (president of Dime Savings Bank) testified before the committee.[44] All of them agreed that the financial markets would be adversely affected by a New York City default and were in favor of a federal loan or guarantee program.[45]

The last witness before the committee that day was the financial journalist and author Martin Mayer. He made the case for the city filing bankruptcy, and the city's debt holders and pension holders having their claims reduced so that the burden of setting the fiscal house in order would not fall disproportionately on the city's taxpayers by way of higher taxes and the city's poor, who would receive fewer services.[46] The union leaders and the bankers, knowing Mayer's analysis was spot-on, never ceased their continuous drumbeat regarding the horrors that bankruptcy would bring to the city, the national economy, and the markets. The politicians, wanting a federal judge nowhere near the room where the ladling of the pork was decided, eagerly joined in that drumbeat. Most of the public in New York, unknowledgeable about the process of municipal bankruptcy and believing that filing bankruptcy was a shameful act that brought ruin, reflexively dismissed the prospect out of hand, believing it was a right-wing plot to punish the city, not help its taxpayers and poor.

While they were in Washington for the Senate committee hearings, Kenneth Axelson and Ira Millstein met with Treasury Secretary Simon at his office. According to Simon, both Axelson and Millstein told Simon that they in truth believed, like Martin Mayer, that the city should default and file bankruptcy because that would allow an orderly resolution of the city's finances.[47] Of course, neither Millstein nor Axelson would say that publicly. Millstein provided a memo for the Proxmire committee outlining the disastrous consequences that would befall the city if it were forced to file bankruptcy.[48] Like any good lawyer, Millstein was aware of who approved the payment of his bills, and that person was Beame.

On October 20, the House Subcommittee on Economic Stabilization of the Committee on Banking, Currency, and Housing began its hearings on the New York City fiscal crisis with Abe Beame, Kenneth Axelson, Ira Millstein, and Richard Bing, New York City assistant director of the budget, as the first witnesses. They essentially parroted their earlier testimony before the Proxmire's Senate committee.[49] Elmore Patterson of Morgan Guaranty Trust of New York and Brenton Harries, president of S&P, testified in the afternoon session, each in favor of federal financial assistance.[50]

On October 21, Senator Proxmire took a vote of his committee to determine whether it should proceed with marking up a bill for consideration by the full Senate. By a vote of seven to six, the committee agreed to proceed. All the Republicans on the committee, along with Democratic Senator Robert Morgan of North Carolina, voted against proceeding. All the remaining Democrats voted in favor.[51] Because of the close vote, Proxmire agreed to another day of hearings (on October 25) to hear from Arthur Levitt, Harrison Goldin, Simon Rifkind, and other witnesses.

The House subcommittee hearings continued that day as well, with Governor Carey, Felix Rohatyn, Arthur Levitt, David Burke, Carey's secretary, and Peter Goldmark, state budget director, appearing.[52] In arguing against requiring the city to file bankruptcy, Carey told the subcommittee that the laws of twenty-seven states and the District of Columbia prevented fiduciaries in those states from investing in entities that had filed bankruptcy for periods from five to twenty years after the bankruptcy filing. Accordingly, a city bankruptcy filing might close the municipal bond market to the city for over five years, Carey warned.[53]

On October 23, the House subcommittee heard testimony from Paul Volcker, president of the Federal Reserve Bank of New York. Volcker told the subcommittee that the effect of default on the nation's banking system was likely to be limited. The value of the city's debt securities would not go to zero, and in fact those securities were already trading at a substantial discount that reflected the effects of default.[54] Even those banks that invested heavily in city securities would likely remain solvent, as the Federal Reserve stood ready to provide liquidity to those banks.[55]

House Speaker Carl Albert came out strongly for federal guarantee legislation on October 25. "We have to prevent default by the New York City government—I just don't think the country can take it," Albert said in a news conference in his Capitol office.[56] The House subcommittee concluded public hearings with testimony from Albert Shanker and Victor Gotbaum.[57] Following the hearings that day, Representative Henry S. Reuss, chairman of the House Banking, Currency, and Housing Committee, polled the Democratic members of the committee and found that a strong majority supported federal loan guarantee legislation.[58]

A majority of the senators on Proxmire's committee agreed on a bill to put to a vote of the committee. It was a compromise bill worked out with Illinois Senator Adlai E. Stevenson III, the key swing vote on the committee. The legislation would provide for $4 billion of US Treasury bond guarantees for New York City. As a condition to receiving the federal guarantees, a three-member federal board headed by Treasury Secretary Simon would oversee the city's finances, with power to lay off workers, end rent control, and take other aggressive actions to eliminate the city's deficit.[59] Private investors would be required to purchase an additional $1 billion in city bonds without the federal guarantee as a condition to the issuance of the guaranteed bonds.[60] A vote by the committee on the bill was deferred until Thursday, October 30, as the White House had announced that the president would be making a major address on the New York City fiscal crisis on October 29 at a speech at the National Press Club in Washington, DC.[61] The game of chicken was over. Ford was finally going to agree to bail out New York City.

Before Ford could announce that he would bail out New York City, he concluded that he had to throw a scalp to the conservative Republican base, and that scalp belonged to Nelson Rockefeller. Nelson's last-chance presidential aspirations would be the first of three to be felled by the fiscal crisis. Before his scheduled speech at the National Press Club, President Ford had a private meeting with Rocky. It would be a tough meeting for both men. Although many in Ford's inner circle had been advising him to dump Nelson for months, and some of them publicly, Ford had stood by him. In truth, Nelson had been a loyal, hard-working and effective vice president. Ford found Nelson impossible not to like, on a personal level. But Nelson had also alienated the Nixon people in 1960, the Goldwater people in 1964, and the conservatives always. The soon-to-be announced New York City bailout was going to be a major issue in the fight for the 1976 Republican nomination. Rockefeller, while governor of New York, had done a great many things to enable, and arguably even cause, the fiscal crisis. If Rockefeller, the New Yorker and titular head of the liberal wing of the Republican Party, remained on the ticket, the New York City crisis would be an albatross around Ford's neck, costing him not only support among the conservative base, but among moderates as well. Ronald Reagan would remind Republican primary voters at every opportunity who Ford had at his right hand. Ford told Rockefeller he would not be the vice presidential nominee in 1976. Rocky took it with class and agreed that he would announce that he had decided on his own to not be on the ticket in 1976.

The purpose of Ford's National Press Club speech was to announce a major shift in administration policy: Ford would agree to provide federal financial assistance to New York City. There would, of course, be conditions to New York City getting the money, and those conditions would need to be negotiated with Carey. The speech was to be the opening round of those negotiations. Ford's threshold condition was that the city file bankruptcy. If it did that, and private-sector financing was not sufficient to fund the city's operations with the breathing room that bankruptcy provided, Ford would have the federal government fund the city's operations. The ball would then be in Carey's court to come back with a counterproposal, and so on until a mutually acceptable, politically viable agreement was reached. That was how things were done in Washington (and still are).

Ford began his speech laying blame for the city's fiscal crisis at the feet of New York City officials. "Let's face one simple fact: most other cities in America have faced these same challenges, and they are still financially healthy today. They have not been luckier than New York; they simply have been better managed."[62] "No city can expect to remain solvent if it allows its expenses to increase by an average of 12 percent every year, while its tax revenues are increasing by only 4 percent to 5 percent per year," Ford continued.[63] Ford went on to talk about how most of the nation's municipal employees had to contribute 50 percent or more of their pension costs, while in New York City, many employees contributed nothing to their pension costs; the city had eighteen municipal hospitals, but 25 percent of the beds were empty; and 10 percent of city welfare recipients were frauds, ineligible to receive benefits.[64]

Ford said that while a New York City default might cause temporary disruptions in financial markets, talk of catastrophe was simply a tactic to get the federal government to bail out the incompetent city leaders.[65] Ford then laid out the conditions to which he would approve aid to the city: "I can tell you—and tell you now—that I am prepared to veto any bill that has as its purpose a federal bailout of New York City to prevent a default."[66] Ford stated that a bailout before default would only enable city officials to continue their irresponsible ways, encourage other cities to behave similarly, and benefit rich investors who bought New York City securities—and received sky-high interest rates—passing the risk on to the nation's taxpayers.[67]

Ford outlined his alternative: First, the Congress should promptly pass the proposed new Chapter XVI of the Bankruptcy Act, similar to bills currently in committee, that would allow cities to file for bankruptcy protection without prior approval of a majority of creditors—and New York City should file for bankruptcy protection. Second, with the breathing space that bankruptcy provides, New York City should reorganize its debts. Third, under the new bankruptcy law, New York City could sell debt certificates to private investors that rank ahead of pre-bankruptcy debts. If those steps were taken and New York City could not sell those debt certificates to private investors, Ford promised that the federal government would provide financial assistance to the city to pay for essential city services like police, fire, and sanitation.[68]

Ford braced himself for what he thought would be a barrage of criticism—from the Reaganites and the conservatives. But then something weird and unexpected happened. The press ignored the major change in policy—that Ford had agreed to provide financial assistance to the city. Instead, the coverage focused nearly exclusively on Ford's bankruptcy filing condition, notwithstanding that the press knew it would be subject to negotiation and would very likely be softened. Ford's speech was described as heartless and cruel, his requirement of bankruptcy draconian or worse. O'Neill and Carey were one step ahead of Ford. They knew the battle was not just one of public relations but of the hearts and minds of the men and women of the press corps who shaped public opinion. The hearts and minds of the Washington and New York City reporters were Democratic, and O'Neill and Carey had done their homework with those reporters. John Scanlon had worked the phones relentlessly in advance of Ford's speech, and this may well have been his finest hour. It didn't matter what Ford said, it would be spun by the Monk as punishment of the decent, hardworking people of New York City—indeed of working Americans everywhere.

The New York progressives were predictably hysterical. "He has branded New York as diseased and now he wants to pull the plug on our city," wailed Manhattan Congresswoman Bella Abzug.[69] "An irresponsible diatribe that Richard Nixon at his worst could never have uttered. In retrospect, it makes one wonder whether impeachment was really such a good idea," spat City Council President Paul O'Dwyer.[70] Illinois Senator Adlai E. Stevenson III, always eager to curry favor with his boss, advised New Yorkers that, "the best solution for your problems would be the loan of Chicago Mayor Richard J. Daley."[71] Moody's, uncertain of how the negotiations over federal assistance would play out or the timing thereof, lowered its rating on New York City general obligation bonds from BA to CAA.[72]

The most remembered response came from *Daily News*' managing editor, William Brink, who decided the headlines for the paper's October 30, 1975, edition. The front page headline would be 144-point type reserved for the most major news events—that Brink knew for sure. The first draft read: "FORD REFUSES AID TO CITY." Brink didn't like it. He tried: "FORD SAYS NO TO CITY AID." Too mundane, thought Brink. Then came inspiration: "FORD TO CITY: 'DROP DEAD.'"

CHAPTER TWELVE

THE PAIN IS JUST BEGINNING

CAREY READ THE NEXT DAY'S PAPERS AND ADMIRED JOHN Scanlon's handiwork. He could not believe his good fortune that the Ford people had been caught so flat-footed. Did they have any communication plan for rolling out the administration's proposal? Not only had Ford agreed to bail out the city, but he was being pilloried by most of the press for not simply handing over the check without condition. The bailout was on, and the wind was at Carey's back for a successful negotiation of its terms. Success, for Carey, meant avoiding a bankruptcy filing for the city and, hopefully, avoiding a default on its debt obligations as well. This would require an out-of-court restructuring of the city's debt. Simon Rifkind was hard at work on this task, Second, Carey would need to shake the trees for more money—from Anderson for more state money, from Jack Bigel and the union leadership for the public employee pension fund money, and from the banks. Rohatyn was the shaker-in-chief on that front.

Perhaps Rohatyn was shaking too hard.

A glitch had developed. A glimmer of hope that the union leadership might be on board with a plan floated by Rohatyn to provide the city with the financing it needed for the next two years nearly derailed the Washington bailout. On the day of the *Daily News'* famous headline, the *New York Times* carried a story by Fred Ferretti disclosing that MAC executive director Herb Elish and Jack Bigel were working out the details of Rohatyn's plan whereby the city's five public employee pension funds would pledge their $8.5 billion in assets as collateral for a guarantee of up to $4 billion of MAC bonds, the proceeds of which would have allowed the city to meet its cash needs for two years.[1] A pension fund guarantee, as opposed to an outright purchase of MAC bonds, would not raise the same diversification of investments concerns and would be easier to agree to from a fiduciary duty perspective, it was reasoned. Ferretti reported that the plan was kept quiet by state, city, and MAC officials because if Congress knew there was a viable option available to the city besides a federal loan or guarantee, Congress would not vote to approve such federal assistance.[2] Ironically, Shanker said publicly he was "not opposed in principle" to the guarantee plan,[3] his agonizing over the fiduciary duties of pension fund trustees apparently having ended when Carey called his bluff a couple weeks earlier.

The Republican members of Proxmire's Senate committee were furious. Senator Bob Packwood of Oregon called the New York leaders who testified earlier that the city had no financing options left a "bunch of liars."[4] Senator Jesse Helms of North Carolina and Jake Garn of Utah stormed out of the hearing room in protest.[5] Nevertheless, the Senate Banking Committee approved the Stevenson–Proxmire loan guarantee bill by a vote of eight to four.[6] In the House, Speaker Albert said the Democratic leadership was "100% committed to get a guarantee-type bill."[7] On October 31, the House Economic Stabilization Subcommittee voted ten to six to approve legislation that authorized $7 billion in loan guarantees to New York City.[8] It was clear that the congressional Democrats were going to call Ford's bluff and force him to veto the guarantee legislation.

Not all Democrats were aligned with the congressional leadership. Two 1976 Democratic presidential contenders opposed the guarantee legislation. One of them, conservative Governor George Wallace of Alabama, unsurprisingly opposed the measure. The other, then thought to be only a slightly more viable candidate than Wallace, was the former governor of Georgia, Jimmy Carter. Carter said he saw no reason why "the small towns of Georgia" should pay the tuition for New York City college students.[9]

The same day the House subcommittee approved the loan guarantee legislation, officials at Citibank and Morgan Guaranty Trust Company met with Rohatyn on the pension fund guarantee plan. The bankers told Rohatyn they had no appetite to make any more loans to or underwriting more bonds of the city or the MAC, even with a pension fund guarantee.[10] This, with the guarantee legislation moving ahead in Congress, was music to Rohatyn's ears. Rohatyn quickly told reporters the plan only had a 20 to 25 percent possibility of working—and that it wasn't even really a plan just "the beginning of an exploration, and there are serious problems with it."[11]

Ford's fixation on a bankruptcy filing wasn't motivated simply by looking tough for the conservatives. There were basic principles of fairness suggesting that course. Namely, that the pain of restructuring the city's finances should be as evenly distributed as possible. That meant reducing rich pension benefits and obtaining concessions from the city's bondholders through modification of debt terms like reductions in interest rates and extensions of maturities. Those actions could not be taken under applicable law (absent voluntary agreement) except pursuant to a federal bankruptcy proceeding. The banks and other large financial institutions might agree to debt reorganization, but they held less than half of New York City's debt, both the long-term bonds and the more problematic short-term notes. Considering the thousands of individual remaining bondholders and noteholders, to get voluntary agreement from enough of them so that the burden to be borne by banks in the debt restructuring would be acceptable to the banks was nearly an impossible task. And getting the retired union workers to agree to a reduction in their pension benefits was too laughable to even consider.

It is most unlikely that Carey resisted Ford's insistence on a bankruptcy filing to protect individual bondholders—and his legislative program in November would prove that. Protection of union members' pensions was another matter altogether, given how important that constituency was to Brooklyn Democrats like Carey. And there were other reasons to keep the city out of bankruptcy. Who knows what might happen if a federal bankruptcy judge started asking too many questions about where the money went in Brooklyn? That would be like having a Maurice Nadjari that Carey couldn't fire.

With the pension fund guarantee firestorm extinguished, Carey began his public relations campaign to keep New York City out of federal bankruptcy court while still getting the federal dollars the city needed. In a statewide televised address, Carey made his case: "I am here tonight to say that I agree with Gerald Ford. Washington should not bail out New York. I am here to tell

New Yorkers, and all Americans, that the bill we seek will impose on New York City the obligation to pay its bills in full, and to put its fiscal house in order. It is the Ford bankruptcy plan that would cost the cities, states, and taxpayers of this nation billions of dollars that need not be spent."[12] After acknowledging that blame for the city's financial crisis must be shared by Democrats and Republicans alike, Carey emphasized that the federal loan guarantee program he sought wouldn't cost taxpayers a dime (assuming New York City paid its bills, which at that moment it could not do), but that Ford's plan would cost taxpayers billions, because once the city filed bankruptcy, it would become the federal government's responsibility to fund New York, as no one would loan a bankrupt city money.[13] Carey also insisted, dubiously, that a New York City bankruptcy would cause a collapse of the municipal bond market nationwide, bankrupting other cities.[14]

Carey spent the next week out on the road, from Washington, DC, to Los Angeles and San Francisco, evangelizing for the federal guarantee legislation and warning of the dangers of a bankruptcy filing.[15] New York City business leaders were drafted by Carey into this effort as well.[16] Charles F. Luce, chairman of the Consolidated Edison Company, telegrammed President Ford that the utility might be forced to cut off service to New York City or withhold up to $400 million in tax payments if the city filed for bankruptcy (the legal basis for taking any such action was omitted in the telegram).[17] Even Mayor Beame's assistance was enlisted. On November 5, he gave a speech at the National Press Club in rebuttal to Ford's "Drop Dead" speech given there a week earlier. "Subjecting America's largest city to humiliation and impoverishment does not enhance the economy or the moral fiber of our nation. It is unimaginable to me that any other head of state in the world would abandon the premier city of his nation or punish its people as an object lesson," Beame said, in his best speech of the crisis.[18]

Carey's friends in Washington were doing their part. Senate Majority Leader Mike Mansfield told reporters that he had the votes to pass the Senate version of the federal loan guarantee legislation despite a threatened filibuster by Senator James Allen of Alabama.[19] On November 3, the House Banking, Currency, and Housing Committee approved the $7 billion loan guarantee legislation by a vote of twenty-three to sixteen.[20] The following day, Speaker Carl Albert scheduled the bill for a vote of the full House early the following week.[21]

The speedy consideration by the House ran into trouble on November 9, though, when George Meany, president of the AFL-CIO, came out against the bill because it would empower the federal oversight board it created to unilaterally abrogate union contracts and pension benefits.[22] There were no *Daily News* headlines declaring that George Meany told New York City to drop dead. It was apparently not a despicable act of racist punishment of urban America when national labor leaders opposed bailing out New York City for their own selfish interests. Speaker Albert agreed to postpone the House vote to address the union's concerns.[23]

During the first week of November, Simon Rifkind worked through possible schemes to reorganize the city's short-term debt outside of a federal bankruptcy proceeding. What was clear from the beginning was that current New York law would have to be changed, either by way of new legislation or, ideally, through some judicial action that would avoid Governor Carey having to go back yet again to Warren Anderson in Albany. The first scheme in this regard, Rifkind's brainchild, was to negotiate a settlement in the pending federal securities fraud class action lawsuit brought by Burton M. Abrams so that it included a remedy that compelled an extension of the city's short-term debt. Rifkind's plan was to settle the lawsuit by agreeing to give the city's noteholders MAC bonds worth more than the city notes they held, but with maturities of fifteen years, and making the exchange of the city notes for those MAC bonds mandatory for the individual holders of $1.6 billion in city notes.[24] This required the cooperation of not only Burton Abrams, the class action lead plaintiff, but also the federal district court judge overseeing the case, and that judge must be special indeed, because there was no legal precedent or authority for a judge in a securities class action settlement mandating anything resembling such an exchange. It was quite likely—almost a certainty—that such a ruling by a judge would be overturned on appeal by objecting city noteholders who, expecting their principal back within a year, would be forced to take MAC bonds maturing in fifteen years. This didn't trouble Rifkind, for such an appeal would take more than a year to resolve in the courts, and that was precisely the outcome he desired: delaying the maturity of short-term city notes.

This sort of legal chicanery wasn't particularly nice, or even ethical, and certainly not in accord with the distinguished mien Rifkind worked hard at presenting to the public; but Rifkind was, and remained, a Tammany sharpie at heart.

Rifkind first entered the consciousness of the New York City press during the curious case of Judge Joseph Force Crater of the New York Supreme Court who disappeared on the night of August 6, 1930, after leaving a dinner at Billy Haas's restaurant on West 45th Street in a taxi. Crater had been appointed to the bench by Governor Franklin D. Roosevelt at the urging of US Senator Robert F. Wagner, Tammany's man in Washington (and the father of the future mayor). Crater and Wagner shared a law office. A week after Crater was last seen, his wife, spending August in Maine, called Simon Rifkind, Senator Wagner's legislative assistant, alarmed that her husband had gone missing. As reported by Stephen J. Reigel in his 2022 book *Finding Judge Crater*, Rifkind told Crater's wife that Crater was fine and not to worry.[25] When Crater failed to show for the opening of the Supreme Court session on August 25, a concerned colleague called Mrs. Crater in Maine to inquire about his whereabouts. Now panicked, Mrs. Crater returned to New York. Then nearly three weeks after his disappearance, Rifkind nonetheless convinced Mrs. Crater not to report her husband as a missing person to the police, according to Reigel.[26] Not until September 3, nearly a month after he disappeared, did Rifkind report Crater's disappearance to the police.[27] Rifkind never publicly explained his conduct regarding Crater, whose body was never found. It would later come out that Crater liked the company of women who were not his wife (and were much younger) and enjoyed time in nightclubs with gangsters like Arnold Rothstein who fixed the 1919 World Series. These sorts of behaviors were hardly aberrant by the standards of the Democratic Party of Mayor Jimmy Walker's Jazz Age New York, but Supreme Court judges disappearing without a trace raised the eyebrows of even the most jaded of the city's tabloid reporters.

Whatever Rifkind knew about Crater's disappearance, he kept to himself. He too was rewarded by Tammany with a judgeship, appointed by then-President Franklin D. Roosevelt to the

US District Court for the Southern District of New York in 1941. Rifkind liked money, however, which was in modest supply for federal judges (even those from Tammany Hall not opposed to outside income), so he resigned from the bench in 1950 to join the Paul, Weiss firm, where he made many, many millions of dollars representing corporate interests and where he insisted on everyone calling him "Judge" until his death in 1995.

It became clear to Rifkind that the judge in the Burton Abrams litigation was not going to play ball. That judge was Richard Owen, a Nixon appointee and a straight arrow. This meant the legislative route to a debt reorganization had to be taken if a federal bankruptcy were to be avoided. On November 3, Carey told legislative leaders to be prepared to be in Albany the following week for an emergency session.[28]

Over the course of the next week, Carey engaged in back-channel negotiations with the Ford administration to finalize a deal to avoid bankruptcy but get federal financial support. Finally, the end had arrived. Thanks to the creative headline writing of William Brink at the *Daily News*, the superb spin-doctoring of John Scanlon and the skillful political maneuvering of Carey in New York and across the country, the political tide had turned against punitive measures for the city. In November, Ford was hearing from key political advisors like James Baker, who would become his 1976 campaign manager, that forcing New York into bankruptcy would likely cost Ford New York State in the 1976 general election and possibly other urban industrial states as well. With Rockefeller jettisoned from the ticket, Ronald Reagan was denied the easy opportunity to tie Ford to the New York mess, and the conservative base was at least temporarily sated. The terms would involve concessions (and more money) from the banks and public employee pension funds, new state taxes, and default by another name. On November 12, Ford took the deal. Carey called the legislature back into session on November 15 to put in place his end of the bargain.[29]

The lynchpin of the deal Carey agreed to with Ford was another Rifkind idea—taken from the days of the Great Depression. In 1935, the State of Minnesota passed a law extending the time homeowners could repay their mortgages to avoid foreclosure. The banks sued, claiming the law violated Article 1, Section 10, of the US Constitution, known as the "Contracts Clause," which prohibits states from passing laws impairing existing contract rights. The case went all the way to the US Supreme Court, which upheld the law, known as the Mortgage Moratorium Act, holding that the Contracts Clause did not prohibit state action during a grave emergency, and the Great Depression was such an emergency. Rifkind thought the same argument might be applied to a reorganization law with respect to New York City debt obligations. And even if the courts ultimately held that the New York City fiscal crisis was not quite the same emergency that the Great Depression was, the litigation challenging such a moratorium law would take at least a year to resolve—and any remedy ordered by a court thereafter would also buy time.[30] Carey thought it a genius idea.[31] President Ford liked it too—for it gave him the ability to say he was true to his word not to help New York City until it defaulted. Ford would claim that Rifkind's moratorium law was default by another name, indeed bankruptcy by another name. The following day, Ford said publicly he would consider short-term aid to the city outside of a federal bankruptcy proceeding.[32]

On November 14, 1975, a New York delegation headed by Governor Carey, Felix Rohatyn, Stanley Steingut, and Warren

Anderson met with Treasury officials to hammer out the last details of the federal bailout bill. After the New York Moratorium Act was passed, the MAC would make an exchange offer to the city's individual noteholders to exchange their $1.6 billion of city notes for ten-year 8 percent MAC bonds. Those city noteholders not accepting the MAC exchange offer would, pursuant to the Moratorium Act, receive 6 percent interest after the maturity of their notes, notwithstanding the higher stated interest rates on those notes, and would not be able to seek repayment for three years (which period could be extended by the state legislature, if the New York City fiscal emergency continued at that time). The large banks and financial institutions would voluntarily agree to exchange their city and MAC notes for ten-year 6 percent MAC bonds. The city's public employee pension funds would agree to invest $2.5 billion in new city bonds over the next three years and roll over their existing $1.2 billion city and MAC notes into ten-year 6 percent MAC bonds.

In addition, the city would be required to implement an additional $200 million of annual taxes, and city employees would be required to contribute 2.5 percent of their salaries to pension contributions, amounting to approximately $85 million per year. The state would also be required to balance its budget and provide funding for the four state moral obligation agencies that were on the brink of insolvency: the Housing Finance Agency, the Medical Care Facilities Financing Agency, the Dormitory Authority, and the Environmental Facilities Corporation. Additionally, the state would purchase $250 million of MAC bonds, fulfilling its funding obligations under the September $2.8 billion rescue financing plan.

Once those actions were taken, Ford agreed that the US Treasury would provide up to $2.3 billion of seasonal loans to the city for three years to replace the proper use of anticipation note borrowing that the city was unable to do because the municipal bond market was closed to it.[33] It was believed that if the city's three-year plan was fully executed, it would be able to reenter the municipal bond market by 1978.

On the same day the deal was finalized in Washington, Carey introduced the Moratorium Act to the special session of the legislature in Albany.[34] The following day, it was approved by the Assembly by a vote of 109 to 31 and by the Senate, 45 to 13. Carey also introduced bills that day to provide funding to the four troubled state moral obligation agencies and a new addition to the insolvency roster—the City of Yonkers, which needed a $21 million loan to avoid default on its maturing short-term notes.[35] Ron Nessen, Ford's press secretary, told the reporters that the Moratorium Act was, in fact, a default and a state-law version of bankruptcy, therefore satisfying Ford's precondition before providing federal assistance.[36] Carey sent Rifkind out to reporters to correct the record: "This does not constitute default by the City of New York. This does not constitute a sort-of default or a sham default. It is not any kind of breach of contract."[37] Reporters then sought out comment from Rohatyn, who weeks earlier said, "An involuntary moratorium is default, and default in our view is not an acceptable option."[38] Rohatyn was brief in explaining his earlier comments: "I was wrong."[39]

The bankers and the MAC Hawks, through John Scanlon, had been planting stories in the press since August that Beame should fire Cavanagh, but Beame would have none of it. The idea of him turning his back on Cavanagh, a loyal friend and ally for three decades, was out of the question. But in early November, Cavanagh took a fishing trip, a short vacation, his first since becoming first deputy mayor, and he thought more about his friend Beame than he did the fish. Cavanagh would never purposely hurt the mayor, who he loved like a brother, but he realized on that vacation that his continued presence at City Hall was doing just that. Cavanagh knew Beame would never fire him, and that was why Cavanagh knew he must resign. Upon his return, Cavanagh went straight to Gracie Mansion and told Beame he would announce his resignation the following day. Both men had tears in their eyes. Beame, in that moment, hated all the bankers and Ivy League types who took pleasure at bad-mouthing the wonderful man in front of him, but lacked the guts to criticize him to his face—or to Beame's face. In the midst of the rapid-fire developments in Washington and Albany, Cavanagh put out a press release announcing his resignation, effective on December 31, 1975. The papers, covering the announcement in great detail, all spoke of Cavanagh as a symbol of the old, discredited budget practices. With the MAC and the Emergency Financial Control Board in place, they portrayed the once-feared and irascible Cavanagh as an object of pity, an irrelevancy.[40] A few weeks later, a testimonial dinner to honor Cavanagh was held at the Americana Hotel. Mayors Beame and Lindsay presided over the occasion, which drew over a thousand who came to pay their respects to Cavanagh. Praise of Cavanagh came from the old clubhouse warhorses, as expected, but also came from unexpected admirers. Joseph Papp, director of the New York Shakespeare Theatre, gave the most memorable speech: "Bankers and financiers, though essential to the working of our economy, cannot provide the human leadership chosen by the people. Efficiency and economic considerations alone will lead only to a fascist desert. And James Cavanagh must not be made a scapegoat of history."

On November 17, the Flushing National Bank in Queens filed a class action lawsuit challenging the Moratorium Act under the US Constitution and the New York State Constitution.[41] The clock had been started on the period of time the Moratorium Act would delay the payment of principal on $1.6 billion of city notes. In Albany, the $200 million in additional annual city tax revenue Carey requested was facing resistance, as the Democratic rank and file did not see the need for the additional taxes, and there was no agreement regarding what types of tax increases and new taxes would comprise the tax package.[42] In Washington, Ford announced that he would soon submit his bill for New York City assistance and requested that the House of Representatives postpone a floor vote on its federal guarantee legislation.[43]

To seal the deal with the banks, Carey agreed to expand the size of the Emergency Financial Control Board to provide for a seat for a representative of the banks.[44] Likewise, to secure the support of the city unions for his plan, they too would be given a seat on the Emergency Financial Control Board.[45] Once James E. Greenridge, chairman of the New York City Council Against Poverty, heard of this, he publicly called for a representative of the Black and Puerto Rican communities to be appointed to the Emergency Financial Control Board as well.[46] Carl McCall, a Black member of the New York State Assembly from Manhattan, took up that cause and vowed that the twenty-member Black and Puerto Rican legislative caucus would withhold its support of Carey's $200 million city tax bill unless such a representative was appointed.[47]

At the last minute, when Carey was trying to put forth the details of his city tax plan to a Saturday session on November 22, the banks also threw a monkey wrench into the process: they stated that they would refuse to honor their commitment to exchange their notes and bonds unless there was a more definitive program for the state to close its own $700 million budget gap. Carey had thought his promise of a balanced budget would be enough.[48] With that, Carey had the legislative session adjourned until the following Monday.[49]

On Monday, Carey's headaches got worse. Shanker was again threatening to renege on a financial commitment, this time balking at approving the purchase by the teachers' pension fund of its $860 million portion of $2.5 billion new money pension fund financing.[50] Shanker was not pleased about the requirement for teachers to contribute 2.5 percent of their salaries to help fund their pensions. Carey offered to postpone from January 1, 1976, to April 1, 1976, the effectiveness of the pension contribution and further agreed to pass legislation having the state indemnify the teachers' pension fund trustees for any claims of breach of fiduciary duty that might arise out of the purchase.[51] This bought peace with Shanker.[52]

Finally, on Tuesday, November 25, Carey was able to pass the city tax legislation. The Republicans required that the Emergency Financial Control Board certify the need for the taxes, which the board promptly did. To satisfy the Black and Puerto Rican caucus, the majority of the tax increase would be in the form of a 25 percent increase in the city income tax (approximately $75 million per annum), a 2 percent increase in the bank tax (approximately $40 million per annum), and a 50 percent surcharge on city estate taxes (approximately $35 million per annum), which did not directly affect poor city residents.[53] Sales taxes, which do affect the poor, accounted for only $30 million per year of the new taxes.[54] Carey also agreed to give "strong consideration" to appointing a Black or Puerto Rican to fill the next vacancy on the Emergency Financial Control Board.[55] Finally, with the ball on the one-yard line, the banks agreed to commit to exchange their notes and bonds based on the governor's vow to eliminate the state budget deficit. With that, the Senate and the Assembly passed the remaining legislation to implement the plan.

On Wednesday morning, Carey sent a telegram to President Ford informing him that all the conditions had been met pursuant to their agreement of November 14 for the $2.3 billion of federal aid Ford had promised.[56] True to his word, Ford called a press conference for 7:30 p.m. that evening to announce his proposal for financial aid to the city—the New York City Seasonal Financing Act of 1975.[57]

In advance of the press conference, Ford handed out a summary of the act. The US Treasury would provide the city with a $2.3 billion revolving credit facility to provide for the seasonal liquidity needs of the city, but all borrowings under the facility must be repaid by the last day of each fiscal year (June 30, 1976, 1977, and 1978). According to the city's estimates, the amount of loans outstanding at any time would not exceed $1.3 billion in fiscal 1976, $2.1 billion in fiscal 1977 and $2.0 billion in fiscal 1978—the extra $200 million funding commitment was to provide a cushion above those estimates. Loans would bear interest at the latest Treasury borrowing rate plus 1 percent. Loans would only be made if the secretary of the Treasury determined there was a reasonable prospect of repayment, and the secretary could require collateral for loans as he deemed appropriate. If any loans were not repaid by a fiscal-year end, the secretary could apply any federal aid otherwise due to the city to repay such loans.[58]

During the press conference, Ford, in brief opening remarks, emphasized the progress New York City had made in putting its fiscal house in order, as well as the banks agreeing to exchange their notes and the unions providing $2.5 billion in pension fund loans and their members agreeing to bear part of the cost of their pensions going forward. When asked if his program was a bailout of New York City, Ford responded brusquely: "The answer is very simple. New York has to bail itself out."[59]

After the president's press conference, Carey released a statement thanking the American people for their compassion and announcing the crisis over: "Bankruptcy for New York City is now behind us. Talk of collapse and chaos should now disappear. In its place we shall talk of the work of rebuilding and restoring confidence in New York City, of insuring New York's place in this nation."[60]

The day after the press conference, at the new FBI headquarters at 935 Pennsylvania Avenue, a ten-minute walk from the White House, a case was being opened, called UNIRAC, short for union racketeering, targeting Mafia influence in the International Longshoremen's Association. The case would make the career of a young special agent in New York named Louis Freeh, who would go undercover to investigate Genovese and Gambino crime family figures who controlled the New York waterfront. Freeh would go on to become director of the FBI. The ultimate target of UNIRAC was the man who controlled the mobsters who controlled the waterfront: Anthony Scotto. It would become Louis Freeh's obsession to see Anthony Scotto brought to justice. And there began three years of wiretaps and painstaking evidence-gathering that culminated in Anthony Scotto's racketeering trial and conviction.

There was little time to spare for Congress to approve the New York City Seasonal Financing Act of 1975, and the related appropriation—two pieces of legislation were required to actually get the funds to the city. The city faced another *Perils of Pauline* fiscal deadline on December 31, when internal sources of funds were projected to run dry. The city needed to borrow $130 million by that day. On the day before Thanksgiving, the Democratic congressional leaders agreed to substitute Ford's legislation for their loan guarantee legislation and pledged floor action on Ford's bill the following week and to pass the appropriation shortly thereafter.[61] Tip O'Neill's timeline was spot-on.

On December 2, the House of Representatives passed the New York City Seasonal Financing Act of 1975 by a vote of 213 to 203, with Governor Carey and Mayor Beame watching from the House gallery.[62]

At 4:00 a.m. on December 5, the legislature in Albany passed the Shanker's pension bill (by a vote of 48 to 2 in the Senate and 107 to 32 in the Assembly), which was signed immediately into law by Governor Carey. Immediately thereafter, the pension trustees approved the purchase of $120 million of New York City bonds, the first tranche of the $2.5 billion in total committed by the pension funds.[63]

The next day, the US Senate voted to approve the New York City Seasonal Financing Act of 1975 by a vote of fifty-seven to thirty. A filibuster attempt by Jesse Helms of North Carolina and other Southern senators failed the prior day when a cloture motion passed by a vote of seventy to twenty-seven.[64]

On December 9, without ceremony, President Ford signed into law the New York City Seasonal Financing Act of 1975.[65]

On December 10, the Senate approved the $2.3 billion appropriation to fund the act (the House had approved the appropriation prior to passing the act).[66] The following day, a Senate-House conference committee approved a reconciled appropriation bill.[67] The reconciled appropriations bill passed the House by a vote of 275 to 130 on December 15, and also passed the Senate the same day on a voice vote.[68] On December 18, Ford signed the appropriations bill, again without ceremony, and later that day, the US Treasury wired $130 million to the city's account at Chase Manhattan Bank.[69]

"It was over that abruptly,"[70] wrote Fred Ferretti of the *New York Times*. "The pain is just beginning," said Rohatyn. Judge Rifkind presented his bill for four months' work: $500,000 (approximately $3 million in 2024 dollars).[71]

CHAPTER THIRTEEN

THE AFTERMATH

JANUARY 6 WENT OFF WITHOUT A HITCH FOR THE FORD PEOPLE. With only a ripple of dissent from a few Reagan loyalists, the Republican State Committee met in Albany and pledged all thirty-seven delegates to the Ford slate. Technically, they were uncommitted and led by Nelson Rockefeller, out of respect to Rocky as he had bowed out as a vice presidential candidate as promised, but all knew they were going for Ford and not Reagan. Ford went on to win the Iowa caucuses and the New Hampshire primary, then the primaries in Florida and Illinois, and it looked like he might run the table on Reagan. But then he hit a brick wall in North Carolina in Jesse Helms, who organized the state for Reagan and pulled off a surprise 52 percent to 46 percent victory. From then on, Ford and Reagan traded primary victories. By the time the Republican National Convention began on August 16, both Ford and Reagan had around 1,000 delegates each (it would remain a moving target right up until the floor vote) with about 150 delegates up for grabs (1,130 votes were needed for nomination). It would be the last presidential convention at which there was any real drama.

The uncommitted delegates requested that Ford and Reagan each announce his candidate for vice president. Ford selected Bob Dole. Reagan, in a bid to win over moderates, selected liberal Senator Richard Schweiker of Pennsylvania. The move backfired. A number of ardent Reagan supporters, including Jesse Helms, started a movement to draft conservative New York Senator James Buckley for vice president. In the midst of the dissension, the key uncommitted Mississippi delegates went over to the Ford side. It was over for Reagan. On the first roll call, Ford won the nomination by a vote of 1,180 to 1,069.

Nelson Rockefeller did his part at the convention, giving the nominating speech for Bob Dole. Rocky also demonstrated that he hadn't lost any of his fire. When a Reagan supporter crossed his path on the convention floor near the Ford command post, waving a Reagan sign at him, Nelson grabbed the sign out of his hands and ripped it to shreds. In retaliation, the Reagan man tore the Ford command post phone out of the cubicle wall. Nelson snatched the destroyed phone away from him and with a look of mischievous glee in his eyes paraded the work of the Reagan vandals in front of the press cameras.

The general election ended up being as close as the contest for the Republican nomination. Jimmy Carter, the surprise Democratic nominee, left the Democratic Convention at Madison Square Garden in New York City with an overwhelming 30 percentage point lead, but the race quickly tightened. By Election Day, it was too close to call. The popular vote as well as the electoral margin were razor-thin. Carter ended up with just over 50 percent of the popular vote; Ford just over 48 percent.

The electoral tally was Carter 297, Ford 240. The difference was New York State's 41 electoral votes.

Carter's margin of victory in New York State was 4.43 percent, but his margin in New York City was 32.74 percent. It was the third largest margin of victory in New York history up to that point (after the national landslide victories of LBJ in 1964 and FDR in 1936). If Ford had performed on par with prior Republican presidential contenders in New York City, he would have won New York State and the election. The fiscal crisis had claimed its second victim among the men who would be president.

Simon Rifkind's moratorium scheme accomplished its purpose. It wasn't until November 19, 1976, that the New York State Court of Appeals struck down the Moratorium Act as unconstitutional, violative of Article VIII, Section 2, of the New York State Constitution, the "full faith and credit" clause for the payment of principal of New York City debt.[1] The court of appeals rejected out of hand Rifkind's argument that the emergency clause in the New York State Constitution overruled the "full faith and credit" clause with respect to the fiscal crisis: "The invocation of the emergency clause in the State Constitution is of little avail," the court of appeals stated.[2] "Its purpose was to provide for a functioning and continuing government, even if many of the officers of the several branches of government and their quarters have been atomized in nuclear Armageddon, free and clear of constitutional limitations."[3] The court of appeals concluded that: "Obviously, it does not mean that the Constitution is always suspended in every emergency in a world and life that is a succession of emergencies, natural and man-made."[4] But—most importantly—the court of appeals did not require that the city immediately repay the unredeemed notes. It allowed for a period of time—until March 31, 1977, for the city to arrange for the repayment of the notes held by individual noteholders and until September 30, 1977, to repay institutional noteholders.[5] Not a bad outcome, from Rifkind's perspective.

Of the approximately $1.6 billion of short-term city notes outstanding at the time of the enactment of the Moratorium Act and subject to the exchange offer, about $600 million had been exchanged. To retire the remaining $1 billion, Mayor Beame unveiled a plan on March 9, 1977, whereby $410 million would be raised from the sale of city-held mortgages on Mitchell-Lama properties, $340 million would be raised from the sale of MAC bonds ($90 million of which were purchased by the city's public employee pension funds), and the remaining $250 million was raised from a hodgepodge of sources, including bond sinking funds and federal aid advances.[6]

The SEC issued its 800-page report on the fiscal crisis on August 26, 1977, following a nineteen-month investigation.[7] The scathing report found incompetence and possibly fraud by virtually everyone involved in the sale of city securities: the underwriters, the lawyers, the ratings agencies, and, most pointedly, city officials all the way up to the comptroller and the mayor. The day after the report was issued, Beame released a statement vehemently denying any wrongdoing—and blaming the banks for misleading investors.[8] Beame also accused the SEC of meddling in city politics, because the report was released three weeks before the 1977 New York City mayoral Democratic primary.[9]

Beame was in a hard-fought contest for reelection against New York Secretary of State Mario Cuomo, whom Governor Carey was supporting, Congressman Ed Koch, Congresswoman Bella Abzug, and a number of lesser candidates. On September 8, 1977, Koch and Cuomo, with less than 10,000 votes separating them, advanced to the runoff. Beame missed the runoff by less than 7,000 votes. Most political observers agree the SEC report was Beame's undoing.

In November 1977, New York City attempted to offer to the public $200 million of short-term notes. Moody's assigned the notes a low rating, and the underwriters canceled the offering. Some thought that the Moody's rating was too pessimistic—a defensive rating to atone for the criticisms leveled against the ratings agency in the SEC report. Notwithstanding the rating, most market professionals believed the offering would have failed in any event because the city was still years away from a truly balanced budget—with hundreds of millions of expenses still stuffed into the capital budget.[10]

It was clear after the failed notes offering that New York City was not going to be able to finance itself after the expiration of the New York City Seasonal Financing Act on June 30, 1978. Until the city's budget was actually balanced under generally accepted accounting principles—meaning no more expenses in the capital budget—the municipal bond market would remain closed to the city. By late 1977, the MAC was struggling to sell bonds as well, barely placing an offering of $250 million of bonds in December.[11]

The city had deferred necessary capital expenditures for years in order to preserve cash, but the limits of such deferrals had been reached by fiscal 1978. The city had $1.7 billion of genuine brick-and-mortar capital needs in fiscal years 1979, 1980, and 1981 that simply had to be made or bridges and tunnels would literally start falling apart—and it had no way of financing them.[12] Over the same period, it also needed to finance $900 million of operating expenses in the capital budget, $750 million of debt service owing to the MAC, and

$500 million owing to the State of New York for prior advances of aid.[13] In addition to these $3.8 billion of long-term financing needs, the city's seasonal short-term financing needs of approximately $1.5 billion per fiscal year would need to be met after the federal seasonal loan program expired on June 30, 1978. The MAC revenue stream was not large enough to support those borrowing needs. Arthur Levitt continued to hold firm on the state's public employee pension funds not purchasing any more MAC bonds, and, with the city's public employee pension funds already holding nearly 30 percent of their assets in MAC and city securities, their trustees were balking at purchasing any more MAC bonds. The banks indicated that they had no appetite to hold more than $1 billion of new long-term MAC bonds and $500 million of new short-term, seasonal city debt.

What was needed was another bailout from Washington, and with Democrats Jimmy Carter in the White House and Tip O'Neill as the speaker of the House, this would prove to be much easier to obtain than the one three years earlier.

In May 1978, Treasury Secretary Michael Blumenthal met with Mayor Koch in New York and hammered out a plan for the federal government to save New York City again.[14] The $3.8 billion long-term financing plan ultimately worked out with Congress provided for a US Treasury guarantee of $1.4 billion of long-term city and MAC bonds, $900 million of which would be purchased by the New York City public employee pension funds and $500 million of which would be purchased by the New York State public employee pension funds. The banks would purchase $1 billion of MAC bonds without a US Treasury guarantee, and public offerings would be made of an additional aggregate of $1.4 billion MAC bonds also without a federal guarantee.[15]

The city's short-term seasonal borrowing needs were to be financed by up to $500 million in the aggregate of MAC and city notes to be purchased by the city's public employee pension funds, up to $250 million of which would be guaranteed by the US Treasury, $500 million in the aggregate of MAC and city notes to be purchased by the banks without a federal guarantee and $500 million in the aggregate of MAC and city notes to be sold in public offerings without a federal guarantee.[16] The city was required to pay the US Treasury a guarantee fee of 0.5 percent per annum of the principal amount of notes and bonds guaranteed and was further required to have a balanced budget in accordance with generally accepted accounting principles beginning in fiscal 1982.[17]

The 1978 bailout passed the House by a ninety-two-vote margin and the Senate by a vote of fifty-three to twenty-seven.[18] Unlike in 1975, when President Ford signed his bailout with no fanfare, President Carter signed the 1978 legislation at City Hall in New York City on August 8 with an elaborate public ceremony with thousands of New Yorkers cheering him on.[19]

The litigation against the City of New York, its officials, and the underwriters of its debt continued long after the fiscal crisis subsided. It wasn't until August 27, 1979, that the US Department of Justice finally concluded that Beame and Goldin would not be charged criminally for their roles in the crisis. "The chances of a successful criminal prosecution are too remote to warrant a continued commitment of resources," said Robert Fisk, the US Attorney for the Southern District of New York.[20] The civil litigation was not resolved until January 25, 1980, when Judge Richard Owen in the US District Court for the Southern District of New York decided that the federal securities laws that were in effect exempted municipalities and their officers from the antifraud provisions of those laws.[21] Beame, Goldin, and New York City were off the hook. Not so for the underwriters. Owen ruled that they were subject to the antifraud provisions and, worse, the indemnity they received from the city was unenforceable because it violated public policy.[22] The underwriters went on to settle the litigation for $13 million.[23] As part of the 1975 Securities Acts amendments, Congress amended the antifraud provisions to make them applicable to municipalities.[24] Congress declined to require that municipal securities be subject to registration under the federal securities laws despite considering legislation to do so in 1976,[25] and, to this day, there are no mandatory disclosure requirements for municipal securities.

The lean years in New York City—1975 through 1979— brought austerity that was not evenly distributed. As journalist Martin Mayer predicted before Congress, most of the budget cuts disproportionately affected the most needy New Yorkers: five city hospitals were closed, seventy-seven day care centers were shuttered, foster care funds were reduced by one-third, twenty neighborhood health-care clinics and fifty-nine dental clinics were closed, six chest X-ray facilities were closed, and most of the city-provided outpatient mental health services were eliminated.[26] Public education was hard-hit as well: forty schools were closed, class sizes were increased, the length of the instructional day was shortened, and special education programs for the developmentally disabled were neglected and failed to meet federal requirements.[27]

While Mayor Koch told the press that 61,000 positions had been eliminated from the city payroll, like Mayor Beame before him, Koch played fast and loose with layoff numbers. In truth, when rehired employees and employees shuffled to federal programs were taken into account, only approximately

25,000 jobs had been eliminated between 1975 and 1978.[28] Because of seniority rules, most of the actually laid off employees were younger workers, disproportionately female and Black or Hispanic.[29] Koch would often speak of the wage freeze and how, after it lapsed, wage increases were tied to productivity improvements. In truth, when cost-of-living adjustments and seniority pay increases were taken into account, city workers who were not laid off fared rather well, averaging about a 5.5 percent annual increase in pay from 1975 through 1980, and most of the "productivity improvements" were illusory, so much so that even the pretense of them offsetting compensation costs was abandoned by 1980.[30] The city's expense budget continued to increase—it was 20 percent higher in 1978 than in 1975[31]—and most of that increase went to a somewhat smaller, but better paid, unionized city workforce.

There were some genuine reforms implemented during this period. The city reduced the percentage of welfare cheats from 17.3 percent to 8.6 percent.[32] The state took over a greater share of CUNY's expenses—75 percent[33]—and took over all the expenses of the city court system in 1980.[34] Undoubtedly, the city hospital system was inefficient and corrupt and in need of wholesale revamping. For example, Lincoln Hospital in the South Bronx experienced chronic theft of equipment and its drug treatment program had been taken over by a Puerto Rican street gang, the Young Lords, who bilked the city for millions of dollars. "Hospitals are for sick people, not for thugs," Mayor Koch proclaimed after shutting down the program.[35]

Nelson Rockefeller spent the two years after he left the vice presidency tending to his philanthropies and his art collection. He had been given a book deal to write about his art collection, and on the evening of January 26, 1979, after having dinner with his family, he left the Fifth Avenue apartment and was driven down to the townhouse on 54th Street to work on the book, he said. He was not alone there. Assisting him that evening was a blond, twenty-five-year-old woman named Megan Marshack. What is not in dispute is that Nelson died of a massive heart attack that night. The initial announcement of Nelson's death by a family spokesman said that Nelson had died at his Rockefeller Center office, with no mention of Marshack. Later, after police reports were issued, that statement was revised, twice, to give the right location of and attendee to his death. Also revealed was that Marshack had a friend with her at the Rockefeller townhouse that night—local New York television personality Ponchitta Pierce. Given Nelson's well-known appetites, scandalous rumors proliferated: Nelson was having an affair with Marshack; Nelson died *in flagrante* with Marshack; Nelson died *in flagrante* with both Marshack and Pierce. Another rumor had it that Nelson's buddy and neighbor Bill Shea was called by Marshack, and Shea arranged it so that the police report was much more discreet than it could have been.

In the immediate wake of the fiscal crisis, Carey had achieved a celebrity status never before obtained by a Brooklyn politician, and it was bound to diminish. At first, his every off-hour move was chronicled by the New York tabloid press as if he were politics' answer to Reggie Jackson. One of New York's most eligible bachelors, he began dating Anne Ford Uzielli—the glamorous daughter of Henry Ford II to whom he was introduced at a dinner for Frank Sinatra at Patsy's Italian Restaurant—to the delight of the press. Carey was regularly feted at Elaine's, the celebrity nighttime haunt, by the likes of Clay Felker, Pete Hamill, Shirley MacLaine, and Woody Allen. Carey and Rohatyn would be seen having dinners at the 21 Club and P.J. Clarke's, followed around by reporters who covered their late-night tête-à-têtes like super-power summit meetings.

With the city's fiscal situation stabilized, Governor Carey was easily renominated in the 1978 gubernatorial Democratic primary and went on to defeat Assembly Minority Leader Perry Duryea in the November general election with 51 percent of the vote to Duryea's 45 percent.

But Carey's second term was anticlimactic. He never recaptured the glory bestowed upon him by the press and the Manhattan smart set for his handling of the fiscal crisis. None of the praise and attention heaped on Carey sat well with the resentful brown-suited, wide-tie crowd in the Albany legislative leadership. They held up Carey's appointments and overrode his vetoes, the relationship between the governor and the legislature during Carey's post-crisis years being among the worst in New York history. Eventually the press turned on him too. Jimmy Breslin was first and foremost. Seeing a way to break out from the deep pack of talented city tabloid columnists of that era, Breslin decided to savage Carey. He took to calling him "Society Carey" in his columns, forty times in one famous piece.

The more the press beat up on Carey, the more Carey brooded, and the more Carey brooded, the more the press beat up on him. Quite often during that second term, Carey thought of the fuck-you money. He thought about how pleasant life might be playing golf at Gardiner's Bay Country Club near his home on Shelter Island whenever he wanted. He thought about a life that did not include Jimmy Breslin.

Perhaps if the fiscal crisis had hit in Carey's second term rather than his first, it all could have ended differently. He would have been poised to be the Democratic Party's presidential nominee in 1984. Timing is everything in politics. On January 16,

1982, Carey stunned the political world when he announced he would not be running for a third term. The hero of the fiscal crisis would be its last victim.

New York City was able to re-access the municipal bond market for short-term notes in January 1979, with an offering of $125 million of revenue anticipation notes.[36] The federal bailouts that showed that New York City was, at least in the 1970s, too big to fail and the city's continued progress toward a balanced budget had finally opened the market that had been closed to the city for four years.

New York City shocked the world by balancing its budget—without gimmicks—a year ahead of schedule in fiscal 1981, ending that year with a surplus of over $200 million.[37] On March 23, 1981, the city successfully closed its first offering of long-term bonds ($75 million) since the crisis began six years earlier.[38] At the time the MAC was created, Felix Rohatyn told New Yorkers that it was hoped the city would be back in the municipal bond market within four months. With that bond sale—five years later than the MAC promised—the fiscal crisis truly was over.

It was not the MAC or the Emergency Financial Control Board or the 1975 New York City Seasonal Financing Act or the New York City Loan Guarantee Act of 1978 that catapulted the city from the depths of 1975 to its golden era of the first two decades of the twenty-first century. New York City's remarkable comeback began not in Washington or in Albany or in New York City itself, but rather in an office building at 1901 Avenue of the Stars in Century City, Los Angeles, that was rented in 1978 by the investment bank Drexel Burnham Lambert Inc. at the request of its star banker, Michael Milken. Milken's financial innovation—the junk bond—provided the fuel that drove the explosive growth of mergers and acquisitions that enriched

Wall Street during the 1980s and created the mammoth private equity industry, headquartered, like the rest of the financial services industry, in New York City. That industry, which accounted for less than 5 percent of gross domestic product in 1978, by 2000 accounted for nearly 8 percent. That growth poured trillions of dollars into New York City's economy over that period, and hundreds of billions of tax revenues into its coffers. It was the first trickle of those dollars in 1980 that enabled the city to balance its budget ahead of schedule. If Anthony Scotto was the felon who personified the city's descent to insolvency in the 1970s, Michael Milken was the felon who personified its ascent in the 1980s.

BACK TO BUSINESS AS USUAL

EVERY SUMMER IN EAST HAMPTON, NEW YORK, THERE IS HELD A preposterous event known as the Artists and Writers Annual Softball Game. Like many gatherings in the Hamptons, it is an orgy of masturbatory status-flaunting. It started, in the 1940s, as an actual informal, pick-up softball game, played by real artists like Willem de Kooning and Jackson Pollock from the flourishing artistic community in the Hamptons in those days. The Hamptons, before the 1970s, was a relatively low-key summer colony for society types who divided their time among the Southampton Bathing Corporation, the Meadow Club and Maidstone, surfers and fishermen in Montauk, the aforementioned artists, and potato farmers who lived there year-round. By the late 1970s, it had become something quite different. It was no longer a refuge from Manhattan, but an extension of it. An ambitious scrum of Wall Street types, media people, and up-and-coming politicos invaded every summer to get in on the *scene* and, more importantly, *be seen.* The conceit of the Artists and Writers Softball Game, like so many of the status-flaunting Hamptons events, was to raise money for charity, and it became one of the hottest tickets of the season. Certainly not to watch— as a less-athletic assemblage would be difficult to imagine—but to play in, because being invited to play in the game meant you had arrived, you made the cut, the reigning establishment of that ambitious scrum had let you in. The doyenne of that ambitious scrum was John Patrick Scanlon, the announcer and sometimes player at the Artists and Writers Softball Game. Other players in the game included MAC board members Donna Shalala and Felix Rohatyn, Ken Auletta, Pete Hamill, Ben Bradlee, Mort Zuckerman, Senator Daniel Patrick Moynihan, Carl Bernstein, and Dick Cavett.

In 1978, a publication called *Hamptons* magazine was born, published and distributed from West Hampton to Montauk each week from Memorial Day to Labor Day. Its sole purpose, besides selling advertisements for real estate and overpriced personal care products for the ambitious scrum, was to cover their comings and goings out East, in page after page of photographs of tan, too-thin women and their short, balding, paunchy men with the money to bejewel them. *Hamptons* editors had the brilliance to come up with a section of the magazine called simply The List. Each week The List would set forth the names of individuals deemed shiny enough for readers to have heard of. Good sources have it that particularly vulgar strivers pay a gasping amount of money to PR agents to plot and scheme their way onto The List, even buying ad copy to seal the deal. On Father's Day 2012, *Hamptons* magazine profiled Anthony Scotto and his family at his Southampton home. "Heavenly aromas of marinara waft into the air, wine glasses are never empty," the author wrote.

Anthony Scotto began his five-year prison sentence on July 23, 1981, at the Federal Correctional Institution in Danbury, Connecticut, but was later transferred to prisons in Sandstone, Minnesota, and Otisville, New York. He was released early, on October 9, 1984, for good behavior. He was fifty years old when he left prison. He spent the immediate years after prison spending time with his family, with Marion, sons Anthony Jr. and John, and his daughters Elaina and Rosanna, a local morning television newscaster. Within a few years, however, the powerful politicians were back to pay homage to Anthony Scotto. The Scotto family opened a restaurant on East 52nd Street in Manhattan named Fresco by Scotto, in 1993 and in no time it became, and remains, a power-dining establishment (also with some of the best Italian food in town). Bill and Hillary Clinton came whenever they were in town. Rudy Giuliani, Andrew Cuomo, Al D'Amato, George Pataki, and Chris Christie were regulars. Beame, even at age ninety, would come. George Steinbrenner came too, with Roger Clemons and Jorge Posada. Barbara Walters would compete for attention with Jennifer Anniston. Leonardo DeCaprio and Robert DeNiro would be at one table; Sly Stallone at another. It was just like old times for Anthony Scotto. Scotto died in 2021 at age eighty-seven.

John Scanlon did not live a long life, dying of a heart attack at age sixty-six in 2001. His damage-control services were in high demand right up until his death. Ivana Trump hired Scanlon for the divorce from Donald. Jesse Jackson hired him in February 2001 after news broke that he had fathered a child out of wedlock. In the late 1980s, CBS head Laurence Tisch hired the Monk to get a retraction after *Spy* magazine referred to Tisch as a "churlish dwarf billionaire." Scanlon called Graydon Carter, the editor and founder of *Spy* who later became the celebrity editor of *Vanity Fair*, and said "Look, Graydon, you've really gone too far this time. To begin with, Larry is technically not a dwarf." Scanlon got his retraction. The next issue of *Spy* prominently placed the correction: "Laurence Tisch is not technically a dwarf." Tisch was reported to be displeased with Scanlon. Graydon Carter, on the other hand, waxed poetic about Scanlon to the *New York Times* for its obituary of Scanlon: "What he was brilliant at was rhetoric. He could take a white tennis ball and, at the end of an hour, make you think it was black."

AN UNUSUAL COALITION AROSE OUT OF THE 1975 FISCAL CRISIS. The city's politicians and bankers and union leaders who had fought among themselves prior to Ford bailing out the city came to realize they all shared one very lucrative common interest: getting more money from Washington. This was on full display during the 1978 congressional hearings for the Carter administration's New York City loan guarantee legislation when the city's political, banking, and union leaders heaped praise on one another. What had emerged was, in Ken Auletta's memorable phrase, a "public/profit complex."[1] Another phrase that comes to mind is "Back to Business as Usual."

As described by Auletta in *The Streets Were Paved with Gold*: "The same absence of opposition, of rigorous checks and balances, which helped cause the fiscal crisis now rendered it almost impossible to cure. Former adversaries were now on a first-name basis. Labor leader Victor Gotbaum hosted a dinner party at his Brooklyn Heights home for Ellmore C. Patterson, Chairman of the Morgan Guaranty Bank. Felix Rohatyn and Gotbaum celebrated a joint Southampton birthday party in 1978. William Ellinghaus, the Vice President of AT&T and former member of MAC and the Control Board, agreed to chair a New School dinner in honor of Gotbaum. Rohatyn and Carey are feted as celebrities at chic watering holes like Elaine's. Gotbaum is featured in Scavullo's latest book. Jack (Bigel) is a friend of Walter's (Wriston). Barry and David and Jack and Felix and Abe and Punch and Mike and Jay and Max and Tex and Victor and Don and John are all friends."[2]

The public/profit complex was institutionalized through organizations such as the Municipal Unions Financial Leadership Group, whose board was co-chaired by Walter Wriston and Jack Bigel and included David Rockefeller, Donald Platten, Felix Rohatyn, Victor Gotbaum, Albert Shanker, and Barry Feinstein. The group was engaged nearly exclusively in various creative efforts to gather more money from Washington for New York City (read union workers). This merger of high finance and big labor was symbolically sealed when Joshua Gotbaum, son of Victor, was hired by Rohatyn as a junior banker at Lazard.

Rohatyn's breakfast vision came true. Virtually every media mention of Rohatyn following the fiscal crisis would refer to him as "The Man Who Saved New York" or some derivation thereof. In a lengthy puff-piece profile of him in the *New York Times Magazine* in August 1984 entitled "Life at the Top," no less than seven times was it mentioned that Rohatyn saved the city—amid a tsunami of name dropping the "Friends of Felix" who were graced with his presence that week: Henry Kissinger, William Paley, Oscar de la Renta, Marella Agnelli, Mort Janklow, Leslie Wexner, Joseph Flom, Marty Lipton, Francois Mitterrand, Mario Cuomo, Lee Iacocca, Lew Wasserman, and H. Ross Perot, to name a few. Rohatyn became the eminence he dreamed of being, a trusted advisor to the titans of industry and heads of state, his ITT exploits nearly forgotten. He would even be briefly considered for grooming to become chairman of the Federal Reserve Board as the successor to Alan Greenspan by President Clinton, but the Senate Republicans wouldn't cooperate. Rohatyn had to settle for ambassador to France.

With five decades elapsed since the fiscal crisis, it is possible to judge the performance of the major players in the drama. Hugh Carey, Warren Anderson, and Jack Bigel certainly played their parts extraordinarily well. Mayor Beame certainly did not. Neither did President Ford, who received no credit among liberals or moderates for bailing out the city, but took the blame for doing so among conservatives. Harrison Goldin was neither ruined by the crisis nor elevated by it, remaining city comptroller through 1989. Shanker and Rohatyn skillfully obtained for themselves more credit than they deserved. Gotbaum probably deserved more than he got. Rifkind was the most brilliantly cunning; Levitt the most honorable. The real winners, though, were those who benefited from the cozy corruption that made the fiscal crisis possible to begin with, and who skipped not a beat with the rise of the public/profit complex—the barons of business as usual: the real estate moguls and bankers and businessmen and union chieftains and politicians and judges and clergymen proudly displayed on the client rolls of Bunny Lindenbaum and Bill Shea and Roy Cohn and Simon Rifkind.

There will be another New York City fiscal crisis. And there will be another federal bailout thereafter. It might be blamed on a pandemic or on immigrants or on working from home or on inflation or higher interest rates. It might result, in part, from an exodus of financial services industry jobs to the friendlier climates (weather and taxes) of Florida and Texas—similar to the exodus of industrial jobs out of New York City in the 1950s and 1960s. Public employee union members still can elect the winner of the New York City Democratic mayoral primary, which is now tantamount to electing the mayor. A brief perusal of the releases of good government groups like the Citizens Budget Commission will show that the same temptations to fiscal excess exist now as they did in the 1970s.

It is uncertain whether there is, in fact, less government corruption these days or whether it is simply better hidden. In the 1970s, there were "no-show" jobs and dimwitted relatives on the city payroll that were discoverable by an intrepid investigative reporter. Today, a complex myriad of contractors and "not-for-profit" corporations receive billions for providing services to the city, but their payrolls are not public. In the 1970s, a retiring politician might be rewarded with a cozy partnership at Shea & Gould; Paul, Weiss; or another friendly law firm. Today, they do not have to work, having managed to accumulate, somehow, tens of millions of dollars in their investment portfolios.

What is certain is that everyone still likes their parking tickets fixed. And politicians will always spend all the taxpayers' money they have and more, until there is no more.

ENDNOTES

Chapter One

1. Congress of the United States. "New York City's Fiscal Problem: Its Origins, Potential Repercussions, and Some Alternative Policy Responses" (background paper no. 1, Congressional Budget Office, October 10, 1975).
2. U.S. Department of Labor, Bureau of Labor Statistics, "Employment, Hours and Earning, States and Areas, 1939–82, Vol. II, New Hampshire–Wyoming."
3. Rona Stein, "The New York City Budget: Anatomy of a Fiscal Crisis," *FRBNY Quarterly Review* (Winter 1973): 2.
4. Stein, 5–6.
5. Ibid.
6. Ken Auletta, *The Streets Were Paved with Gold* (New York: Random House, 1979), 41.
7. Robert D. Reischauer, *New York City's Fiscal Problems* (Washington, DC: Congressional Budget Office, October 10, 1975).

Chapter Two

1. Securities and Exchange Commission, *Staff Report on Transactions in Securities of the City of New York* ([SEC *Staff Report*] Washington, DC: Securities and Exchange Commission, August 26, 1977), Chapter Three, 14.
2. SEC *Staff Report,* Chapter Two, 29.
3. Ibid., 33.
4. Temporary Commission on City Finances, *Better Financing for New York City: Final Report of the Temporary Commission on City Finances, City of New York* (New York: New York Temporary Commission on City Finances, August 1966), 53.
5. SEC *Staff Report*, Chapter Two, 19, 24.
6. Ibid., 22.
7. Richard Ravitch, *So Much to Do: A Full Life of Business, Politics and Confronting Fiscal Crises* (New York: Public Affairs, 2014), 81.

8. Jack Newfield and Paul Du Brul, *The Abuse of Power: The Permanent Government and the Fall of New York* (New York: Penguin Books, 1978), 121.
9. Wayne Barrett, *Without Compromise* (New York: Bold Type Books, 2020), 25.
10. Newfield and Du Brul, 208.
11. "List of Major Donors and Lenders to Carey Campaign," *New York Times*, January 2, 1975.

Chapter Three

1. Robert D. Reischauer, "New York City's Fiscal Problem" (Congressional Budget Office, October 10, 1975).
2. Federal Reserve Flow of Funds Data (August 19, 1975).
3. Security Industry Association, "Municipal Market Developments" (October 1975).
4. *Debt Problems of State and Local Government: The New York City Case*, Hearings Before the Subcommittee on Economic Stabilization of the Committee of Banking, Currency and Housing, House of Representatives, Ninety-Fourth Congress, First Session, Part I, October 20, 1975 (Washington, DC: US Government Printing Office), 784–785.
5. SEC *Staff Report*, Introductions and Summary, 3.
6. SEC *Staff Report*, 14.
7. Ibid., 61.
8. Robert A. McTamaney, "United States Trust Company v. New Jersey: The Contact Closure in a Complex Society," *Fordham Law Review* 46 (1977).
9. Newfield and Du Brul, 113.
10. Ibid.
11. Tom Goldstein, "William Shea Law Firm Makes Business of Power," *New York Times*, December 6, 1978.

Chapter Four

1. Jane Perlex, "Bronx's Friedman Nurtures the Image of Tough Deal Maker," *New York Times*, September 2, 1981, B1.
2. SEC *Staff Report*, Chapter One, 2.
3. Ibid.
4. Ibid., 9.
5. Ibid., 14–15.
6. Ibid., 17.
7. Ibid., 18A.
8. Ibid.
9. Ibid., 21.
10. Ibid., 23.

11. Ibid., 31–32.
12. Ibid., 33–34.
13. Fred Ferretti, *The Year the Big Apple Went Bust* (New York: G.P. Putnam & Sons, 1976), 100–101.
14. Ibid., 102.
15. Ibid., 102–103.
16. Ibid., 105.
17. Ibid., 111.
18. Ibid., 41–42.
19. SEC *Staff Report*, Chapter One, 42–43.
20. Ibid., 43–44.
21. Ibid., 44 45.
22. Ferretti, 99.
23. SEC *Staff Report*, Chapter One, 47–48.

Chapter Five

1. Edward Ranzal, "City to Pay 9.4%, 2D-Highest Rate, on 1-Year Notes," *New York Times*, January 8, 1975.
2. Ibid.
3. Ibid.
4. Fred Ferretti, *The Year the Big Apple Went Bust* (New York: G.P. Putnam & Sons, 1976), 119.
5. SEC *Staff Report*, Chapter One, 57–59.
6. Ibid., 60.
7. Joseph P. Fried, "Banks Assailed by Head of U.D.C.," *New York Times*, January 17, 1975.
8. "Carey Asks $178 Million in Loan for Urban Unit," *New York Times*, January 24, 1975.
9. Linda Greenhouse, "Carey Asking New Taxes, Cut in Agencies to Meet a $10.69 Billion Budget," *New York Times*, January 31, 1975.
10. "Carey and Beame See Rockefeller," *New York Times*, February 7, 1975.
11. Linda Greenhouse, "Banks Refuse Carey Plan to Back Development Unit," *New York Times*, February 25, 1975.
12. Robert Cole, "Default by UDC Hits Bond Market," *New York Times*, April 26, 1975.
13. SEC *Staff Report*, Chapter Two, 96.
14. Ibid., 107–117.
15. Fred Ferretti, "Banks Cancel City's Sale of $260 Million in Notes," *New York Times*, March 1, 1975.
16. Ferretti, *The Year the Big Apple Went Bust*, 149.

Chapter Six

1. Robert E. Tomasson, "Upgrading Moves Ahead in Red Hook," *New York Times*, March 2, 1975.
2. SEC *Staff Report*, Chapter One, 125.
3. Ibid., 128.
4. Ibid., 131–133.
5. Ibid., 140–141.
6. Ibid., 142–145.
7. Ibid., 150–167.
8. Ibid., 169.
9. Ibid., 171–175.
10. Ibid., 186–190.
11. Martin Tolchin, "Beame Bids U.S. Lend City Money Without Interest," *New York Times*, March 6, 1975.
12. "Text of Mayor Beame's Fiscal Statement," *New York Times*, March 24, 1975.
13. Edward Ranzel, "Beame Says City Will Have to Add Taxes in 1975–76," *New York Times*, March 25, 1975.
14. SEC *Staff Report*, Chapter One, 176.
15. SEC *Staff Report*, Chapter Six, 75.
16. SEC *Staff Report*, Chapter One, 255.
17. Fred Ferretti, "State to Advance Funds to City to Pay April Bills," *New York Times*, April 4, 1975.

Chapter Seven

1. Edwin L. Dale Jr., "Federal Aides Reviewing Ways City Might Be Aided," *New York Times*, May 8, 1975.
2. Thomas P. Ronan, "Carey Asks Aid From Congress," *New York Times*, May 8, 1975.
3. Edwin L. Dale Jr., "Simon Says U.S. Won't Aid in Financial Rescue of City," *New York Times*, May 11, 1975.
4. Ronald Smothers, "Simon's Rejection of City's Aid Plan Scored by Beame," *New York Times*, May 12, 1975.
5. John H. Allen, "City Securities Fall in Sharp Reaction to U.S. Aid Denial," *New York Times*, May 15, 1975.
6. "Beame and Carey Ask President Today for Fiscal Aid to City, but Resolution Is Hinted," *New York Times*, May 13, 1975.
7. Fred Ferretti, "Ford Will Study City Aid Request and Reply Today," *New York Times*, May 14, 1975.
8. Ibid.
9. Fred Ferretti, "Ford Rejects a Plan by Beame for Help," *New York Times*, May 15, 1975.

10. "Carey and Beame Voice Anger at Ford's Decision," *New York Times*, May 15, 1975.

11. John Darnton, "Simon Says a City Default Would Not Hurt Economy," *New York Times*, May 16, 1975.

12. Ibid.

13. Ibid.

14. Ibid.

15. Richard D. Lyons, "House Leaders to Press for U.S. Aid to Bail Out City," *New York Times*, May 15, 1975.

16. Ibid.

17. Ibid.

18. Martin Tolchin, "General Negative Feeling Toward City Slows in Congressional Refusal of Aid," *New York Times*, May 25, 1975.

19. "G.O.P. in Albany Rejects Beame's $650 Million Plea," *New York Times*, May 16, 1975.

20. Linda Greenhouse, "G.O.P. Bill Will Offer City a Loan Tied to Budget Cut," *New York Times*, May 18, 1975.

21. Maurice Carroll, "Carey Threatens Veto on Aid to City If State Budget 'GAP' Is Not Filled," *New York Times*, May 21, 1975.

22. Ronald Smothers, "Temporary Plan," *New York Times*, May 30, 1975.

23. John T. McQuiston, "Bankers Offer Loan Plan; Goldin Sees 'Rejection,'" *New York Times*, May 23, 1975.

24. Damon Stetson, "Union Chiefs Call Citibank the City's 'No. 1 Enemy,'" *New York Times*, May 21, 1975.

25. John Allan, "Banks' Own Crises," *New York Times*, May 23, 1975.

26. Fred Ferretti, "Beame Requests 2d Budget Delay," *New York Times*, May 9, 1975.

27. Damon Stetson, "Municipal Unions Warn They Won't Yield Gains," *New York Times*, May 15, 1975.

28. John Darnton, "Beame Threatens 38,000 Dismissals," *New York Times*, May 17, 1975.

29. Steven R. Weisman, "Mayor Seeking New Delay for Submitting of Budget," *New York Times*, May 24, 1975.

30. Ibid.

31. Steven R. Weisman, "City Budget: A Document in Flux," *New York Times*, May 24, 1974.

32. Ibid.

33. Ibid.

34. Ibid.

35. Ibid.

36. "Transcript of Major Beame's Speech Describing an Austerity Budget for City," *New York Times*, May 30, 1975.

37. Ibid.
38. Ferretti, *The Year the Big Apple Went Bust*, 144.
39. Maurice Carroll, "$200 Million Limit Set on Aid from the State," *New York Times*, May 22, 1975.
40. Maurice Carroll, "Carey Says Fiscal Crisis Must Be 'Depoliticized,'" *New York Times*, May 23, 1975.
41. Ibid.
42. Newfield and Du Brul, 178.
43. Maurice Carroll, "Nonpolitical Trust Urged to Direct the City Fiscally," *New York Times,* May 30, 1975.

Chapter Eight

1. Maurice Carroll, "State to Control Panel to Oversee Budget for City" *New York Times,* June 3, 1975.
2. Fred Ferretti, "Mayor Seeks Concessions on State Cert—Flawed Plan" *New York Times,* June 4, 1975.
3. Ibid.
4. Fred Ferretti, "State Aid Agency City's Only Option, Panel Maintains," *New York Times,* June 5, 1975.
5. Ibid.
6. Maurice Carroll, "New State Fiscal Agency Delayed Again in Albany," *New York Times*, June 7, 1975.
7. "Corporation's Provisions," *New York Times,* June 10, 1975.
8. Peter Kihss, "City's Major Businesses Weigh a Plan to Aid City," *New York Times*, May 22, 1975.
9. Ronald Smothers, "Tax Prepayment Voted by Council," *New York Times*, May 28, 1975.
10. Fred Ferretti, "State Agency Setup to Avert City Default" *New York Times*, June 11, 1975.
11. John Darnton, "Goldin Predicts City's Short-term Borrowing Would Grow 11% in Next Fiscal Year," *New York Times,* June 13, 1975.
12. Linda Greenhouse, "Anderson Foresees Need to Buttress City—Aid Unit," *New York Times,* June 15, 1975.
13. Fred Ferretti, "City and State Split on Wording of Aid Measure," *New York Times,* June 15, 1975.
14. Ibid.
15. Joseph P. Fried, "Trump Promises to End Race Bias," *New York Times*, June 11, 1975.
16. Ken Auletta, "Don't Mess with Roy Cohn," *Esquire,* December 1978.
17. Ibid.
18. Ibid.

19. Alfonso A. Narvaez, "1,100 at Waldorf Mark Inauguration of Carey," *New York Times,* January 6, 1975.

20. Steven R. Weisman, "Bankers Here Vow to Buy Half-Billion in City Bonds," *New York Times,* June 26, 1975.

21. "Fiscal Aid Agency Gets Bond Rating," *New York Times,* June 27, 1975.

22. Ibid.

23. John H. Allan, "Bonds to Aid City to Cost State 9%," *New York Times,* July 1, 1975.

24. John H. Allan, "Record Bond Issue Is Sold in the Tax-Exempt Market," *New York Times,* July 2, 1975.

25. Ibid.

26. John Darnton, "Civil Service Rally Assails Bank's Role in City Crisis," *New York Times,* June 5, 1975.

27. Ronald Smothers, "School Fund Cuts Prompt Protest," *New York Times,* June 10, 1975.

28. Alden Whitman, "The Rise and Rise of Albert Shanker," *New York Times,* January 15, 1975.

29. Lee Dembart, "Fiery Yet Quiet Chief," *New York Times,* July 12, 1975.

30. Lee Dembart, "City's Fiscal Ills Create Municipal Union Split," *New York Times,* July 21, 1975.

31. Selwyn Raab, "Police Given a Plan to Cut $100 Million with Safety," *New York Times,* June 13, 1975.

32. Glenn Fowler, "Union 'Guide' to 'Fear City' Is Banned by a Court Order," *New York Times,* June 13, 1975.

33. Ibid.

34. Ibid.

35. Tom Goldstein, "Leaflet Ban Is Called Unconstitutional," *New York Times,* June 14, 1975.

36. Glenn Fowler, "City Officers Win Right to Go Ahead With 'Fear' Drive," *New York Times,* June 17, 1975.

37. Selwyn Raab, "PBA Gives Out Leaflets Again," *New York Times,* July 18, 1975.

38. Ibid.

39. Fred Ferretti, "City Approves Its New Budget of $12.08 Billion," *New York Times,* June 20, 1975.

40. Fred Ferretti, "City's Realty Tax Will Rise by 11.3%," *New York Times,* June 28, 1975.

41. Joseph B. Treaster, "Court Bans Cut of 2,930 Sanitation Jobs," *New York Times,* June 28, 1975.

42. "DeLury, After Court Loss Strike Is 'Inevitable,'" *New York Times,* July 1, 1975.

43. Ibid.

44. Fred Ferretti, "Violence Flares," *New York Times,* July 2, 1975.

45. Ibid.
46. "Text of Statement Broadcast by Mayor Beame," *New York Times*, July 3, 1975.
47. Joseph B. Treaster, "26 Fire Department Companies Closed," *New York Times*, July 3, 1975.
48. "Numerous Garbage Fire Blazes Give Firemen One of 'Busiest Nights,'" *New York Times*, July 3, 1975.
49. Edward C. Burks, "A Strike Over Layoffs Causes Hudson Parkway Traffic Jam," *New York Times*, July 3, 1975.
50. Linda Greenhouse, "Albany Compromise Gives City $330 Million in Taxes," *New York Times*, July 4, 1975.
51. Lee Dembart, "High-Level Talks Ended Walkout," *New York Times*, July 4, 1975.
52. Peter Kihss, "Sanitationmen Start on Big Cleanup," *New York Times*, July 4, 1975.
53. Fred Ferretti, "Beame Restores 2,600 More Jobs; Asks Pay Freeze," *New York Times*, July 8, 1975.
54. Steven R. Weisman, "Adjusting to Cutbacks Will Be Painful," *New York Times*, July 13, 1975.

Chapter Nine

1. John Darnton, "MAC in Trouble, Too," *New York Times*, July 19, 1975.
2. Steven R. Weisman, "Beame Weighing a City Pay Freeze to Aid Bond Sale," *New York Times*, July 17, 1975.
3. John Darnton, "M.A.C. Urges Dramatic Cuts to Reopen Bond Market," *New York Times*, July 18, 1975.
4. Fred Ferretti, "1-Billion Savings," *New York Times*, July 19, 1975.
5. Emanuel Perlmutter, "Teachers Strike to Ask 20% Raise in Pact," *New York Times*, July 21, 1975.
6. Fred Ferretti, "Beame and M.A.C. Agree on 3 Moves to Avert a Crisis," *New York Times*, July 21, 1975.
7. Frank J. Prial, "Carey to Remove M.A.C. Chairman to Toughen Unit," *New York Times*, July 20, 1975.
8. Ibid.
9. Fred Ferretti, "M.A.C. Bonds Drop by 10% on Wall St. as Trading Begins," *New York Times*, July 22, 1975.
10. John Darnton, "Need for Quick Action Unites M.A.C. Board," *New York Times*, July 24, 1975.
11. Fred Ferretti, "Beame and M.A.C. Ask a Quick Rise in Transit Fares," *New York Times*, July 25, 1975.
12. Ibid.

13. Linda Greenhouse, "Levitt Vetoes M.A.C. Sales to State Pension System," *New York Times*, July 25, 1975.

14. Ibid.

15. Ibid.

16. Francis X. Clines, "Carey Tells Union Aides Problem Is Washington," *New York Times*, July 25, 1975.

17. Martin Tolchin, "Simon Tells M.A.C. Aides US Aid to City Is Unlikely," *New York Times*, July 26, 1975.

18. Ibid.

19. Steven R. Weisman, "M.A.C. Offers Plan to Gain Investor Confidence in City," *New York Times*, August 1, 1975.

20. "City Fiscal Developments," *New York Times*, August 1, 1975.

21. Fred Ferretti, "Some Unions Balk," *New York Times*, August 1, 1975.

22. Ibid.

23. John Darnton, "Beame to Order Spending Limits at M.A.C.," *New York Times*, August 7, 1975.

24. John Darnton, "Banks Here Agree to Help City Cut Its Interest Costs," *New York Times*, August 9, 1975.

25. John Darnton, "M.A.C. Head Joins Advisory Board," *New York Times*, August 15, 1975.

26. John Darnton, "M.A.C.'s Package Sealed with Help of Pension Funds," *New York Times*, August 8, 1975.

27. Ibid.

28. Steven R. Weisman, "Interest Rates on M.A.C. Bonds Set at New High," *New York Times*, August 15, 1975.

29. Steven R. Weisman, "M.A.C. Calls on U.S. to Pay for Relief," *New York Times*, August 10, 1975.

30. Edwin L. Dale Jr., "M.A.C.'s Next Hurdle," *New York Times*, August 9, 1975.

31. Ernest Holsendolph, "U.S. Gives Praise to City, but No Aid," *New York Times*, August 9, 1975.

32. Frank Lynn, "Carey Gloomy on Default Unless U.S. Gives City Aid," *New York Times*, August 25, 1975.

33. Ibid.

34. Tom Goldstein, "S.E.C. May Sue If Cities Fail to Reveal Bond Risks," *New York Times*, August 11, 1975.

35. Arnold H. Lubasch, "Investor Alleging Fraud by City Sues Beame, Goldin and Banks," *New York Times*, August 14, 1975.

36. "Carey Estimates a Huge City Debt," *New York Times*, August 21, 1975.

37. John Darnton, "Beame Excluded as Board Meets on Fiscal Crisis," *New York Times*, August 21, 1975.

38. Steven R. Weisman, "M.A.C. Says State Must Supervise City's Borrowing," *New York Times*, August 23, 1975.

39. Steven R. Weisman, "A Freeze on Taxes Offered by Beame in Fiscal Package," *New York Times*, August 24, 1975.

40. Maurice Carroll, "Beame Plan Late, Irking M.A.C. Aides," *New York Times*, August 26, 1975.

41. Steven R. Weisman, "A Rule for Levitt," *New York Times*, August 27, 1975.

42. Steven R. Weisman, "3 Banks Reject City Fiscal Plan; Beame-Carey Accord Is in Doubt, and 'Alternatives' Are Explored," *New York Times*, August 28, 1975.

43. Steven R. Weisman, "Fear of Default Crucial Obstacle to City Bond Sale," *New York Times*, August 17, 1975.

44. Steven R. Weisman, "Irate Beame Bars Any Further Cuts in Vital Services," *New York Times*, August 22, 1975.

45. Steven R. Weisman, "Officials Fashion New Plan Bar a Default by City," *New York Times*, August 29, 1975.

46. Steven R. Weisman, "Governor Is Considering a Session on Fiscal Panel," *New York Times*, August 30, 1975.

47. Weisman, "Officials Fashion New Plan to Bar a Default by City."

48. Steven R. Weisman, "Default: A Fearsome but Imprecise Dirty Word," *New York Times*, August 31, 1975.

49. Steven R. Weisman, "An Albany Session on Crisis in City Set for Thursday," *New York Times*, August 31, 1975.

Chapter Ten

1. "City Gives Breakdown of Financial Package," *New York Times*, September 1, 1975.

2. Fred Ferretti, "M.A.C. Plan Seeks to Restructure City Financially," *New York Times*, September 3, 1975.

3. Maurice Carroll, "Carey Proposes $2-Billion Plan on City Finances," *New York Times*, September 2, 1975.

4. "Text of M.A.C. Letter to Carey," *New York Times*, September 3, 1975.

5. Martin Tolchin, "Carey Visits Ford, but U.S. Aid to City Called No Closer," *New York Times*, September 3, 1975.

6. Ibid.

7. Francis X. Clines, "Text of Carey's Musings on City's Plight," *New York Times*, September 6, 1975.

8. Ibid.

9. Ibid.

10. Francis X. Clines, "Anderson Meets David Rockefeller on U.S. Aid to City," *New York Times*, September 7, 1975.

11. Maurice Carroll, "Anderson Pleads City's Case Today with Ford's Aides, " *New York Times*, September 8, 1975.

12. Francis X. Clines, "Carey Plan to Help City Voted on by Assembly, 80–70; Senate Taxes Up Debate," *New York Times*, September 9, 1975.

13. Francis X. Clines, "Negotiations On," *New York Times*, September 10, 1975.

14. Steven R. Weisman, "Notes Cost State as Much as 8.70%," *New York Times*, September 11, 1975.

15. Leonard Ruder, "Teachers' Talks Near a Deadlock," *New York Times*, September 4, 1975

16. Leonard Ruder, "Teachers Vote to Strike Today; A Million Pupils Here Affected; Schools to Try to Remain Open," *New York Times*, September 9, 1975.

17. Leonard Ruder, "Tally 10,651–6,695," *New York Times*, September 17, 1975.

18. Ibid.

19. Francis X. Clines, "Carey Puts 3 Executives on Fiscal Control Board," *New York Times*, September 12, 1975.

20. Fred Ferretti, "Beame Appoints a Deputy Mayor for City Finances," *New York Times*, September 13, 1975.

21. Francis X. Clines, "Credit Rater Warns State on Additional Aid to City," *New York Times*, September 16, 1975.

22. Stephen R. Weisman, "M.A.C., City and State Aides Save Agency About to Default," *New York Times*, September 25, 1975.

23. Ann Crittenden, "12 Big Concerns Will Buy $20-Million M.A.C. Bonds," *New York Times*, September 26, 1975.

24. Katharine Q. Seelye, "One of Two Women Who Tried to Kill Gerald Ford Explains Why," *New York Times*, May 28, 2009.

25. Martin Tolchin, "Buckley Opposes U.S. Intervention in City's Crisis," *New York Times*, September 24, 1975.

26. Martin Tolchin, "Chase Bank Urges Temporary Help for City from U.S.," *New York Times*, September 28, 1975.

27. Ibid.

28. Sgaglione v. Levitt, 37 N.Y.2d 507 (1975).

29. Francis X. Clines, "Court Voids Law Ordering 2 Funds to Buy City Bonds," *New York Times*, September 30, 1975.

30. Fred Ferretti, "Carey Puts Teachers' Pact in Doubt Because of Cost," *New York Times*, September 30, 1975.

31. Ibid.

32. Linda Greenhouse, "Banks Resisting New State Issue of Notes for City," *New York Times*, October 1, 1975.

33. Ibid.

Chapter Eleven

1. Linda Greenhouse, "City Urged to Tap Its Pension Funds for a Crisis Loan," *New York Times*, October 2, 1975.

2. Ibid.

3. John Darnton, "Trustees of City Pensions Wary of More City Bonds," *New York Times*, October 2, 1975.

4. Ibid.

5. Steven R. Weisman, "Pension Tapping Urged on Carey," *New York Times*, October 5, 1975.

6. Martin Tolchin, "Carey Lobbies for Federal Help Here," *New York Times*, October 2, 1975.

7. Ibid.

8. Eileen Shanahan, "Burns Says City's Crisis May Harm U.S. Recovery," *New York Times*, October 3, 1975.

9. Martin Tolchin, "Reuss Proposes $7-billion for City," *New York Times*, October 8, 1975.

10. Eileen Shanahan, "Ford Is Adamant on City Crisis Aid," *New York Times*, October 4, 1975.

11. Edwin L. Dale Jr., "Simon Proposes City's Banks Call Debt Moratorium," *New York Times*, October 5, 1975.

12. Peter Kihss, "Rockefeller Asks Congress to Weigh Some Aid to City," *New York Times*, October 6, 1975.

13. Martin Tolchin, "Burns Eases View on Federal Role in City's Crisis," *New York Times*, October 9, 1975.

14. Francis X. Clines "Bankers Urge State Aid to Finance Unit in Credit Squeeze, but Carey Resists Idea," *New York Times*, October 3, 1975.

15. Fred Ferretti, "Beame Planning to Trim Budget $200-million in '75," *New York Times*, October 7, 1975.

16. Francis X. Clines, "Beame Ready to Give Order for Further Budget Cuts," *New York Times*, October 8, 1975.

17. Leonard Ruder, "Financial Board Rejects City Pact with School Union," *New York Times*, October 8, 1975.

18. Fred Ferretti, "City Unions Weigh a General Strike," *New York Times*, October 9, 1975.

19. Ibid.

20. New York City Financial Crisis, Hearings Before the Committee on Banking, Housing and Urban Affairs, United States Senate, Ninety-Fourth Congress, First Session on S. 1833, S. 1862, S.2372, S. 2514, and S. 2523, to Furnish Loan Guaranties to Municipalities Suffering Financial Adversity to Enable Them to Achieve Fiscal Balance and Financial Health at Minimum Cost and Disruption to the Nation, October 9, 10, 18, and 23, 1975 ([the "Senate Banking Committee Hearing"]; Washington, DC: US Government Printing Office, 1975), 34.

21. "President Sees No Justification for Help to City," *New York Times*, October 10, 1975.

22. Edwin I. Dale Jr., "Simon Plan Calls for Shift in Law," *New York Times*, October 11, 1975.

23. Ibid.

24. Senate Banking Committee Hearings, 299–348.

25. Ibid., 396.

26. Steven R. Weisman, "Teachers Reject $150-Million Loan City Needs Today," *New York Times*, October 17, 1975.

27. Linda Greenhouse, "A Night of Anxiety on Brink of Default," *New York Times*, October 18, 1975.

28. Ibid.

29. Ibid.

30. Ibid.

31. Ibid.

32. Richard Ravitch, *So Much to Do—A Full Life of Business, Policies, and Confronting Fiscal Crises* (New York: Public Affairs, 2014), 91.

33. Ibid., 90.

34. Ibid., 91–92.

35. Ibid., 92.

36. Ibid., 93.

37. Seymour P. Lachman and Robert Polner, *The Man Who Saved New York—Hugh Carey and the Great Fiscal Crisis of 1975* (Albany: State University of New York Press, 2010), 143.

38. Ferretti, *The Year the Big Apple Went Bust*, 340.

39. Ibid.; Jeff Nussbaum, "The Night New York Saved Itself from Bankruptcy," *New Yorker*, October 16, 2015.

40. Steven R. Weisman, "$150-Million Pact," *New York Times*, October 18, 1975.

41. Ibid.

42. Martin Tolchin, "Ford Again Denies Fiscal Aid to City," *New York Times*, October 18, 1975.

43. Senate Banking Committee Hearings, 440.

44. Senate Banking Committee Hearings, 640.

45. Senate Banking Committee Hearings, 646.

46. Senate Banking Committee Hearings, 712.

47. William E. Simon, *A Time for Truth* (New York: Reader's Digest Press, 1978), 164.

48. Ibid., 165.

49. Debt Financing Problems of State and Local Governments: The New York City Case, Hearings Before the Subcommittee on Economic Stabilization of the Committee on Banking, Currency and Housing, House of Representatives, Ninety-Fourth Congress, First Session (["House Economic Stabilization Subcommittee Hearings"] Washington, DC: US Government Printing Office, 1975).

50. Ibid.

51. Martin Tolchin, "Senators Agree to Consider Bill to Assist the City," *New York Times*, October 22, 1975.

52. Ibid.

53. Ibid.

54. House Economic Stabilization Subcommittee Hearings, 1432.

55. Ibid.

56. Martin Tolchin, "Congress Is Urged by Albert to Act on Bill to Aid City," *New York Times*, October 24, 1975.

57. House Economic Stabilization Subcommittee Hearings, 1687–1766.

58. David E. Rosenbaum, "Support for Loan Guarantees for City Grows in House," *New York Times*, October 29, 1975.

59. Martin Tolchin, "Proxmire and Stevenson Agree on City Aid Action," *New York Times*, October 29, 1975.

60. Ibid.

61. James M. Naughton, "Ford to Propose Bill to Help City After a Default," *New York Times*, October 29, 1975.

62. "Transcript of President's Talk on City Crisis, Questions Asked and His Responses," *New York Times*, October 30, 1975.

63. Ibid.

64. Ibid.

65. Ibid.

66. Ibid.

67. Ibid.

68. Ibid.

69. Richard L. Madden, "President Is Commended and Assailed on Stand," *New York Times*, October 30, 1975.

70. Francis X. Clines, "Beame and Carey Decry Ford Plan," *New York Times*, October 30, 1975.

71. Madden, "President Is Commended and Assailed on Stand."

72. Michael C. Jensen, "Ford's Stance Criticized by 8 of 10 Financial Men," *New York Times*, October 30, 1975.

Chapter Twelve

1. Fred Ferretti, "Pension Funds Near Pact on Backing Loans to City," *New York Times*, October 30, 1975.

2. Ibid.

3. Fred Ferretti, "Shanker Doesn't Oppose Aid from Pension Funds," *New York Times*, October 31, 1975.

4. Joseph Lelyveld, "Hard Day for the City on Capitol Hill," *New York Times*, October 31, 1975.

5. Ibid.

6. Martin Tolchin, "Senate Unit, 8 to 5, Backs Loan Guarantee for City Despite Threatened Veto," *New York Times*, October 31, 1975.

7. Ibid.

8. "House Unit Votes Loan Guarantees to Assist the City," *New York Times*, November 1, 1975.

9. R. W. Apple Jr., "City a '76 Issue for Ford; Democrats Doubt Its Value," *New York Times*, October 31, 1975.

10. John Darnton, "Bankers Discuss Pension Loan," *New York Times*, November 1, 1975.

11. Ibid.

12. "Text of the Governor's Speech on New York City's Financial Crisis," *New York Times*, November 2, 1975.

13. Ibid.

14. Ibid.

15. Douglas E. Kneeland, "Carey, on Coast, Critical of Ford," *New York Times*, November 8, 1975.

16. Maurice Carroll, "Carey Lobbies in Washington for Help, Then Heads for Coast to Gain Backing," *New York Times*, November 7, 1975.

17. Francis X. Clines, "Con Ed Warns Ford of Impact Default Would Have on Utility," *New York Times*, November 5, 1975.

18. "Text of Address by Beame Describing City Situation and Calling for Federal Aid," *New York Times*, November 6, 1975.

19. Martin Tolchin, "City Aid Measure Gains in Senate," *New York Times*, November 11, 1975.

20. Martin Tolchin, "House Banking Committee Backs Guarantee for City," *New York Times*, November 4, 1975.

21. Martin Tolchin, "House Unit Slates Action on City Aid Bill Next Week," *New York Times*, November 5, 1975.

22. Martin Tolchin, "Labor Fights Bill to Allow the City Loan Guarantees," *New York Times*, November 7, 1975.

23. Ibid.

24. John Darnton, "State Fails in Bid to Raise $150 Million for City Bills," *New York Times*, November 7, 1975.

25. Stephen J. Riegel, *Finding Judge Crater: A Life and Phenomenal Disappearance in Jazz Age New York* (New York: Syracuse University Press, 2022), 18.

26. Ibid.

27. Ibid., 19.

28. Linda Greenhouse, "Be on Hand," *New York Times*, November 4, 1975.

29. Linda Greenhouse, "Carey Calls Legislature, Citing Signal That Ford Eases Stand on City Help," *New York Times*, November 13, 1975.

30. Martin Tolchin, "President Sees 'Progress' Toward Financial Reform," *New York Times*, November 13, 1975.

31. Martin Tolchin, "White House Now Ready to Consider Aid for City," *New York Times*, November 14, 1975.

32. Memorandum from Stephen S. Gardner to President Gerald Ford, Subject: New York Plan, November 14, 1975 (Gerald R. Ford Presidential Library).

33. "Text of Purpose of Planned Legislation," *New York Times*, November 15, 1975.

34. Linda Greenhouse, "Debt Moratorium of 3 Years in City Passed in Albany," *New York Times*, November 15, 1975.

35. Steven R. Weisman, "Note Moratorium Held No Default," *New York Times*, November 15, 1975.

36. Ibid.

37. Ibid.

38. Ibid.

39. Ibid.

40. Thomas P. Ronan, "Cavanagh Will Quit Dec. 31 as Beame's First Deputy," *New York Times*, November 16, 1975.

41. "Bank Sues Over Debt Moratorium," *New York Times*, November 18, 1975.

42. Linda Greenhouse, "Revolt Reported on City Tax Rates," *New York Times*, November 18, 1975.

43. Martin Tolchin, "Ford Considers Three-Year Plan for Helping City," *New York Times*, November 18, 1975.

44. John Darnton, "Unions and Banks Will Get Role in Governing of City," *New York Times*, November 19, 1975.

45. Ibid.

46. Ibid.

47. "Minority Group to Press Carey for Posts on New York Fiscal Units," *New York Times*, November 20, 1975.

48. "Demand by Banks Perils City Plan," *New York Times*, November 23, 1975.

49. Linda Greenhouse, "Legislature Fails to Pass Package of Taxes for City," *New York Times*, November 23, 1975.

50. John Danton, "A 3-Year Accord," *New York Times*, November 26, 1975.

51. Ibid.

52. Linda Greenhouse, "Compromise Won," *New York Times*, November 26, 1975.

53. "List of Taxes Voted for City," *New York Times*, November 26, 1975.

54. Ibid.

55. Linda Greenhouse, "Compromise Won."

56. Ferretti, *The Year the Big Apple Went Bust*, 244–345.

57. Ibid.

58. Ibid., 347–398.

59. "Transcript of the President's New Conference on Domestic and Foreign Matters," *New York Times*, November 27, 1975.

60. Fred Ferretti, "Carey Sees a Vindication of 'Merit of Our Position,'" *New York Times*, November 27, 1975.

61. "8% Interest Rate," *New York Times*, November 27, 1975.

62. Martin Tolchin, "$2.3 Billion Loan for City Voted by House 213–203," *New York Times*, December 3, 1975.

63. Linda Greenhouse, "Albany Votes Protection for Pension Funds' Trustees," *New York Times*, December 6, 1975.

64. Martin Tolchin, "Package in Place," *New York Times*, December 6, 1975.

65. Martin Tolchin, "Ford Signs Aid Bill; Bankruptcy Change for City Advances," *New York* Times, December 10, 1975.

66. Martin Tolchin, "Senate-House Panel Backs Aid for City," *New York Times*, December 10, 1975.

67. Ibid.

68. Martin Tolchin, "$2 billion City Loans Clear Congress," *New York Times*, December 16, 1975.

69. "City Receives First U.S. Loan as Ford Signs the Legislation," *New York Times*, December 19, 1975.

70. Ferretti, *The Year the Big Apple Went Bust*, 409.

71. Fred Ferretti, "M.A.C. Head's Prediction: City's 'Pain' Just Starting," *New York Times*, December 10, 1975.

Chapter Thirteen

1. Flushing Natl. Bank v. Municipal Assistance Corp. for City of New York, 40 N.Y.2d (1976).

2. Ibid.

3. Ibid.

4. Ibid.

5. Gayle Gutekunst-Roth, "New York—A City in Crisis: Fiscal Emergency Legislation and the Constitutional Attacks," *Fordham Urban Law Journal* 6, no. 1 (1977).

6. Charles Kaiser, "New York Offers Plan to End Its Debt Crisis Without Aid from Banks," *New York Times*, March 10, 1977.

7. Securities and Exchange Commission, "Commission Issues Staff Report on Transactions in New York City Securities" press release, August 26, 1977.

8. "Beame's Statement on the S.E.C. Report," *New York Times*, August 28, 1977.

9. Ibid.

10. Senate Banking Committee Hearings, 193.

11. Ibid.

12. Ibid., 594.

13. Ibid.

14. Ibid., 145.

15. Ibid., 137.

16. Ibid.
17. Public Law 95-339, 95th Congress (August 8, 1978).
18. Lee Dembart, "Senate Votes, 53–27, to Provide Loan Guarantees to New York; Efforts to Cut Aid Defeated," *New York Times*, June 30, 1978.
19. "Thousands See Carter Sign N.Y. Aid Bill," *Washington Post*, August 9, 1978.
20. Maurice Carroll, "Book Finally Closed on City Fiscal Blame," *New York Times*, August 28, 1979.
21. In Re New York City Municipal Securities Litigation, 507 F.Supp. 169 (S.D.N.Y. 1980).
22. Ibid.
23. Ann Judith Gellis, "Mandatory Disclosure for Municipal Securities: Issues in Implementation," *Journal of Corporation Law* (Fall 1987): 72.
24. Ibid., 66.
25. Ibid., 76.
26. Senate Banking Committee Hearings, 304–305.
27. Ibid.
28. Auletta, *The Streets Were Paved with Gold*, 295.
29. Ibid., 293–294.
30. Ibid., 311–315.
31. Senate Banking Committee Hearings, 24.
32. Ibid., 148.
33. Ibid., 56.
34. Ibid., 55.
35. "The Region," *New York Times*, December 3, 1978.
36. Anna Quindlen, "City Notes Sell Out with Interest Cut to 8% from 8.25%," *New York Times*, January 23, 1979.
37. Edward A. Gargan, "City Surplus Put at $243 Million for Fiscal Year," *New York Times*, May 11, 1981.
38. Clyde Haberman, "City Acts on Own to Sell Issue of $75 Million," *New York Times*, March 24, 1981.

Epilogue
1. Auletta, *The Streets Were Paved with Gold*, 320.
2. Ibid.

ACKNOWLEDGMENTS

I WANT TO THANK MY PRODUCTION EDITOR JEFF FARR, MY COPY-editor and proofreader Cindy Durand, and my photo editor Ruth Mandel for their hard work and dedication.

I also want to thank Judith Regan for her patient guidance and support in telling this story.

Before the era of social media, and before we started bragging about how low our bad cholesterol is and how high our sleep scores are according to the latest app, we spent late nights out and about on the town with reporters, politicians, lawyers, judges, cops, and robbers.

Through the haze of cigar smoke at 21, Neary's, Elaine's, and other lesser establishments in New York City, the older generation would regale us with outrageous, yet mostly true, tales of what happened in the city way back when. I don't think that happens much anymore, and if it does, I don't know where, or maybe I'm not invited. Sadly, I believe we are worse off for it.

I miss those wonderful characters and the places we frequented. I know I got in just under the wire and am so grateful to have known that New York.

INDEX